The Death of Christ

The Death of Christ

The Bible and Popular Culture vs Archaeological and Historical Evidence

Steven Rutledge

PEN & SWORD
HISTORY

First published in Great Britain in 2022 by
Pen & Sword History
An imprint of
Pen & Sword Books Ltd
Yorkshire – Philadelphia

ISBN 978 1 39908 877 0

A CIP catalogue record for this book is available from the British Library.

Typeset by Mac Style
Printed and bound in the UK by CPI Group (UK) Ltd,
Croydon, CR0 4YY.

MIX
Paper from responsible sources
FSC® C013604

Pen & Sword Books Limited incorporates the imprints of Atlas, Archaeology, Aviation, Discovery, Family History, Fiction, History, Maritime, Military, Military Classics, Politics, Select, Transport, True Crime, Air World, Frontline Publishing, Leo Cooper, Remember When, Seaforth Publishing, The Praetorian Press, Wharncliffe Local History, Wharncliffe Transport, Wharncliffe True Crime and White Owl.

For a complete list of Pen & Sword titles please contact

PEN & SWORD BOOKS LIMITED
47 Church Street, Barnsley, South Yorkshire, S70 2AS, England
E-mail: enquiries@pen-and-sword.co.uk
Website: www.pen-and-sword.co.uk

Or

PEN AND SWORD BOOKS
1950 Lawrence Rd, Havertown, PA 19083, USA
E-mail: Uspen-and-sword@casematepublishers.com
Website: www.penandswordbooks.com

Contents

Preface and Acknowledgements

Much always goes into writing a work such as this and it is often difficult to know where to begin to credit those who have been of such great assistance along the way, but before I express my gratitude, just a brief note to the reader. First, in my citation of Biblical passages I have used almost exclusively the King James version of the Bible, simply because of a personal love of the majesty of its language and its style. For translations of Josephus and Philo I have relied primarily on the Loeb editions by H. St. J. Thackeray (for *The Jewish War*), Louis H. Feldman (for *Jewish Antiquities*), and C. D. Yonge (for *Against Flaccus* and *The Embassy to Gaius*); similarly for translations of Cassius Dio I have relied on Earnest Cary's translation of his *Roman History*. Latin translations are for the most part my own, and I have tried, probably as with any translator, with varying degrees of success to navigate between being faithful to the author's grammar and syntax but also trying to convey what I believe the sense of the Latin is attempting to communicate as well, never an easy task and one that carries with it a number of problems. Any infelicities of translation or factual errors rest solely with me. As to those to whom I owe a debt of thanks, Professor Robert Wagoner (emeritus Juniata College), an old and dear friend, is perhaps first and foremost. Many years ago he steered me away from all manner of prejudices and presumptions concerning not just Christianity but religion in general, and I could never thank him enough for the myriad of different ways in which he has helped me to view the complicated subject of religion and its place in human culture over time. I would also like to thank Professor Thomas Mertes (History, Linfield University) who lent me encouragement and had helpful suggestions on a draft of this work. Brennen Guillory, a minister at a local combined Methodist and Lutheran Church (McMinnville, Oregon), is also owed a debt of gratitude, first for inviting me initially to speak to his congregation on this subject, and then for generously looking at my manuscript with numerous suggestions from the perspective of someone of theological background in this area. Above all, as always, I owe my greatest debt to my life partner, Lori, who has now been a help and a support for nearly four decades, and who has suffered through every word of my writing, from my early undergraduate essays to the current work at hand. There simply is no greater love.

List of Abbreviations of Ancient Works and Sources

With a few exceptions, almost all abbreviations of ancient authors and works in this history follow the *Oxford Classical Dictionary* or the *Oxford Latin Dictionary* usage.

App.	**Appian**
BCiv.	*The Civil Wars*
Hisp.	*The Wars in Spain*
Mith.	*The Mithridatic Wars*
Aur. Vict.	**Aurelius Victor**
De Vir. Ill.	*De Viris Illustribus* (On Famous Men)
BAf.	*De Bello Africano* (The African War, author unknown, attributed to Caesar)
BAlex.	*De Bello Alexandriae* (The Alexandrine War, author unknown, attributed to Caesar)
Caes.	**Caesar**
BCiv.	*De Bello Civili* (The Civil Wars)
BGall.	*Commentarii De Bello Gallico* (The Gallic Wars)
Cass. Dio	Cassius Dio's Roman History
Cic.	**Cicero**
Att.	*Epistulae ad Atticum* (Letters to Atticus)
Brut.	*Brutus*
Fam.	*Epistulae ad Familiares* (Letters to his Friends)
Har. Resp.	*De Haruspicum Responso* (On the Response of the Haruspices)
Verr.	*In Verrem Orationes* (Speeches against Verres)
CIL	*Corpus Inscriptionum Latinorum* (Corpus of Roman Inscriptions)
Dio Chrysostomus	

Or.	*Orationes*
Diod. Sic.	**Diodorus Siculus**
Eus.	**Eusebius**
Hist. Eccl.	*Historia Ecclesiatica* (History of the Church)
Eutrop.	**Eutropius**
Brev.	*Breviarium ab urbe condita* (A summary of history since Rome's foundation)
Flor.	**Florus**
Epit.	*Epitome* (Epitome of Roman History)
Front.	**Frontinus**
Str.	*Strategemata*
Fronto	
Ad M. Caes.	*Letters to Marcus Aurelius Caesar*
Hdt.	**Herodotus** (*The Histories*)
Hor.	**Horace**
Od.	*Odes*
ILS	*Inscriptiones Latinae Selectae* (Selections of Latin Inscriptions)
Jos.	**Josephus**
AJ	*Antiquitates Judaicae* (Jewish Antiquities)
Ap.	*Contra Apionem* (Against Apion)
BJ	*Bellum Judaicum* (The Jewish War)
Juv.	**Juvenal** (*The Satires*)
Livy	
Per.	*Periochae* (Summaries)
Macrob.	**Macrobius**
Sat.	*Saturnalia*
Nep.	**Cornelius Nepos**
Att.	*Atticus* (Life of Atticus)
Oros.	**Orosius** (History Against the Pagans)
Ovid	
Fast.	*Fasti*
Pont.	*Epistulae ex Ponto*
Trist.	*Tristia*
Philo	**Philo Judaeus**
Flacc.	*In Flaccum* (Against Flaccus)
Leg.	*Legatio ad Gaium* (Embassy to C. Caligula)

Philostr.	**Philostratus**
VA	*Vita Apollonii* (Life of Apollonius of Tyana)
Plin.	**Pliny the Elder**
HN	*Historia Naturalis* (Natural History)
Plin.	**Pliny the Younger**
Ep.	*Epistluae* (Epistles)
Pseudo-Brutus	
Epist. ad Cic.	*Epistles to Cicero*
Quint.	**Quintilian**
Inst.	*Institutio oratoria* (Education in Oratory)
Sall.	**Sallust**
Cat.	*Bellum Catilinae* (War with Catiline)
Sen.	**Seneca the Younger**
Ben.	*De Beneficiis* (On Benefits)
Dial.	*Dialogi* (Dialogues)
Epist.	*Epistulae Morales* (Moral Epistles)
Suet.	**Suetonius**
Aug.	*Augustus*
Caes.	*Caesar*
Cal.	*Caligula*
Claud.	*Claudius*
Dom.	*Domitian*
Galb.	*Galba*
Tib.	*Tiberius*
Vesp.	*Vespasian*
Vit.	*Vitellius*
Tac.	**Tacitus**
Agr.	*Agricola*
Ann.	*Annales* (Annals)
Hist.	*Historiae* (Histories)
Tert.	**Tertullian**
Apol.	*Apologeticus* (The Apology)
Val. Max.	**Valerius Maximus**
Veg.	**Vegetius**
De Re Mil.	*De Re Militari* (On Military Matters)
Vell. Pat	**Velleius Paterculus**
Xen.	**Xenophon**
Hell.	*Hellenica* (History of Greece)

Abbreviations of Roman Names:

A. = Aulus
C. = Gaius
Cn. = Gnaeus
D. = Decimus
L. = Lucius
M. = Marcus
P. = Publius
Q. = Quintus
Ser. = Servius
T. = Titus

List of Illustrations, Maps, and Family Trees

Illustrations

Fig. 3.2: The so-called Grand Cameo of France. A sardonyx cameo of the first century AD. From the collection Cabinet de Médailles; originally purchased by King Louis IX (St. Louis) in 1247 from Constantinople and deposited to Sainte-Chapelle; deposited in the Cabinet de Médailles by Louis XVI in 1791. (*Attribution GFDL © Marie-Lan Nguyen (user:Jastrow) / Wikimedia Commons; source/photographer Janmad based on photo by Jastrow and Cabinet des Médailles, CC BY-SA 3.0 [http://creativecommons.org/licenses/by-sa/3.0/], or CC BY-SA 2.5-2.0-1.0 [https://creativecommons.org/licenses/by-sa/2.5-2.0-1.0], via Wikimedia Commons*)

Fig. 4.1: The inscription recording Pilate as prefect of Judaea; it reads (restored), [DIS AVGVSTI]S TIBERIEVM … PONTI]VS PILATVS/[… PRAE]FECTVS IVDA[EA]E/[… FECIT D]E[DICAVIT] which translates: 'To the Divine Augustus (this) Tibereium Pontius Pilate, Prefect of Judaea, has built (and) dedicated'. The Tibereium referenced is likely a temple to Tiberius. Dedicatory inscription found reused in the staircase of the theatre at Caesarea, Israel Museum, Jerusalem. (*Attribution by Carole Raddato from FRANKFURT, GERMANY Carole Raddato from FRANKFURT, Germany, CC BY-SA 2.0 [https://creativecommons.org/licenses/by-sa/2.0], via Wikimedia Commons*)

Fig. 4.2: A scene from Trajan's Column in which Roman troops arrive at the scene of a sacrifice, including standard bearers. (*Attribution by Apollodorus of Damascus, graphics by Conrad Cichorius [1863–1932], Public domain, via Wikimedia Commons*)

Fig. 4.3: Caesarea Maritima, Israel, with an aerial view including the hippodrome. (*Attribution by Abraham Gracier, Own work, CC BY-SA 4.0 [https://creativecommons.org/licenses/by-sa/4.0], via Wikimedia Commons*)

Fig. 4.4: A paleochristian sarcophagus belonging to Marcus Claudianus (AD 330–335) with scenes from the Old and New Testament from the Via della Lungara next to S. Giacomo in Settimania, Rome. (*Attribution by Jean-Pol Grandmont, Palazzo Massimo alle Terme, CC BY-SA 3.0 [https://creativecommons.org/licenses/by-sa/3.0], via Wikimedia Commons*)

Maps

Family Trees

Chapter 1

Introduction

Tacitus, the greatest and perhaps most moralistic of ancient historians, makes no mention of the most singular event in human history, the crucifixion of Jesus. How could this be? How could this most stentorian voice of liberty, virtue, and justice from pagan antiquity fail to take notice of the greatest event in humanity's most dramatic epoch? It remains possible that the response to that question was made by a pious but destructive copyist somewhere amidst Europe's dark scriptoria in late antiquity or the early Middle Ages: It cannot be. It must not be. And thus was history suppressed, deleted, and erased.

Tacitus' *Annals* (*Annales* in Latin) breaks off just a few chapters into Book V, in AD 29, not resuming until the winter of 31. His historical masterpiece encompassed the period from AD 14 until AD 68, covering a grand sweep of Roman history including some of its most colourful characters: the brooding and morose Tiberius, his mad nephew Caligula, the inept, pathetic, and alcoholic Claudius (Caligula's uncle), Claudius' voraciously adulterous empress Messalina, and the knavish yet murderous artist-actor-poet-charioteer-champion-wannabe, Nero. The break at Book V, however, is odd because of how ancient manuscripts were written and how ancient authors, in turn, structured their works: Tacitus himself had organized his *Annals* into what were known as hexads, with every six books (what we would consider the equivalent of perhaps several modern book chapters) covering the reigns of one or two emperors. Hence, the first six books represent a discrete section of the period covering the reign of Tiberius, from AD 14 until 37. The next six covered the reigns of Caligula and Claudius, and although roughly half of this second hexad survives, the loss of the first half represents one of the most egregious losses of antiquity. We miss the history of the whole of Caligula's reign from a master historian, an incalculable loss. We also miss about half of Claudius' reign, including what was doubtless a fabulous treatment of the absurd succession of Claudius after he was discovered cowering behind a tapestry in the imperial palace after Caligula's assassination. However, the manuscript does resume in time for us to catch up with the shocking fall of Messalina and the rise of Nero, whose reign completes the third of what were almost doubtless three hexads. Almost, because the reign of Nero breaks off about half way through Book XVI, in the year AD 66 – another wrenching loss, since sometime in that year was the start of the Jewish rebellion against Rome that was to lead not just to the defeat of the Jews but the destruction of the Temple in AD 70. It is not peculiar that we have lost the first part of one hexad – the reign of Caligula and part of Claudius', and the last part of another – that about Nero. Because of the nature of how ancient manuscript scrolls were handled on a purely physical level, it is not unusual to miss the beginning and the conclusion to works whose survival was precariously based on fragile materials – the ends of manuscripts on scrolls would often receive the most wear and tear, and it is not particularly remarkable to be missing the beginning of works here and there, such as the opening of Caesar's *Civil War Commentaries* (*De Bello Civili*). But to miss a large segment in what would have been somewhere in the middle of a manuscript is not, generally speaking, the norm. The loss in this instance means that we are missing the violent and dramatic fall of Sejanus, Tiberius' praetorian prefect who possibly tried to overthrow his emperor, something to which Tacitus had been building since his introduction of the prefect at the very opening of Book IV. We will never know with certainty why we have lost it, and it means that we miss from his hand events from about the late spring of AD 29 until the winter of AD 31. It has been suggested, however, rather conspiratorially, that there was a nefarious theological reason behind the loss.

The inspiration for the subject and focus of this book is based in part on a theory suggested some forty years ago that posited that Tacitus' fifth book was deliberately suppressed by a scribe in the late antique or Medieval period since it did not mention Jesus' crucifixion.[1] Sceptical scholars have duly noted the difficulties with the argument. Among the most effective arguments against wilful suppression is that the loss of Book V was due to other more plausible factors, likely accidental and certainly not intentional.[2] Yet that begs another question: since this portion of the work is missing, how can we in fact be so sure that Tacitus indeed did not discuss the Christians and the crucifixion?

The answer to that is that Tacitus appears to first introduce the Christians and Jesus in Book XV of his *Annals* where he discusses Nero's persecution of the Christians after the Great Fire of AD 64 in Rome.[3] The argument, exemplified here by Van Voorst's, is a compelling one: Tacitus was nothing if not economical, and his language in the passage about the Christians and their persecution in the wake of the Great Fire indicates that he had not yet mentioned them elsewhere in his work:

> There was no human effort, no bestowal of imperial largesse, no appeasements of the gods whereby the malicious talk could be made to stop the belief that Nero had ordered the fire. Therefore, to abolish the rumour, Nero put up as fake defendants those who the commonality called Christians – people hated for their disgraces – and afflicted them with the most exquisite punishments. Christ was the originator of this name who, under Tiberius' rule, had been put to death by the procurator Pontius Pilate; the destructive superstition, repressed for the moment, again burst to the surface not only throughout Judaea, the origin of this evil, but even Rome, where everything from everywhere that is horrible and disgraceful converges. (Tac. *Ann*. 15.44).

There are a number of things that are noteworthy about this particular passage: first, Tacitus feels compelled to explain to his audience who Christ is, what his origins are, and where this religion first emerged. It is doubtful that he would have felt the need to explain to his audience who these Christians and Christ were, had he mentioned them in a previous book of the *Annals*. He almost certainly would not have felt compelled to rehearse the history of the religion, mentioning the governor, Pilate, and the emperor under whom Christ conducted his ministry had he mentioned them before, and he has absolutely no mention of Pilate or his governance of Judaea, much less his recall in AD 36 by Tiberius, a year he covers in Book VI of his *Annals*. It is hard to argue, given all of this, that this is not quite possibly the single existing mention of Christians in the entire Tacitean corpus. Indeed, it is quite telling that Tacitus, writing this passage probably sometime between AD 110 and 120, feels compelled to explain to his Roman audience who the Christians were even during the early decades of the second century AD. Pliny the Younger, Tacitus' friend and contemporary, had to do the same when corresponding with Trajan, even going into details about how benign the practices of the early Christians appeared as they merely broke bread together, sang hymns, and swore to keep faith to God's law (see pp. 68–72).

In fact, it bears noting that we simply do not know the precise year Christ died, although there are plenty of theories.[4] That is rather remarkable. One of the individuals who introduced the most profound changes in terms of religion, culture, ethics, even the shape of history, from the introduction of Jewish-based ethics into the bloodstream of a pagan empire, to the monastic movement, to the Reformation and attendant development of the nation state, and we know little of his life. He himself left nothing behind. No poems, memoirs, letters – absolutely nothing. In this, he shares something with Socrates, who believed knowledge fluid, and something that could not be committed to writing. And yet the legacy of his ministry is profound.

There are numerous theories and possibilities, of course, for the date of Christ's death, the most likely candidates ranging from AD 29 to AD 33. However, it is not my intention to resolve this or even attempt to resolve it, despite the subject of the book. The purpose of this history, rather, is to give a snapshot of the world at approximately the time of Christ's death, with a sharp focus on the politics, personalities, and world between roughly the early twenties to late thirties AD, with some necessary breaking of this tidy chronological delimitation, since history is never a hermetically sealed box but rather a seemingly limitless and ever-expanding web of connections. Hence, some of this chronological snapshot will naturally leak through the semi-permeable membrane of this period in order to elucidate some of the events and characters who parade through the pages of the New Testament. These were years that were eventful not only for Rome, but, needless to say, subsequently for the entire world.

The further inspiration for this study stretches back to several years ago, when I was asked by a local church during Advent to discuss some basic background to the world and story of the New Testament in a series of conversations with the pastor in front of his congregation. The intent of this work is to give those interested in the life of Jesus a larger context of the world as it was at the time of his death. What forces shaped the personalities who governed the Roman Empire? Who were the major players that shaped the world at the time during which Jesus lived, preached, and was executed? Who were the significant personalities that impacted and influenced policy from Rome to Judaea and beyond? Where does Jesus' ministry fit in the larger context of the Roman world and its values system? From that perspective it is designed to be a snapshot of the events that occurred during his life and a few years after, and the personalities who were both at the forefront and in the background of Roman political life. It is, therefore, intended to give a macro context to the political culture of the Roman Empire during the time in which he ministered. It is certainly not intended to be a history of Roman Judaea, or Jesus' life per se, but rather of those who governed the empire in which he lived and who influenced and assisted in its governance – from the imperial head of state, Tiberius, to the Roman centurion and local tax collector. And while it will deal with a number of personalities grounded in Roman daily life, it is not its intention to rehearse the quotidian details of the Romans' existence.

The first chapter is a sketch of the man whom fate had appointed as the ruler of the Roman Empire during Jesus' ministry, the emperor Tiberius, one of ancient history's more tragic and enigmatic figures. Of necessity this chapter will have a long chronological scope that surveys Tiberius' personality and his life that spanned some 78 years. Over his reign loomed a creature of limitless and, as it happened, disappointed ambitions, Lucius Aelius Sejanus, his praetorian prefect, a personality perhaps best described, at least as presented in our sources, as Richard the Third in a toga and sandals, but with greater charm and sex appeal. Sejanus, his meteoric rise and precipitous and dramatic fall in one of the years proposed for Jesus' crucifixion, is the subject of the second chapter of this history. Sejanus is also significant, since he may have been responsible for the appointment of Pontius Pilate to his position as prefect of Judaea. Pontius Pilate will be the subject of the third chapter of this work, and we will seek to put him in his larger overall historical context not just as the governor of Judaea but also as a Roman governor of a typical, albeit small, Roman protectorate, and to further put him in his context as a Roman provincial administrator in general; the chapter also seeks to put him in his larger cultural and political milieu in the early decades of the first century AD. The local client ruler of Galilee, known officially as a tetrarch, under whose jurisdiction Jesus lived and conducted his ministry, Herod Antipas, a significant figure in the history of the gospel accounts, will be the subject of Chapter 4. The fifth chapter will attempt to understand and contextualize Jesus' activities as a resistance movement, not so much in its Jewish milieu but in its much larger context of rebellions against Roman power: it will attempt to understand the nature of resistance to Rome, specifically resistance that could possibly be understood as having a religious element in its inspiration, motives, or leadership. If we accept the gospel accounts, Jesus' movement can be understood as a markedly radical form of resistance that is both shocking and unique in terms of its messages of peace and inclusion, with no comparable text in the Greek or Roman world of which he was a part. The final chapter will consider collaborators drawing on three examples from the New Testament: the centurion who asks Jesus to cure his servant; the *publicanus* (tax collector) Matthew; and the informant Judas Iscariot. Each of these was an important civic functionary in Roman society, essential for the governance and maintenance of order and stability for the empire, and starting from each one we will expand to consider their larger roles in Roman society and governance.

There is, of course, no shortage of studies – ranging from articles to massive tomes – on Jesus, ancient Judaea, Pilate, Herod Antipas, Tiberius, Sejanus, or any of the other topics and individuals the current work will explore, although they have not yet been drawn together in such a way as to set Jesus' life and times in their larger historical or political context. Any scholar, theologian, or writer approaches the subject, as they should, with a numbing humility before the sheer volume of works that have explored the life and times of this heretical rabbi. Yet while Jesus' life has often been understood and approached in the micro-context of Jewish discontent and revolution in Judaea, it has more rarely been put in its larger historical context against the backdrop of resistance movements in the first century AD; it is hoped that by presenting this larger context a new and deeper perspective of Jesus' place against the macro-historic background of his own time will give the reader a new way to think about his life and ministry. Whatever one's personal beliefs or lack of them might be, whether the believer understands him to truly be the Son of God, or the non-believer rejects him entirely as such, whether one accepts Jesus as a historical figure or whether his very existence is denied, there is no doubt that either as concerns Jesus himself or the mind that created him as a fiction, we are dealing with an entity that for his time – and still for our own time – was and remains remarkably radical. By understanding the nature of the worldly powers and forces that surrounded Jesus we can more deeply appreciate the profundity of that radicalism and the spiritual genius behind the ethics he preached. Hence, while Jesus will rarely appear in the text of this study, he will, however, be ever present as an alternative and a reproach to Rome's embrace of a material, transient, and fallen world.

Chapter 2

Tiberius: The Man on the Coin

In the last week of Jesus' life, the Pharisees put him to the test (*Matthew* 22: 17–22):

> Tell us therefore, What thinkest thou? Is it lawful to give tribute unto Caesar or not? But Jesus perceived their wickedness, and said, Why tempt me, ye hypocrites? Shew me the tribute money. And they brought unto him a penny. And he saith unto them, Whose is this image and superscription? They say unto him, Caesar's. Then saith he unto them, Render therefore unto Caesar the things which are Caesar's; and unto God the things that are God's. When they had heard these words, they marvelled, and left him and went their way.

The image of the man on the coin (fig. 2.1) was of the Roman emperor, Tiberius, and in some respects his appearance on the coin was one of the most unlikely of events, a product, as history often is, of a power struggle that included its share of human irrationality, as well as shifting alliances, and pure dumb luck.[1] Perhaps the best, but also most damning, sketch of Tiberius' personality and life, at least prior to the chance that found him on the imperial throne, is Tacitus' rapid-fire description of him in the opening chapters of his historical masterpiece, the *Annals*. It consists of an unforgettable painting in a series of staccato sentences in a Latin that is compressed, terse, and has helped to condemn Tiberius' reputation for nearly two millennia. The author strategically deploys a simple but unsubstantiated phrase here, a series of rumours re-circulated there, with innuendo added in for good measure. Describing Augustus' worry about the succession over who will actually replace him, Tacitus notes that Tiberius was deemed qualified due to his maturity and his proven competence as a military commander, but then come the qualifications: first, he was of that inborn and ancient arrogance that

Fig. 2.1: A silver denarius of Tiberius reading on the obverse: Caesar Augustus Tiberius, son of the Divine Augustus, and on the reverse Pontifex Maximus with Livia as Pax or Peace. It was possibly this very sort of coin to which Jesus would have referred. (Classical Numistmatic Group via *Wikimedia Commons*)

marked his family, the Claudians; in addition, there were numerous indications of cruelty, and although repressed, they persistently burst forth.[2] Tacitus continues that Tiberius had been put forward as a candidate for succession secretly by the wiles of his ambitious mother, Livia, for whom he would play the compliant son. Add to that that while on the island of Rhodes, where Tiberius spent time in self-imposed exile, he had meditated on nothing but his anger, practised hypocrisy, and indulged in hidden vices. The nature of Latin itself is to be economical, capable of saying and expressing much in a few words, and Tacitus' is particularly compact and brief. Through a short, sharp introductory portrait, Tiberius is condemned before he can even make his case, and the reader's opinion of him thoroughly corrupted and tainted. Of course, the reality about Tiberius is far more complex, though perhaps no less interesting.

Tiberius' Early Life

His father, Tiberius Claudius Nero, and his mother, Livia Drusilla, were from the bluest of blue-blooded Roman clans: he was descended on both his father's and mother's side from the Claudian clan, a family that was known for producing two types of fruit, the sweet and the sour, and Tiberius was to eventually prove himself decidedly of the latter.[3] His father had been a loyal partisan of Julius Caesar, but on the day after Caesar's assassination, which had taken place on the Ides of March in 44 BC, he had proposed in the Senate not just amnesty, but honours for Caesar's murderers.[4] Two years later, in 42 BC Tiberius was born; it was the year of Philippi, where the leading assassins of Caesar – Marcus Brutus and Gaius Cassius – fell to the swords of Marc Antony and Gaius Octavius, later known to the world as Augustus. The first of these men had been Caesar's second in command during his dictatorship, a position known as the *magister equitum*, or Master of Horse, while Octavian was Caesar's precocious great-nephew and, according to the terms of Caesar's will, his heir. In the fraught and violent period following Philippi, when the temporary and convenient alliance between Octavian and Antony was suffering under the strains of the ambition of both, Tiberius Claudius Nero sided with Antony, now commanding in the East, and was forced to flee Italy when Octavian defeated Antony's brother, Lucius, at Perusia (modern Perugia) in 40 BC, when Lucius Antonius attempted to challenge Octavian's power. With his wife and toddler son Tiberius in tow – just as Joseph had fled from Herod's own political persecution to Egypt with Mary and the infant Jesus – he undertook a hair-raising flight, via Neapolis (modern Naples) and Sicily, to Greece, where he joined Marc Antony's retinue. The young family was in extreme peril at several points during their flight: the infant Tiberius' wailing nearly betrayed the family at Neapolis while the family was in hiding, and, still pursued even in Greece, they escaped from Sparta only to be nearly burnt to death when trapped by a chance forest fire. Once Antony and Octavian made peace (which was destined to be tense and not to last) Tiberius Claudius Nero returned to Italy with his family.[5] There Octavian met Livia and, smitten by her charm and beauty, created a public scandal when he refused to wait but forced her to divorce her husband and led her to the altar when six months pregnant, bulging with Tiberius' brother, Drusus, who was destined to become the father of the emperor Claudius, grandfather of Caligula, and great-grandfather of the emperor Nero. The public derision at the scandalous affair still excited gossip decades later at Augustus' funeral in AD 14.[6]

Tiberius was immediately welcomed into Octavian's family. In 30 BC Octavian celebrated his triumph at Actium over Antony and Cleopatra, the Ptolemaic Greek queen of Egypt. Now an adolescent of 12, Tiberius was allowed to ride a trace horse to the left of Octavian's triumphal chariot, Octavian's nephew Marcellus riding to the right. In 27 BC, the same year that Tiberius assumed the *toga virilis* (the 'gown of manhood'), Octavian became Augustus, a name that was singular and resonant with meaning for the Romans.[7] His rivals dead, Augustus planned for the future, and looked to establish himself as the *princeps* – the first man of the state – an informal republican title given to the one senator who, by virtue of seniority, wisdom, and experience, held greater authority and political influence than his fellow senators. Augustus thereby eschewed the mistakes of his great-uncle, Julius Caesar, who was aggressive about the supremacy of his position as dictator, parading in the garb of Rome's ancient and hated monarchs, studiously contemptuous of the Senate, and who flirted with divine honours, none of which suited the ancient habits of free republican government. Augustus was to be the iron hand in the velvet glove, maintaining the façade of the republic even as he set in place a military dictatorship for himself and claimed ownership of the empire.[8] One of the means by which he achieved this was to secure his power, in part, through a series of marriage alliances. However, Augustus had only a single daughter, Julia, from a previous marriage to a woman named Scribonia, a relative of a former rival, Sextus Pompeius, who had been executed in Asia in 36 BC. Augustus wed Julia to his nephew Marcellus, but he died in 23 BC.

Tiberius, in turn, was married to Vipsania Agrippina in 15 BC, daughter of M. Vipsanius Agrippa and Caecilia Attica, herself daughter of the renowned expatriate T. Pomponius Atticus, who, like Agrippa, was an equestrian (i.e., a 'knight', a step in rank just below that of senator), but who also was a wealthy financier whose love of all things Greek led him to set up residence in Athens.[9] A friend of Cicero's, Vipsania's grandfather was a voluminous correspondent with the greatest of Roman orators, with sixteen books of letters between the two men surviving, thereby making Cicero perhaps the best-known individual to us who ever lived – including Moses, Jesus, Socrates, and Mohammed – up until the Renaissance. Agrippa, Augustus' lifetime friend and lieutenant, had been closely connected to Augustus' family; Tiberius' marriage, arranged when both he and Vipsania were still children, was to tie the two friends in an even closer nexus.[10] The marriage was a tragic one by virtue of its happiness: Tiberius reportedly was deeply in love with Vipsania who bore him his only son, Drusus. Three years into the marriage, however, in 12 BC, Agrippa, Tiberius' father-in-law, died. After Marcellus' death in 23 BC, Julia had been married to Agrippa and the union produced four children: Gaius and Lucius Caesar, Agrippina the Elder (so called to distinguish her from her own daughter, Agrippina the Younger), and Agrippa Postumus, who was born, as his name implies, after his father's death.

Of the four, only one, Agrippina, survived long enough to produce any children. Julia, now widowed for a second time, was still relatively young (in her early twenties), and Tiberius was compelled to divorce Vipsania and marry her. Our sources indicate that the experience embittered Tiberius, and Suetonius relates a moving story that one day Tiberius saw his now former wife, Vipsania, in public, and followed her home, weeping. Tiberius' action embarrassed the imperial family and he was forbidden to see her again. Tacitus goes so far as to assert that Vipsania's new husband, Asinius Gallus, subsequently became the object of Tiberius' animus and was persecuted accordingly in the course of Tiberius' reign. Julia's notorious reputation as an adulterous libertine did not help matters according to our sources; indeed, she had reportedly cast an adulterous glance at Tiberius himself while she was still married to Agrippa. When their first child died in infancy, Tiberius reportedly broke off marital relations with Julia for good.

Marriage to Julia and Northern Campaigns

Tiberius was around 30 when he married Julia, and he had already enjoyed, by virtue of his position, what would have been an illustrious and extraordinary career during Rome's republic. He had been quaestor at the age of 19 in 23 BC when he undertook the prosecution of a man named Fannius Caepio for conspiracy against Augustus.[11] Seven years later, in 16 BC, he was praetor, and by the age of 29, in 13 BC he achieved what was once Rome's highest office, the consulship.[12] In conjunction with holding magistracies he also underwent military training. He campaigned in Spain against an Iberian Celtic tribe known as the Cantabrians (in the north and west of modern Spain) before being dispatched in 20 BC to the East to put a king on the throne of Armenia and to negotiate a return of the standards of the legions lost with M. Licinius Crassus – a member of the First Triumvirate that also included Pompey and Julius Caesar

– when he suffered defeat and death at the hands of the Parthians over thirty years earlier, a grave humiliation that still stung.[13] By 15 BC he was campaigning with his brother Drusus in Raetia and Noricum – what today would be Austria and Bavaria – extending Roman power to the Danube which was to become Rome's northern boundary, and the exploits of both were duly celebrated by one of Augustan Rome's greatest poets, the studied, humane, and affable Horace.[14]

Tiberius, by all accounts, took to military life, and (at least according to physical descriptions of him) he was a strong and strapping man, suited to a life in the legions and camps. We can, of course, never know what Tiberius looked like, but coin depictions show a somewhat typological and ordinary man, with a slight aquiline and prominent nose with a gentle bump in its ridge. It was different from the portraiture on his statues, which (like the seated portrait in fig. 2.2) show a baby face, with a receding and weak chin, a large aquiline nose, a broad forehead, and a serene, some would say expressionless, face. The baby face, despite the typological nature of Julio-Claudian portraits, may have had some grounding in reality. 'My little Tiberius', *Tiberiolus*, was the moniker a friend of his had applied to him in conversation in AD 32, while Suetonius, the imperial biographer who penned the lives of the first twelve Caesars, also notes his 'fresh-complexioned' face, though this admittedly is mere conjecture.[15] But Julio-Claudian Roman emperors, of which Tiberius was the second (third, if we count from Julius Caesar) are often portrayed at the peak of physical maturity, either eternally youthful, as was the case with Augustus, or serenely dignified, as with Tiberius and his nephew, the emperor Claudius. By the time of Jesus' death, if we can believe the reports, Tiberius no longer was as remotely robust and baby-faced as his statuary; he was by then balding, stooped, his head and face occasionally marked with open sores, his physical deterioration reflective of the toll that years of familial and emotional conflict had taken. Of medium height, broad-shouldered, and powerfully built, he had, according to Suetonius, remarkable grip strength, capable of boring through an apple with a single finger.[16]

Not long after his marriage to Julia, he was sent to suppress a revolt in Dalmatia and Pannonia, an area that encompasses roughly the various states of the former Yugoslavia; the campaign was difficult but successful, and Augustus granted Tiberius the right of wearing triumphal honours in

10 BC.[17] His brother Drusus, meanwhile, campaigned on the Rhine, but died there in 9 BC; upon news that his brother was near death, Tiberius hastened to his side, was with him at the end, and accompanied his body back to Rome.[18] He was then put in command of the war in Germany and successively in 9 and 7 BC won triumphal distinctions and also (in 7 BC) a second consulship.[19] In both campaigns our sources laud Tiberius' caution, his deference even as a commander to those more experienced with the region and enemy, and the firm discipline he instilled among his men. He had proven thus far in his career a capable civic administrator and military commander, competent and comfortable in both the civilian and military spheres – *res domi et militiae* ('affairs at home and on military service') as the great historian Livy would have expressed it. Most importantly, he had proven himself in the eyes of Augustus, who had already seen two of his close male family members perish – Marcellus who was barely 21 years of age when he died, and Agrippa who died at the age of 51. Fate could not be trusted, and in 6 BC Julia's two sons Gaius and Lucius, Augustus' favourites, were still boys, too young as yet for positions of responsibility. As a precaution Augustus bestowed the *tribunicia potestas* – 'the power of the tribunate' – upon Tiberius. Augustus had asserted this ancient and important prerogative as a means to project himself as the champion of the people, and their protector; it also granted him the power to introduce business before the Senate and to interpose vetoes. A cornerstone of Augustus' policy and state organization, it became an exclusive dispensation of the *princeps*, and when the emperor had previously bestowed the *tribunicia potestas* on Agrippa it was understood that he was Augustus' choice for assuming the major share of his governing responsibilities.[20]

Fig. 2.2: A seated statue of Tiberius in marble from the Chiaramonte Museum in the Vatican. (Marie-Lan Nguyen via *Wikimedia Commons*)

Self-Imposed Exile on Rhodes

Then a mystery ensues. Tiberius was no sooner bestowed with this significant title and responsibility in 6 BC than he left Rome and went into retirement and seclusion on the island of Rhodes for ten years. He would not return to the city and fully emerge from that retirement until AD 4. In the interim, his estranged wife Julia was exiled in 2 BC after her father discovered – and was embarrassed by – her adulterous affairs.[21] Augustus had passed priggish legislation concerning family life that, among other things, made adultery a public offence, while he later went so far as to legislate privileges and exemptions on inheritance taxes depending on the number of children one had. Julia's behaviour was more than just humiliating for Augustus – it was enraging. Not only was she exiled, Augustus also prohibited her even from the pleasures of wine (perhaps due to her notorious nocturnal drinking bouts in the Forum), and in addition, to show he meant business, one of her paramours, Iullus Antonius, son of Marc Antony and Fulvia (Antony's third wife), who had been spared after Actium and elevated to high office by Augustus, was executed.[22] Neither Augustus nor Tiberius ever saw Julia again, and she died in exile towards the end of AD 14, just months after her father Augustus had passed away. Her sons by Agrippa had no better luck: Lucius, died in AD 2 of a sudden illness in Massilia (modern Marseilles in southern France) while heading to take command of the armies in Spain. His brother Gaius Caesar died of infection from a wound in Lycia (southern Turkey) while on campaign in Armenia in AD 4, and backroom gossip made the rounds that the empress Livia was involved in their deaths.[23] After the demise of his two grandsons, Augustus was left with no options for help in governance except Tiberius, although rumours abounded that Augustus had bandied about the names of senators he felt were possibilities as candidates to succeed to his role.

What motivated Tiberius' retirement is uncertain. Our sources indicate that he was disgusted with his wife's adulteries but due to his position as the emperor's son-in-law could neither divorce her nor divulge her infidelities. There is a sense of genuine bitterness, however, in his withdrawal from public life: his mother, Livia, pleaded with him to reconsider; Augustus openly criticized his decision in the Senate as an act of desertion; Tiberius thwarted attempts to make him stay by a four-day hunger strike; he left for Ostia without taking leave of many friends, barely acknowledging all but a few who came to say their farewells, before leaving for Rhodes. Landing on this pleasant and historic Greek island, he dismissed most trappings of power, lived in a simple country house, started wearing Greek dress, took strolls to a nearby gymnasium, spoke on familiar terms with the locals, and attended lectures on philosophy.[24]

His choice of place for exile, however, was apt, since Tiberius' interest in Greek language, culture, and literature, are all well attested. This would be generally unremarkable in an educated Roman of the elite but for the fact that he seemed particularly interested in all things Greek, perhaps due to his early exposure to travel in Greece and Sicily as a child, and spent more time immersed in the Greek world and culture than any other emperor, including the supposed philhellene emperors Nero and Hadrian.[25] He was also quite fluent in Greek to the point where he could detect variations in dialect, as one professor of rhetoric found out much to his hurt. He studied rhetoric with Theodorus of Gadara, one of the most famous teachers of rhetoric of his day, who Suetonius states was the first to see Tiberius' cruel nature, calling him 'mud mixed with blood'.[26] Throughout his life he was a champion and patron of some of the greatest and most ancient cities of the Greek East, and early in his career acted as an advocate in the courts for a number of notable ancient cities, and when some requested relief due to damage from an earthquake he acted as their champion.[27] Later as emperor, when a similar catastrophe struck some communities of the Greek East in AD 17, he was again generous to those cities that had suffered. Moreover, he delighted in hearing Greek myths and legends rehearsed on various occasions, as when emissaries arrived from Segesta in Sicily to plead for the restoration of the Temple of Venus Eryx; when Sparta and Messenia disputed over the ownership of a Temple of Diana; and when the great cities of the Greek East argued over who would have the honour of dedicating a temple to his imperial godhead.[28] He also nurtured an apparent love of Greek literature, although his taste for Greek poetry was far from mainstream, and he took pleasure in reading obscure poets such as Euphorion, Rhianus, and Parthenius (scarcely household names, even to professional classicists), and composed his own Greek verses in imitation of them.[29] Indeed, his affection for these poets went so far as to encourage commentaries on their works, and their busts were soon set up in Roman libraries. In addition, he enjoyed stumping learned men with obscure questions concerning ancient myths, such as 'Who was Hecuba's mother?', 'What name did Achilles assume when he hid amongst the maidens on Sciros?', and 'What song did the Sirens sing to Odysseus?' Some scholars were so vain as to suborn spies to find out what he was reading in order to anticipate his questions, and Suetonius tells us one, a certain Seleucus, was executed for his efforts.[30] It was also on Rhodes that he became acquainted with Thrasyllus, a Greek astrologer, and developed a life-long interest in the art that had been imported to Rome via Greece from Persia by *magi*, who connected human fate and destiny to their reading of the stars. Tiberius sadistically punished those astrologers he caught and called out as frauds, tossing them from Rhodian cliff tops; Thrasyllus, however, had impressed Tiberius by virtue of his accurate foresight. Tiberius had decided to cast Thrasyllus from a cliff but allowed Thrasyllus first to consult his horoscope. Looking at it, Thrasyllus expressed extreme alarm when he saw indicated a moment of extreme peril for himself, after which Tiberius embraced him, congratulated him, and kept him in his close confidences for the rest of his life.[31]

Four years into his self-imposed Greek exile, in 2 BC, after Julia's banishment and after Augustus' grandsons came of age, he requested permission to return to Rome, stating that he had left for Rhodes only because he wanted to avoid the appearance of rivalry with Gaius and Lucius, but now that they were of age and Augustus' heirs, he desired to see his son again and return to Rome.[32] But Augustus had reportedly become embittered against Tiberius – perhaps because of Tiberius' retirement, perhaps because unpleasant information had been divulged about him upon Julia's banishment. Whatever the reason, Augustus for the moment was adamant that Tiberius stay put.[33] His retirement had now turned into exile, during which, as Tacitus perhaps anachronistically reports, he indulged in nothing except anger, deceit, and hidden debauchery.[34] That suits better his later retirement to Capri, and may well be a retrospective view in light of Tiberius' final years. Bad feelings against Tiberius may have filtered from Augustus to Gaius, Augustus' grandson, whose animus against Tiberius reportedly reached the point of imperilling Tiberius' future – perhaps Gaius begrudged Tiberius the bad blood he had with his mother, Julia.[35] Gaius' death, therefore, was opportune in more ways than one.

Return to Rome and Assumption of Power

In AD 4 Tiberius was at last allowed to return to Rome. In rapid succession, he was now adopted into the family of the Caesars and granted a five-year term of the *tribunicia potestas*.[36] There was no doubt what that meant – he was to assume Augustus' position upon his death. In addition, he was now placed at the head of the armies and given the significant task of completing the conquest of Germany to the Elbe, where he campaigned in AD 4–5.[37] In the next year, AD 6, the provinces of Pannonia and Dalmatia rebelled; Tiberius was forced to leave off his campaigns in Germany and the rebellion was not suppressed until AD 9, by which time disaster had struck the legions fighting between the Rhine and Elbe in the Teutoberg Forest.[38] The Germanic tribes east of the Rhine ambushed three legions, slaughtering them almost to a man, while their commander, Quinctilius Varus, was killed, his body partially burnt, and his head sent, via a southern Germanic chieftain named Marboduus, to Augustus.[39] Tiberius was forced to return to Rome. While his actions in Pannonia were a success for him, it was tempered as a result of the catastrophe in Germany, to where he was swiftly dispatched. Both capable and vigorous in managing the disaster, by AD 12 Tiberius had returned to Rome and celebrated a triumph for his victories in Pannonia and Dalmatia.

By that date Augustus was a very old man by the standards of the day: he was 75, and reportedly in steep decline. It is here that Tacitus begins the narrative of his *Annals* in vivid and hair-raising detail. Tacitus rapidly reviews the misfortunes Augustus experienced as his family members died one by one, steering the reader's interpretation of events again through the report of rumour and innuendo: the death of Gaius, Augustus' grandson, was brought about, he implies, by the machinations of Livia; so too was the banishment of his brother, Agrippa Postumus; Livia further connived to have her son brought to the forefront as successor, at first secretly, then quite publicly.[40] Tacitus, however, as is also the case with other sources such as Cassius Dio and Suetonius, presents the reign of Augustus in an anachronistic light, since they wrote after nearly a century (and in Dio's case, nearly two centuries) of rule by emperors. It is for that reason that I have tried to avoid terms such as 'heir', 'successor', or 'dynasty' in discussing Tiberius' career up to this point. As Edward Champlin has noted, the political situation in Rome in AD 14 remained highly volatile and uncertain; there was as yet 'no 'throne' to be behind, no 'dynasty', no 'court', certainly no 'emperor' to 'succeed', no 'princes of the blood' or 'heirs apparent' – all of this was to be established over the coming decades as the *princeps* and his house developed over time. It is anachronistic to think otherwise, and these terms as such stand in merely as a convenient way, in retrospect, to discuss the subsequent nature and growth of the *domus Caesarum*, the house of the Caesars.[41] Much of this uncertainty, despite his anachronistic presentation, is present in Tacitus. Because violent wars ensued after Julius Caesar's death, no one was at all sure how the transfer of power would work after Augustus' demise, or whether it would work at all. Would Rome revert to civil wars? Would a challenger to Tiberius appear? Would Tiberius' natural son, Drusus, and Tiberius' nephew, Germanicus (son of Tiberius' late brother, Drusus, and of Antonia, daughter of Marc Antony), tear the empire apart as they vied for power? Would Livia, a 'Ulysses in petticoats', rule imperiously through the men of the imperial house? And what of Tiberius?[42]

Now, despite his military and administrative reputation, there were profound misgivings and numerous strikes against Tiberius among wagging tongues in Rome. He was a member of the Claudian clan, a family as noted above, known for its inherent arrogance. There were the previously mentioned indications of cruelty in his nature. His reasons for going to Rhodes were inscrutable, but that was beside the point; he used his time there, it was said, to nurture his resentments, rehearse the dissimulation he would employ as emperor, and to keep his secret sexual vices as far from public view as possible.[43] Then there was the awkward end to Augustus' reign. Tiberius had been posted to Illyricum, and had only just set out when he received news that Augustus had become seriously ill.[44] Livia posted guards and sent out bulletins concerning the emperor's last illness as he lay on his deathbed at Nola, and may have continued to do so for some unspecified time – hours? A day or two? After Augustus had breathed his last; there was news now hopeful, now grave, until it was simultaneously announced that Augustus was dead and Tiberius in command of the state.[45]

Tiberius' Principate from AD 14–26

If Tacitus' introductory treatment of Tiberius' character is biting, his narrative about the beginning of his reign is no less harsh: *Primum facinus novi principatus*, 'The first crime of the new Principate', is how he introduces the first action Tiberius took upon succession.[46] This was the execution of Agrippa Postumus, Augustus' grandson with whom, Tacitus implies, Augustus had been reconciled shortly before his death; the reconciliation was in vain, since Livia, according to rumours, pulled off a treacherous end-run around the aged emperor and plotted with Tiberius for Agrippa Postumus' execution.[47] The reality is far more mystifying and complex: Did Tiberius fear him as a rival, as Tacitus states? Was it a matter of Livia's malice and ambition for her son? Or did Augustus want to eliminate a threat, and did he give the final command? Scholars still make careers and reputations untangling the murder of Agrippa Postumus.[48] Tiberius demanded an investigation into his death in the Senate but was admonished by an aged courtier, Sallustius Crispus: do not cripple the emperor's – i.e. your – power by referring matters to senatorial adjudication. It is here that we encounter a dynamic – one of several – that will contribute to the tragedy of Tiberius' reign.

The Senate and People of Rome, familiar to any viewer of cinematic Roman epics of the 1950s as SPQR on the legions' standards, was in no small part always a fiction. The Senate was a body that consisted of hundreds of men, sometimes as many as 900, but just a handful of illustrious and ancient families controlled the high magistracies and wielded the real power in Rome. Their names were famous: the Cornellii, the Claudii, the Junii, the Sempronii, the Julii, and others. Their liberties were seriously curtailed under the regime of Julius Caesar, who paid for it with his life. Augustus, as already noted, was more subtle, maintaining the façade of the republic and co-opting noble families with office and position. But he also kept the Senate on a tight rein. Tacitus sums up the situation succinctly:

> Absorbing the offices of the Senate, the magistrates, and the laws into his person, with no one to oppose him since the fiercest had fallen in battle or during the proscriptions, the rest of the nobles, the more each one was more ready for servitude – having been elevated

> by wealth and honours, and increased from the new state of affairs – preferring the safe and present status quo rather than the former and perilous state of affairs.[49]

The Senate had shown itself unfit to govern. Augustus exploited their unfitness, but did so in such a way that he was able to maintain the façade of republican rule due to his *civilitas*, a word that, because it is a cultural concept, defies simple word-for-word translation. Applied to an emperor it implies respect for the Senate, approachability, and at least the appearance of enjoyment in partaking in the simple pleasures of the people: dicing; participation in public festivals and rituals; and the enjoyment of games and spectacle. It was, in short, behaving like a citizen, and not a king, something to which Julius Caesar gave scant regard: Caesar was not only arrogant but enjoyed making a display of it. He was not interested in being a first among fellow citizens, as Augustus styled himself, and Shakespeare was not far off the mark when he referred to him as bestriding the world like a colossus.

Augustus was more politic, and a quick study when it came to avoiding Caesar's mistakes: as noted he was not called *dictator*, a good Latin word and an office during the republic reserved for state emergencies, but styled himself as *princeps*, a title of the republic given to the most prestigious member of the Senate, marking a man as a first among equals, but not their superior, and this quasi-formal title gave the name 'Principate' to the system he established. To that end he was studious in ensuring that he was viewed not as a king, but a fellow citizen: he lived in a relatively modest house on the Palatine; he wore simple garments such as homespun cloth and the traditional broad-rimmed travelling hat; he attempted to ensure his approachability and once even tweaked a fellow citizen who trembled in his presence stating he was behaving 'as if he were giving a peanut to an elephant'; he partook in the pleasures of the Roman people at games and festivals (not reading letters and conducting business during spectacles as his great-uncle Julius Caesar had done to the people's displeasure); he carried on a bantering correspondence with the poet Horace, affectionately referring to him occasionally with an obscene diminutive as *Penulus Meus*, 'My Little Dick'; and he was sure to emphasize his *pietas* – his sense of duty to his family, his state, and his gods. In his early career he was feared, even loathed. Yet, by the end of his life he was arguably loved. He and his *amici* – circle of friends – that formed the *princeps'* administration saw to the cultivation of arts, culture, and architecture; he beautified and restored Rome giving its populace gainful employment; and he established the boundaries of the Roman Empire and put in place a system, imperfect though it was, that was in the end to endure for hundreds of years.

How many, and who, would be able to follow such an act without their reputation and historical legacy tainted by a comparison? Indeed, Tacitus remarks that at Augustus' funeral tongues wagged that he had groomed Tiberius as his successor because he knew Tiberius was at heart arrogant and cruel, and sought to enhance his own reputation to posterity's hurt.[50] Whether that is true or not, the two could not have been more different in terms of their character. This is one of those instances where personality and temperament have a powerful impact on the subsequent narrative history of Tiberius' reign. He was now 56, old by pre-modern standards, and his personality was one of an introvert, more suited to study and the company of scholars (see pp. 16–17) than to courting publicly the goodwill of the people. Theatrical spectacles and gladiatorial contests were not to his tastes.

But there was a still more difficult problem for Tiberius. Augustus had kept the Senate on a tight rein, and, in addition, lived a very long time by ancient standards. He enjoyed sole rule for four and a half decades, outliving many of his contemporaries, and as a result the Senate – as noted – had fallen into the habit of deference towards him. Tiberius attempted to give the Senate greater autonomy, which left the ancient governing body, after years of deference to an autocrat, occasionally at sea as it attempted to guess Tiberius' wishes. According to Tacitus, the situation was further exacerbated by Tiberius' inscrutable personality and cryptic manner of speech, and taken as a whole created a very confusing situation for the Senate. The combination of keeping his cards close to his chest and his peculiar character traits were interpreted by Tacitus as reaffirming his ability to play a dissembling, hypocritical tyrant. More generously, we could interpret Tiberius' behaviour and policy as one of a tired old man who was dedicated to the Augustan vision of rule and empire but was less interested in being the one to govern it.

Another important contrast is that under Augustus an enormous amount of construction and restoration took place in Rome itself. In an age that lacked a social safety net, employment in construction was a welcome means by which citizens in Rome could obtain a somewhat steady income. To Augustus' credit, numerous structures were variously built, completed, or restored, including his own forum (the Forum of Augustus), as well as that of his adoptive father, Julius Caesar (the Forum of Caesar); the Temple of the Divine Julius Caesar and the Julian Basilica (the *Basilica Julii*), both located in the Roman Forum; the Theatre of Marcellus, the Temple of Apollo on the Palatine, and the Theatre of Balbus; these are by no means all the projects he undertook, famously boasting at the end of his reign that he had entered Rome a city of brick and left it one of marble. Tiberius, on the other hand, undertook substantially less construction activity, the build-up of the Palatine into an imperial palace that could house the budding bureaucracy and the Temple of the Divine Augustus standing as notable exceptions. Instead, as Augustus had also done on several occasions, he left it to the ancient families of the aristocracy to restore decrepit structures, and undertook little himself.

Rarely, even when trying to give the Senate greater freedom and autonomy, does Tiberius escape Tacitus' barbs. Hence, when in the ancient manner of the republic he used his power as tribune to convene the first senate meeting after Augustus' death (the sole purpose of which was the arrangement of Augustus' funeral), Tacitus sees Tiberius' action as little more than a sham and a fraud, hiding the tightening chains of autocracy behind the façade of republican governance.[51] In addition, he let the consuls take the initiative in swearing allegiance to him, as though there were still a free state. In the meantime, Tacitus continues, he already had in place the trappings of an imperial court: imperial bodyguards and escorts accompanied him everywhere; he sent letters to the armies and gave them their marching orders; he gave the watchword to the praetorian guard, Rome's police force. At the next senate meeting, soon after, he spoke about the burdens of empire:[52] Augustus was up to sole rule and, because Augustus had assumed him as partner in that rule, he was aware how difficult and perilous the role of emperor was. There were more than enough distinguished men, he remarked, so that the state ought not to concentrate power in a single individual. The senators protested. Tiberius waivered according to Tacitus and demurred that while he did not consider himself capable of shouldering alone the onerous burden of government, he would undertake the tutelage of whatever part of state governance they would entrust to him.

It was at this juncture than an impolitic senator, Asinius Gallus, posed the embarrassing question, *'Caesar, quam partem rei publicae mandari tibi velis?'* – 'Caesar, what part of the state do you wish to be entrusted to you?' It was a fly on the wall moment, shutting Tiberius down into silence for a few minutes before he could collect his thoughts and at last reply that, though he preferred to be excused from such a burden on the whole, he was too diffident to refuse or to choose any one part. Gallus guessed his offence and sought to make amends, but Tacitus says that his words struck Tiberius deep and from then on he nurtured an animus against him – and that it did not help that Gallus had, as previously mentioned, married Tiberius' ex-wife Vipsania whom he had so loved and been forced to divorce.

There were other similar instances of flattery and men provoking Tiberius' resentment at the opening of his reign, as, for example, when Quintus Haterius, a man of consular standing, made a call to the imperial palace and threw himself at Tiberius' knees while trying to beg forgiveness for an impertinent question during the first senate meeting. Tiberius literally fell over Haterius as he either grovelled at Tiberius' feet or embraced his knees, and Haterius was very nearly killed by the imperial guards.[53] As the first meeting concluded, the charade played out to its conclusion, in which Tiberius, supposedly exhausted by senatorial entreaties to take up the burdens of empire, did not accept power but did cease to refuse it. The senators were likely equally exhausted by the charade, since one reportedly shouted out, 'Oh let him take it or leave it!'[54] Despite Tacitus' presentation, the demurring demeanour of Tiberius and the fraught nature of the days after Augustus, rather than Tiberian hypocrisy, are as likely indicative of what was simply a volatile and uncertain situation. The death of Rome's last autocrat, Julius Caesar, saw the empire devolve into nearly fifteen years of political instability and civil war, and power had been up for armed grabs since at least the time of the aristocratic Sulla, who marched on Rome and took temporary control of the state in 88 BC. In the late summer and early autumn of AD 14 no one could tell what might happen, though there was likely a good reason Augustus had always put in the hands of family members, close friends, and associates, Rome's most powerful armies.

Several of the major events of Tiberius' reign comprise the subject of other chapters in the present work, including the trial of M. Scribonius Libo Drusus in AD 16, the death of his nephew Germanicus in 19, his fraught interaction with Germanicus' widow, Agrippina the Elder, and her family that followed in the 20s, and the rise and fall of his praetorian prefect, Sejanus. Some of the other significant events early in his reign include mutinies among the armies of the Rhine and in Pannonia upon Augustus' death, mutinies that were successfully checked with the help of Germanicus and Tiberius' son, Drusus. Between AD 15 and 16 Germanicus led a not entirely successful punitive expedition against Arminius, leader of the ambush in the Teutoberg Forest some seven years previously.[55] In the same year as Libo's trial and execution, an imposter claiming to be Agrippa Postumus led an incipient rebellion against Tiberius but was quickly intercepted and quietly dispatched.[56] In the next year, AD 17, a North African rebel, Tacfarinas, started a long guerrilla war that was protracted until the year AD 24, when he at last died gallantly, throwing himself into a thicket of Roman lances.[57] In the interim there was a brief rebellion in Gaul led by two men, Julius Florus and Julius Sacrovir; it was quickly suppressed and the two rebels executed.[58]

Tiberius' Retirement to Capri

This was followed in 26 by two noteworthy events: a well-known historian, Cremutius Cordus, was tried and his works were ordered destroyed when he praised Brutus and Cassius, Julius Caesar's lead assassins, as 'The Last of the Romans'.[59] Cordus did not wait around for a verdict but decided to die by starving himself to death. Then, in that same year, Tiberius went again into a form of self-imposed exile, this time not to Rhodes, but to the island of Capri off the Sorrentine Peninsula on the southern end of the Bay of Naples. On his way, he experienced a near-fatal accident: stopping at his villa at Sperlonga (called *Spelunca* or simply 'The Cave' in Latin) on the coast, he was almost killed by a rock fall.[60] Sperlonga today is a popular seaside town halfway between Rome and Naples on the coast, several miles north of Formia (ancient Formiae), where in December of 43 BC the great Roman orator Cicero bared his neck to a centurion's sword and bravely met his end. On the rocky south portion of the beach at Sperlonga is a grotto that is protected just enough to form

Fig. 2.3: Remains of Tiberius' villa at Sperlonga with a view of the grotto that served as a dining room. (*Carole Raddato via Wikimedia Commons*)

a lovely pool at high tide. An imperial villa was built on the site, whose remains are readily visible today (see fig. 2.3), and the grotto itself, we know, served as a magnificently apportioned dining room (or *triclinium* in Latin), and the remains of the sculptures that adorned the dining room are now in the local museum on the site.[61] Indeed, the sculptures serve as yet another testament to Tiberius' profound love of Greek culture, and their subject is the hero Odysseus.[62] The smallest of the sculptures includes Odysseus stealing the Palladium (a talismanic statue of Athena that protected the Trojans) from Troy with the Greek hero Diomedes assisting him (fig. 2.4).

Fig. 2.4: The theft of the Palladium by Odysseus and Diomedes that adorned Tiberius' villa at Sperlonga. (Carole Raddato via *Wikimedia Commons*)

The centrepiece is a riotous, dynamic, swirling mass of sculpture depicting Odysseus and his men on their ship under attack from the multi-headed Scylla (fig. 2.5). Equally imposing – and perhaps the most impressive of all – is a monstrous sculpture of the Cyclops, Polyphemus, sprawling in a wine-soaked stupor as Odysseus and his men (in a series of life-sized statues) are about to blind him (fig. 2.6). The group takes on the added irony in a life-imitates-art sort of way, since Odysseus had been trapped in the Cyclops' cave with his men, a fate Tiberius nearly shared in reality. Finally, there was a sculpture of Odysseus bearing the body of the slain Achilles from the field of battle.

Such décor will have been much to Tiberius' taste. As well as being a lover of Greek language, literature, and philosophy, Tiberius was also a lover of Greek art. Indeed, Tiberius' fondness for Greek art at one time landed him in a spot of trouble with the Roman people: in an impolitic and inept move, he removed a statue that was a favourite of the people with the tongue-twisting name, the *Apoxyomenos*, or 'Athlete scraping himself with a strigil', from the Baths of Agrippa (located in Rome's Campus Martius) for his own personal collection (see fig. 2.7). It was a work of the

Fig. 2.5: A sculpture group of the monster Scylla attacking Odysseus and his men from Tiberius' villa at Sperlonga. (*Carole Raddato via Wikimedia Commons*)

Fig. 2.6: A cast reconstruction of the Blinding of Polyphemus from Tiberius' villa at Sperlonga. (Carole Raddato via *Wikimedia Commons*)

renowned fourth-century BC artist Lysippus, the only sculptor Alexander the Great allowed to execute his portrait in marble. It was also, unfortunately, a favourite of the people, and when they protested in the theatre publicly he was forced to restore it to its original venue.[63] In addition, under Augustus he had been in charge of the refurbishment of the Temple of Concord in the Roman Forum near the senate house.[64] The temple was originally built in the third century BC, restored in the late second, and now, over a century later, was due for modifications and repair; included in Tiberius' restoration of the temple now were

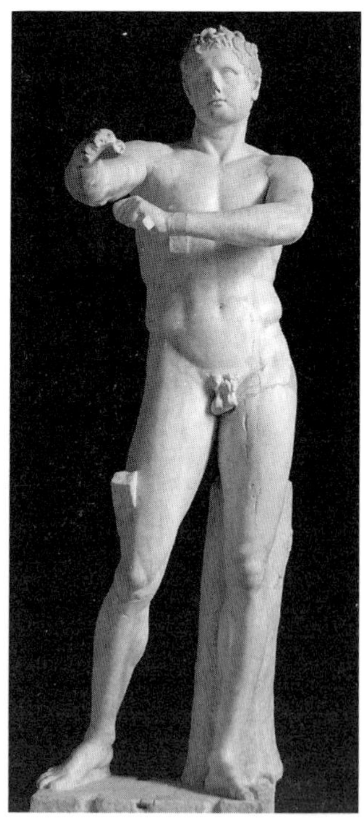

Fig. 2.7: The *Apoxyomenos*, a Roman marble copy of a bronze original by Lysippos, and a favorite statue of both Tiberius and the Roman people. (Marie-Lan Nguyen via *Wikimedia Commons*)

Fig. 2.8: A bronze *sesterces* coin depicting the Temple of Concord and its elaborate statuary; the entrance is flanked by statues of Hercules and Mercury; the pediment is decorated with statues of Jupiter, Juno, Minerva, and Victories; the wings of the temple served as art galleries. (Hermann Junghans, Own work, via *Wikimedia Commons*)

two wings, annexes that were to display masterpieces of Greek sculpture and painting (see fig. 2.8). It was, apart from Augustus' temple, Tiberius' one significant contribution to the cultural life of the city, and he likely oversaw the assembly of its collection.

It was from this city that Tiberius left in 26 (the same year Pilate arrived at his post in Judaea) and to which he never returned again – not for the funeral of his mother, Livia Augusta, who died in AD 29; not in the aftermath of Sejanus' fall from grace; not to announce his ultimate successor, Caligula.[65] His decision to reside on the central Italian coast was not an unusual or peculiar choice (except for its permanence) for a wealthy or elite Roman. Long since, even during the republic, the Bay of Naples had become the vacation play spot of rich and prominent grandees. Cicero, Lucullus, Caesar's father-in-law Calpurnius Piso, all were known to have estates or sumptuous and luxuriously apportioned villas in the region known as Campania, with its beautiful shoreline and coast particularly favoured. By Tiberius' day the Bay of Naples and its islands were dotted with spectacular rambling villas often centred on pleasure gardens or massive swimming pools or fish ponds, richly adorned with mosaics, fountains, paintings, and sculpture. Today one can get a good idea of their appearance thanks to the catastrophic eruption of Vesuvius in AD 79 which buried the towns of Pompeii and Herculaneum, whose remains still impress; also preserved in the eruption were grand villas such as the so-called Villa of the Mysteries in Pompeii, the villas at Boscoreale and Oplontis (which may have been owned by the family of Poppaea Sabina, later known to the world as the emperor Nero's mistress, then wife), and the so-called Villa of the Papyri at Herculaneum, now reproduced as a full-scale replica at the Getty Museum near Malibu, California (see fig. 2.9). Frescoes painted on the walls of some of the townhouses and villas in this region also occasionally depict such seaside villas as they would have appeared in Tiberius' day.

In addition, at Stabiae on the southern end of the Bay of Naples are a series of magnificent villas that dot the shoreline. Indeed, it was so built-up that some ancient authors lamented the environmental impact, remarking that the shore had become one vast line of ostentatious construction. It is on that very shoreline that the great Roman polymath, Pliny the Elder, met his end as he tried to rescue some friends from Vesuvius' destructive swath; his cavalier attitude about the danger Vesuvius presented led to his own ultimate demise, probably by asphyxiation, on Stabiae's beach.

Fig. 2.9: The Getty Villa in Pacific Palisades, California, is in fact a reconstruction after a villa at Herculaneum, the so-called Villa of the Papyri, which belonged to one of Rome's movers and shakers. (Bobak Ha'Eri via *Wikimedia Commons*)

Although the Romans were fully aware of the exhalations of sulfur and the dangerous pits of boiling mud and springs from what they called the Flegreian Fields, believed the nearby Lake Avernus noxious, and even believed the region to harbour one of the entrances to the underworld, few in Tiberius' day were aware that Vesuvius, given its lengthy dormancy, was a dangerous volcano. The region was also a richly diverse place culturally: originally occupied by Italic peoples known as the Samnites who spoke a language known as Oscan, it was heavily colonized from an early date by Greeks. In fact, Ischia (ancient Pithekoussai), an island on the northern end of the Bay of Naples, has yielded the very first real Greek anywhere, with an artefact that is known as the Ischia Cup or the Cup of Nestor, with our very first instance of what we can recognize as genuine classical Greek written in the Greek alphabet and dating to the early eighth century BC. The writing states simply, 'I am the cup of Nestor, good for drinking. Who drinks from me straightaway desire of golden-crowned Aphrodite will seize.'

Wandering through the ancient homes, villas, apartment buildings, shops, baths, and brothels today, one finds copious graffiti not just in Latin, but in Oscan and Greek as well. When an emperor came to the region and attended the theatre, he could expect in venues such as Naples that the performance would be in Greek. Today the Bay of Naples is sprawling, over-populated, polluted, and beset with all manner of social and environmental challenges, including Mafiosi whose story is related vividly in Roberto Saviano's *Gomorrah*.[66] For all its challenges, however, the area still remains a beautiful region, where gardens pop up in the most unlikely spots along the metro line known as the *Circumvesuviana* that rings the region, with numerous delicious wines produced on the slopes of Vesuvius such as *Lacrymae Christi* (Tears of Christ), whose Sorrentine Peninsula produces *Gragnano di Surrento*, a lovely lightly fizzy (*frizzante* in Italian) red; whose bay yields still excellent seafood – also celebrated in numerous ancient mosaics and still-life paintings; and whose herds of cattle are milked to make outstanding mozzarella.

Tiberius chose as his specific place for retirement the island of Capri, which had been purchased by Augustus and had long since become imperial property and built up with several imperial villas; the best known of these today is at the top of the island's second highest peak, the so-called *Villa Jovis*, or Villa of Jupiter (see figs. 2.10 and 2.11).[67] Nearby is Tiberius'

Leap, a precipitous cliff from which hapless victims of the emperor's wrath were cast some 334 metres into the craggy and rocky sea below. It was up this side of the island that one day a fisherman clambered up to present Tiberius with some of his catch, including a giant mullet. Alarmed at this perceived security breach, he had the fish rubbed in the man's face.[68] When the fisherman remarked that he was glad he had not presented the emperor with the crab he had caught, he had the man's face ripped to shreds with it. By way of contrast we might note that while Jesus began to build his church on the rock of the fisherman Peter, Tiberius was more inclined to toss fishermen from his rock atop Capri. As for the imperial villa itself, built on Capri's northern peak, it spans over one and a half acres and its eight levels cover some 40 metres in elevation.[69] The walk up to it is one of hairpin turns on steep, narrow cobbled streets in which one passes beautiful houses rich in splendid Mediterranean flora, including bougainvillea, citrus, and all manner of flowers and succulent plants.

The reasons for his retirement will ultimately defy our grasp: Suetonius states he let affairs of state slide after his retirement to Campania, and he gives the impression of one disinterested in ruling. Tacitus presents several theories, almost all sinister: he attributes Tiberius' withdrawal in part,

Fig. 2.10: The remains of Tiberius' villa on Capri. (Izoe Kriv via *Wikimedia Commons*)

Fig. 2.11: The view from Tiberius' villa on Capri looking south towards the southern end of the island known as Anacapri. (Mister No via *Wikimedia Commons*)

following, he states, the consensus of other historians, to the machinations of his sinister praetorian prefect, Lucius Aelius Sejanus (see Chapter 3, p. 50); but, he adds, Tiberius stayed in retirement six years after Sejanus' demise – likely, he conjectures, to hide his cruelty and immoral passions. Tacitus also offers a third possibility: now thin, bent, balding, and his face covered in sores, he wanted to hide his appearance from the public.[70] Tacitus also presents two other alternatives: he had grown accustomed on Rhodes to seclusion and never appeared particularly sociable; add to that that he supposedly could no longer endure his imperious mother, Livia, and was desperate to escape her influence.[71] Whatever the reason or possible combination of motives, Tiberius' impetus for self-imposed exile once again eludes historical explanation, and has had a deleterious effect on his subsequent reputation.

His reclusiveness merely exacerbated the talk and gossip over his behaviour, and it is hard to ascertain the truth of any of the accusations: his propensity towards hard drinking was already derided early in his career with the moniker 'Biberius Caldius Mero' (instead of Tiberius

Claudius Nero) which means 'an imbiber of heated neat wine', and that he was attended on Capri by drinking companions did not help – one of them was reported to have earned the office of quaestor by winning a drinking contest.[72] Tiberius thereby joined the ranks of famous imbibers from the ancient world such as Alexander the Great and Marc Antony, who reportedly performed his duties as consul hungover and wrote a treatise about his alcoholism titled *De ebrietate sua*, or *On His Drunkenness*. But this was not Tiberius' only vice according to our sources, which also allege assorted sexual perversions.[73] He was reported to have ordered the empire searched for attractive young girls to perform group sex in his presence; he collected erotica, including some notorious pornographic manuscripts from Elephantis in Egypt; he had a painting in his bedroom by Parrhasius (who Pliny the Elder credits with the invention of still-life) depicting the Greek mythological heroine Atalanta performing an obscene act on the hero Meleager; he had young boys and girls dress as Pans and nymphs and prostitute themselves in his pleasure gardens; and most obscene of all, had small children he called his *pisculi* (little fishes) perform oral sex on him while swimming. By modern standards he would have doubtless been charged with sexual assault, if not rape, as the case of Mallonia, a high-born woman, illustrates: she was summoned to his bed, was compelled to horrific acts, and then persecuted for her resistance until she could no longer emotionally endure it and took her own life – not without denouncing him as a 'filthy mouthed, stinking, hairy old man'. If that were not enough, the name Capri literally means Goat Island; the animal was known in antiquity for its insatiable sexual appetite most notably embodied in the mythical satyr. Connections between Tiberius, the 'caprine' moniker of his place of seclusion, and his salacious sexual activities were made in a joke at his expense at a theatrical performance and went the rounds: 'The old goat goes for the does with his tongue.'

Tacitus is equally critical, except his account is far more restrained. Suetonius on the other hand unflinchingly reports at times an 'anatomically correct' autopsy on the sex lives and proclivities of Roman emperors. But Tacitus is quite clear when he speaks of Tiberius' immorality that he was guilty of the same sort of behaviour described by Suetonius, and tells us that in his final years following Sejanus' demise (AD 31–37) he gave his passions full rein, ordering that attractive children of noble families be sent to him for deflowering, and creating new names for exotic sexual acts.[74] How much of this we should choose to believe is problematic. Sexual depravity is often a stock accusation in classical literature against ancient figures deemed tyrannical, and we find all manner of salacious and titillating accusations spread throughout our ancient sources, such as the Greek historian Herodotus and Roman historians such as Sallust and Livy. Yet that the present book is being written in a time when numerous men in public life, some loathed, some once revered, have been exposed as less than enlightened in their attitudes towards women and sexuality, we should by no means dismiss out of hand stories of powerful men abusing their positions to seek sexual gratification.

However, while the whole matter is horribly complicated by the nature of our ancient historical sources, they at least give us a window into the sort of rumours, with or without foundation, which circulated concerning the emperor and collectively serve to give us 'a people's history', as it were, of Tiberius' reign. In addition, we should be clear to qualify that ancient sexual attitudes were no less complex than they can be in any given society at any time. For elite Romans what will have been shocking is his treatment of those of his own class. Roman law was quite clear in its regulation of behaviour that was thoroughly grounded in class and status. Hence, for example, men of high status were by law to divorce their wives within a stated time if their wives were found to have committed adultery, and same sex practices were regulated such that men of high status were in theory not to play the passive partner, although they could be the active partner, with those of lower status. We also must remember that slaves were treated as sexual chattel in their own right, with no legal claim whatsoever to maintain their person as inviolate.

Tiberius' Final Years (and Rather Absurd End)

Tiberius spent the years between AD 26 and 37, the end of his life, dividing his time between Capri and the mainland. The course of the first five of those years, during which Sejanus persecuted the family of Agrippina before Sejanus himself finally succumbed to his own ambitions, is the subject of Chapter 3. Doubtless these years were very bitter for Tiberius. By the end of 31 his trust in those around him, given his experience with Sejanus, must have been slim, and most of his family and many friends had succumbed variously to illness, death, and persecution. Finally, circumstances compelled him to look to Agrippina's sole remaining son, his great-nephew Gaius – i.e., Caligula – as heir, and a surviving grandson, named Gemellus, who was to live only briefly into Caligula's reign before Caligula had him executed as a rival. In the course of his reign, Tacitus states, the restraints on Tiberius were gradually removed: the first of these he asserts, was Germanicus who had died under suspicious circumstances in AD 19; the second of these was his son Drusus who died in AD 23; so long as his mother, Livia, was alive, Tacitus says the reins were still in place, but she died in AD 29; his cruelty metastasized as he came under the influence of Sejanus, but Tacitus asserts that his more grotesque behaviour still remained hidden from view; after Sejanus' demise in AD 31, states Tacitus, he gave full force to his own depraved nature.[75]

It is soon after AD 31 that we hear the apocryphal and likely fictional story from Tertullian and Eusebius that Pilate wrote to Tiberius concerning Christ's godhead.[76] Tiberius, Eusebius reports, showed indifference to Pilate's missive, and referred the matter to the Senate, but Eusebius' characterization of Tiberius as apathetic is unconvincing. He in fact took stern measures against foreign religious practices and communities, going so far as to expel the Jews from Rome when members of their community were involved in an embezzling scandal with a noble Roman woman in AD 19; 4,000 men of the community were sent to Sardinia for military service.[77] This should not necessarily be taken as anti-Semitism on Tiberius' part, since elsewhere Philo is complimentary of Tiberius' relationship with the Jewish community, but something more in the nature of a criminal matter.[78] In the same year, Tiberius expelled followers of the Greco-Egyptian cult of Isis from Rome, destroyed their temple, had three of Isis' priests crucified, and had Isis' statue cast into the Tiber after a cult member sexually violated a Roman noblewoman through deception.[79] But the Romans scarcely needed scandal to take action against different (or in their view, deviant) religions: while they might have been receptive and inclusive of other religious traditions, there were certain qualifications and conditions under which cults such as that of Bacchus, Mithras, Isis, or the Magna Mater (Great Mother) would be tolerated, though Roman involvement was at times regulated and scrutinized depending on the cult. Tacitus, for one, dismissed Judaism out of hand as a mere *superstitio*, mirroring his attitude towards Christianity.[80]

The Jews Tiberius expelled would doubtless have been sympathetic to Tacitus' portrait of Tiberius in the introduction to his *Annals*, cited at this chapter's opening. Taken as a whole, however, Tiberius was far more complex in the final analysis than Tacitus and our other sources allowed. In weighing the scales of how Tiberius performed as emperor the sources, their frequent hostility notwithstanding, are often surprisingly generous. Suetonius, for example, tells us that he did not interfere with the workings of the magistrates, public business, or law, and generally preferred that reports of governors not be referred to him but instead to the Senate.[81] He also expresses admiration for Tiberius' respect for Roman law, and how in general he tried to regulate Roman mores through a variety of social and sumptuary legislation.[82] Even peeling back Tacitus' dislike, it seems evident that Tiberius, though at times inept and impolitic, tried to ensure that the provinces were well governed, and that boundaries were at times placed on senators who, through their desire to curry imperial favour, were themselves eager to tighten the bonds that would impose imperial tyranny. Moreover, as Suetonius notes, Tiberius was generally dismissive of verbal assaults and lampoons against his character, though not entirely.[83] Tiberius' sheer survival and accomplishment is not to be underestimated: it was he who, despite his occasional political ineptitude and problematic personality, helped to solidify and consolidate the system that Augustus had put into place, and established the precedent of a successful succession in which he managed to hold power. He, furthermore, built on Augustan precedent and institutions such as the imperial cult, allowing us as his reign proceeds to use terms such as 'succession', 'throne', and 'imperial house' with perhaps some greater degree of comfort than was the case for discussing what was to come after Augustus, despite the fact that the Romans never entirely worked out a coherent basis on which to choose an emperor. It was under Tiberius, after all, that an imperial palace on the Palatine was constructed, a vast rambling complex to house the burgeoning bureaucracy, and an indication that the rule of the state by an emperor was perhaps not going anywhere anytime soon.

As an epilogue in approaching this chapter's close, by AD 32 Tiberius, according to Tacitus, appears to have become a textbook example of the tormented tyrant, of a man whose soul was tortured and corrupted by power – the very embodiment of Lord Acton's admonition. In that year, Tiberius wrote to the Senate an anguished letter that Tacitus cites possibly verbatim: 'If I knew what I might write to you, Conscript Fathers, or how I might write it, or what I might not write at all at this time, may the gods and goddesses consign me to perdition as I feel myself daily to perish.'[84] Of this Tacitus wrote:

> To such an extent had his own crimes and disgraces turned back on himself as a punishment. Not in vain was he, who was most renowned for his wisdom, wont to affirm that, if the minds of tyrants could be opened up, it would be possible to see lacerations and blows since, as the body is torn apart by thrashing, so is the spirit lacerated by cruelty, lust, and evil counsels.

On this Tacitus further comments, 'Clearly neither fortune nor solitude protected Tiberius from confessing the torture he himself felt inside his heart and admitting his own punishment.'[85] The letter – one of the few instances of verbatim citation in his historical works – and Tacitus' remarks are the essence of tragedy. Tiberius, a capable and in some ways brilliant individual, was reduced in the end by bad judgement, ambitious and flattering courtiers and senators, and his own tragically incongruent (some might say flawed) personality, to an excruciating moment of self-reflection. He was to linger another five years until the spring of 37. During that period, he wrote a brief set of memoirs about his life, defending his conduct as emperor, in particular his persecution of Germanicus' family, in which he transferred the blame for their treatment and ultimate demise on Sejanus, but these are regrettably lost.[86]

His life was to end on a painfully farcical note, according to our sources. Throughout the late winter of 37 his health appeared to be failing. Q. Sertorius Macro, Sejanus' successor as praetorian prefect, was with Tiberius as his health deteriorated; so, too, was Tiberius' great-nephew, Gaius Caligula. As the emperor declined things were set in order for the succession. Then, on 16 March AD 37, he was pronounced dead. He died at Misenum on the northern edge of the Bay of Naples in a grand villa with a history of illustrious owners, including the great republican general Gaius Marius (who was once married to Julius Caesar's paternal aunt), and the Roman gourmand and Sybarite, L. Lucullus; long after Tiberius' reign, in the final days of the western Roman Empire, it was the place of retirement assigned by the barbarian prince Odoacer for Romulus Augustus, the last and finally deposed emperor of the Roman West.

The scene of Tiberius' death is darkly humorous, his end coming with a mordancy that Tiberius would probably have appreciated:[87] as soon as Tiberius was pronounced dead Caligula was surrounded by a group of well-wishers cheering and congratulating him. Then a messenger suddenly interrupted the jubilant crowd and new emperor: it was a fainting fit. Tiberius, his voice and sight recovered, was very much alive and asking for something to eat. Fear and confusion spread over the crowd about how to react – no one could decide whether they should show joy at his recovery or feign ignorance to hedge their bets, and some simply left the scene altogether. Caligula, however, was stunned into silence, but as our sources report it, the praetorian prefect, Sertorius Macro, kept a clear head, went into the imperial bedchamber, and smothered Tiberius under a pile of bedclothes. He was 78 years old. A man of excellent military talent, a capable administrator, variously brooding, morose, introverted, learned, cruel, and tragic, thus ended the life of Rome's second emperor, who appointed the governor under whom Jesus was crucified, and who was the man on the coin.

Chapter 3

The Praetorian Prefect: Lucius Aelius Sejanus

In retrospect, New Year's Day of 31 had not started off well for Tiberius' praetorian prefect, Lucius Aelius Sejanus, despite the celebratory occasion of entering the consulship, an office that during the republic had been Rome's highest elective office, but was now bestowed as an honor by the grace of the *princeps*.[1] A reception couch had collapsed under the weight of attendees sitting in wait to greet the prefect.[2] As he left his house that morning, a weasel ran through the crowd's midst, doubtless exciting observers. Passing by Rome's state prison after a sacrifice on Rome's Capitoline, some of his servants slipped and fell down the stairs where the bodies of executed criminals were cast. Later that day, while taking the auspices, no birds of good omen were to be seen; instead there was a flock of crows that continuously cawed before perching on the prison. Such ill omens initially received little notice on this first celebratory day of January, the traditional day on which the consul entered his office. An astute and ambitious minister, Tiberius had depended on the prefect's counsels for well over a decade and probably longer, honouring him with the title *socius laborum*, 'partner of my labours'.[3] Now he was to be rewarded greatly for his long service to Tiberius. On a cold January morning in Rome, few could foresee the coming catastrophe that was to envelope the prefect ten months later, in October, or the horror to follow. Sejanus had risen to dizzying heights, although his ruin was as harrowing and gruesome as his rise was electric. Such is the depiction by our sources: an outsider who had climbed his way to the top, who enters history from the shadows, unctuously worms his way into the graces of the emperor, seducing his way into the bed of an imperial princess, dismissed by Tacitus as a *municipalis adulter* ('a small-town adulterer') who impugns through the clever and timely deployment of insinuation and rumour Sejanus' rank and worth. In fact, as Edward Champlin has argued, Sejanus was likely very much an insider; one who knew, through his connections, experience, and position, how to work the system, making him by degrees perhaps even more dangerous than the ancient record portrays him.[4]

He first enters history's stage in our sources in AD 14: the emperor Tiberius, according to the rumours reported in Tacitus and other writers as well, disliked and mistrusted Germanicus, his nephew whom Augustus ordered in his will be adopted as Tiberius' son, likely as insurance for the continuation of his line. Sejanus accompanied Germanicus in his mission to assuage the mutinies on the Rhine that had broken out in the wake of Augustus' death, and must have shown himself quite competent in that capacity.[5] He may have had ample experience on the Rhine and in Germania, since he was said to be a friend of Nero Claudius Drusus, Tiberius' brother, who operated there between 14 and 9 BC.[6] In AD 15, Sejanus was back in Rome where he was promoted to his father's position of praetorian prefect, a position created in 2 BC that had grown out of Augustus' personal bodyguard and eventually developed into a large force whose numbers varied, but in Augustus' day was close in size to a legion – around 5,000 men.[7] It was now – according to Tacitus – that, ever the skilled manipulator, Sejanus started to play on Tiberius' envy and jealousy of the popular Germanicus and his family, laying the foundations for an animus which Sejanus was to exacerbate in the coming years.[8] After his father, L. Seius Strabo, was made prefect of Egypt in AD 20, Sejanus succeeded to his father's post as praetorian prefect.[9]

The post had no ancient tradition in Rome; it was new. Difficult as it is for the modern world to comprehend, there was little in the way of an organized police force to maintain public order in Rome prior to the emperors. The disorders of the late republic had demonstrated the need for one, and Augustus recruited and distributed guards in the various districts (he had divided the city into fourteen *regiones*) throughout the city. Now Sejanus moved to convince Tiberius to consolidate the dispersed guards into one large camp, the remains of which are still visible today on Rome's metro on the blue line stop *Castro Pretorio* (the Praetorian Camp).[10] At the same time, Tiberius elevated him to the rank of praetor (an annually elected judicial official), an office whose numbers had varied over the course of Rome's history and now stood at nine in any given year.[11] It was one of the higher magistracies to which a Roman could aspire, and from whose ranks (along with former consuls) governors were selected for Rome's provinces.

Tacitus portrays Sejanus' plan in uniting the guard into a single camp as invidious. His ostensible and purported purpose in undertaking this was to have a large force united in one location in case of emergency; military men scattered throughout the city could become unruly.[12] Discipline would improve, he argued to Tiberius, if they were in a more distant location from the city's enticements. Once in place, he visited the camp often, ensuring that the guards were loyal to him, learning the names of his men, and greeting them personally. To shore up senatorial support he used his position and increased authority to hold out favours to senators as well, winning their loyalty by bestowing offices and provincial commands.[13]

Our sources can lead us to believe that this was quite an accomplishment in the Roman political order for a man of almost (as depicted) no background, whose father was of equestrian status (i.e., wealthy enough to achieve the rank of knight), and not from Rome but from one of Italy's municipalities, Volsinii, near modern Bolsena.[14] In fact Sejanus, as has been well argued, rather than a man of no background was instead one with deep connections to Rome's senate and aristocracy; not the sort of bluff military man as we might be led to believe, but a supremely competent if ambitious administrator, and likely too a sophisticated man of letters, who may have been a patron of Rome's literary circle under Tiberius, and who probably shared in the literary and philosophical discussions at Tiberius' table on Capri.[15] Sejanus, however, appears to have been by any measure ambitious, and it was this ambition that our sources seize upon to paint the portrait of an ascending and energetic villain. Tacitus' introduction of Sejanus encapsulates this, via his brief character sketch which borders on caricature, and is as unforgettable and powerful as it is brief:

> *corpus illi laborum tolerans, animus audax; sui obtegens, in alios criminator; iuxta adulatio et superbia; palam compositus pudor, intus summa apiscendi libido, eiusque causa modo largitio et luxus, saepius industria ac vigilantia, haud minus noxiae, quotiens parando regno finguntur.*

His person was used to endurance, his mind daring; protective of himself, he was an accuser of others; flattery of his betters and

> arrogance against inferiors stood juxtaposed; he pretended modesty, while within was a desire of obtaining the highest position, and for the sake of achieving this he at times bestowed largesse and the accoutrements of luxury, but more often used industry and vigilance, qualities no less harmful than beneficial when used as a pretext for obtaining a crown.[16]

Latin itself is already a more abstract language than English, and certainly much more compact and succinct, and here we get a use of linguistic compression that powerfully outlines Sejanus' personality. We feel we know the type, and we are already uncomfortable in his presence. In fact, Roman readers would recognize him as a stock villain, since the language is very reminiscent of the historian Livy's description of Hannibal, the Carthaginian general who between 218 and 205 BC ravaged Roman Italy, and of the historian Sallust's, of Catiline, a dissolute aristocrat who attempted a coup against the state in 63 BC and whose machinations M. Tullius Cicero, the noted statesman, orator, and philosopher of the late republic, ruthlessly checked when consul.[17] In that sense he appears in our sources as a two-dimensional character, although the reality was far more complex. He was a man well placed, lettered and cultured, who like others, including Augustus himself and Pompey the Great, Caesar's great rival, held the consulship without being of senatorial status. He was also a *novus homo* or 'new man', that is, the first in his family to hold the consulship, as were Cicero and Cato the Elder before him. Finally, as was the case with Maecenas or Agrippa under Augustus, Sejanus would come to hold a powerful position next to the *princeps*, standing as a potential successor as well as a patron of great men of letters, and like them have his own share of scandals.[18] Nothing about Sejanus in any of this was entirely unprecedented, as nearly as we can detect.

Sleeping His Way to the Top

After Sejanus secured the unification of the guard, he proceeded to seduce Livilla, Tiberius' niece and the wife of his son, Drusus, and started a rather lengthy affair with her; the two allegedly nurtured the highest ambition.[19] Livilla (full name Claudia Livia Julia) was reportedly an unattractive child, but had grown to become one of the most beautiful women of her day. She had already been married twice: the first marriage was to a grandson of Augustus', Gaius Caesar, the son of Julia, the emperor Augustus' daughter, and of M. Vipsanius Agrippa, Augustus' close friend and advisor. That marriage lasted from 1 BC–AD 4 when Gaius died in the East.[20] It is quite possible that she met Sejanus during her marriage to Gaius, since Sejanus was one of those among Gaius' retinue when he was appointed to his command.[21] After Gaius' death she married Tiberius' son, Drusus, and by him had three children, Julia Livia, born around AD 7, and in 19 twin boys, Germanicus Gemellus (which means 'twin' in Latin) and Tiberius Gemellus; it is possible that Sejanus was in fact their father.[22] After she started her affair with Sejanus, she reportedly became intoxicated with the notion of joint rule with this charismatic individual, and charismatic he must have been, since he reportedly seduced numerous women of the high nobility in order to collect intelligence and maintain a close network of spies, a move that was by no means unusual. Cicero, in Caesar's day, maintained a similar network through different means in order to gain intelligence on Catiline, but Sejanus, unlike the more restrained Cicero, combined business with pleasure.[23] Indeed, rumour had it that Sejanus had climbed the first rung of the imperial ladder by prostituting himself to Apicius, a wealthy, Sybaritic, and dissolute grandee.[24] Tacitus expresses his utter disgust that she would befoul her noble lineage by climbing into the bed of a 'small-town adulterer' and caustically notes for good measure like the good Roman misogynist he was that 'a woman, once a sense of shame is lost, refuses nothing.'[25] Yet this was nothing unusual if we can believe Suetonius, who noted that Augustus was given to frequent adultery, which was excused on the grounds that he committed it not out of lust but in the interest of what we might readily call 'intelligence gathering'.[26] Nor was the close liaison, even marriage of a man of equestrian status to a member of the ruling family peculiar, given that Augustus had married his daughter, Julia, to his close friend and advisor Marcus Agrippa, who was of the equestrian class.

In AD 23, Tacitus alleges that the diabolical couple plotted – and brought about – the death of Drusus by poison. In Tacitus' view, individuals lurked in the dark corners of the empire who could be suborned for anything.[27] Lygdus, in this case Drusus' alleged poisoner and a noted eunuch, was just one of the parade of names we find in Tacitus who were supposedly specialists at this game. Others include Locusta who was later thought to have been involved in the poisoning of Claudius (his personal physician, Xenephon, and a court eunuch, Halotus, were allegedly involved as well), and Martina, who had already appeared on the pages of Tacitus and been suspected in the death of Drusus' cousin and Livilla's brother, Germanicus, in AD 19.[28] There is often reason to doubt such stories: Claudius, for example, was old, had always been infirm, and was almost certainly an alcoholic. A death in the night after wine and a heavy meal, such as happened with Claudius, could become embellished via court gossip, hence the story of death by a mushroom poisoned in a court conspiracy. The charges of poisoning in the death of Germanicus were ultimately dismissed. But Rome was a rumour mill, and whispering campaigns had previously implicated even Augustus in the poisoning of one consul and the assassination of another, and also implicated his wife, Livia, in the removal of Gaius Caesar, Livilla's late husband, by poison.[29]

In the case of Drusus, similarly, there is also reason for doubt. By the end of our year, AD 31, Tacitus states that Apicata, Sejanus' wife, revealed to Tiberius that Livilla and Sejanus had murdered Drusus; the story was affirmed by Lygdus and Eudemus (a confidant of Livilla's and her personal physician).[30] But as has been pointed out, it is hard to see how Apicata would have had access to know; Eudemus' and Lygdus' stories are suspicious since they were extracted by torture, and on top of everything else, Drusus had suffered from a nearly fatal illness two years previously.[31] Indeed, at the time Drusus had been so ill that a noted poet, Clutorius Priscus, had written a eulogy in the form of a poem, recited it at a gathering, and was consequently put to death.[32] Nevertheless, Sejanus doubtless derived satisfaction from Drusus' demise, since Drusus resented Sejanus' powerful position in the imperial administration, vocally expressed his vexation at the honours and elevation accorded to him (singling out the statues of Sejanus on view in Pompey's Theatre), and the two at one point had even come to fisticuffs, though Drusus reportedly was given to heavy drinking and had a violent temper.[33] In addition, Drusus had a proclivity towards physical abuse of his inferiors, an unseemly enthusiasm for gladiatorial combats, and kept the company of actors, all of which had helped to create a rift between himself and his more reserved father, a void Sejanus exploited and sought to fill.[34] Drusus' comportment likely did not encourage his wife, Livilla, to remain loyal, and she soon started to betray her husband's confidential conversations to Sejanus.[35]

After Drusus died, the consuls took their seats in the Senate on ordinary wooden benches as a sign of mourning, rather than the ivory inlaid curule seats that were a prerogative of higher Roman magistrates. Tiberius, surprisingly to some, continued to attend to state matters and at a meeting of the Senate reminded that body of its dignity and obligations. A brief summation of Tiberius' justification for attending to business so soon in the wake of his son's death survives:

> He was not ignorant that he could be accused for appearing before the eyes of the Senate with grief still fresh; scarcely could the conversations of relatives, scarcely could the light of day be endured by many mourners. Those who grieved ought not to be condemned for their weakness: nevertheless, he had sought a more powerful solace from the embrace of state matters.[36]

With the death of Drusus, the supremacy of Germanicus' children in the imperial pecking order seemed all but assured – upon Germanicus' death his children, Nero and Drusus Caesars, had been adopted by Tiberius' son Drusus, ensuring that they would assume Tiberius' role upon his death, and Tiberius commended the boys' care to the state upon his own son's demise. However, as Sejanus and Livilla watched from the shadows, Sejanus may have realized, if not immediately, then at least in hindsight, that Drusus' death was opportune, and gave him an opening to become the foremost man of Rome's empire.

Spiders and Flies: Sejanus and Agrippina the Elder

Drusus and his cousin Germanicus had got along remarkably well, given the potential for political rivalries to turn violent in Rome; the same could not be said of their spouses. Agrippina, Germanicus' widow, was a strong-willed, violent-tempered woman according to our sources, who was determined to see one of her sons occupy Tiberius' position, and this was to be the case over time with a number of women in the imperial house. In terms of imperial succession as the institution of the Principate developed, one must think of the Roman imperial court in varying degrees of a hot and cold civil war, with women often as the protagonists who were eager to see their children on the throne. In the end, by default, Agrippina was to win a pyrrhic victory when her son, Caligula, to history's (and the Romans') sorrow, won the imperial seat. For the moment, in the early 20s, the drama between the two princesses played out with Livilla hedging her bets with Sejanus over her own husband, Drusus. Perhaps Drusus was too accommodating for her taste with Germanicus' widow, retaining warm feelings for him and his family even after his death; perhaps Livilla was overcome with passion for Sejanus; perhaps she intended to use Sejanus to further her own ambitions for her children; perhaps it was a combination of these and similar factors. Sejanus, too, had agents who would later help create a faction that would pit Livilla and the emperor's mother, the former empress and Augustus' wife Livia (who was now in her eighties) against Agrippina.[37] It was eventually to be a contest over whose children would ultimately succeed Tiberius.

Agrippina was to prove a fearsome opponent. A proud, emotional, and confrontational personality, she was closer by blood to Augustus, a granddaughter of Rome's first emperor, while Livilla was the granddaughter of Augustus' sister, Octavia, and of Augustus' great rival in the final battle for domination over Rome's empire, Marc Antony – a fact about which members of the imperial family could be sensitive. In addition, Agrippina had been more fortunate in terms of children than Livilla, exacerbating the rivalry, for she could boast of six offspring: three boys, Nero Caesar, Drusus Caesar, and Gaius (later Caligula), and three girls, Agrippina (known as 'Agrippina the Younger' to distinguish her from her mother, 'the Elder'), Julia Livilla, and Drusilla. Sejanus was to play on the hatred that Tiberius had started to nurture against Germanicus' children, particularly Nero and Drusus Caesar, and ominously warned Tiberius that the city was split, as though it were in a civil war, with one faction favouring Agrippina and her family.[38]

Over the course of the next five years, after Drusus' death in 23 but particularly after 26, Sejanus was to undertake a series of proxy battles in the cold war between these imperial rivals, often through prosecution in the courts of Agrippina's friends and supporters.[39] The first of these was against a man named C. Silius, whose family had been close to Germanicus' and whose wife, Sosia Galla, was a friend of Agrippina's. Both Silius and Sosia were convicted in AD 25 of – among other crimes – extortion, and complicity with a Gallic rebel named Julius Sacrovir whose revolt started and was put down in 21 (see p. 132). Silius anticipated his condemnation with suicide, and Sosia was banished.[40] It should be noted, however, that this may not have been directed specifically against Agrippina and her family, but may have in fact been a factor in the tensions that would erupt after 26 between Sejanus and Agrippina and play out in the late 20s.[41] Sejanus also enjoyed other successes in 25, including engineering the previously mentioned destruction of Cremutius Cordus (see p. 25), a man of studied animus against Sejanus who joked when Sejanus' statue was erected in Pompey's Theatre that the theatre was now ruined.[42]

The string of successes, however, had reportedly made Sejanus over-confident. In addition, Livilla's pressure for marriage was now intensifying.[43] Not long after Cremutius' demise, Sejanus wrote to Tiberius requesting the hand of Livilla in marriage, all the while insisting that he had no further desire than to work diligently to serve his emperor.[44] Tacitus summarizes both Sejanus' request, and the lengthier response from Tiberius, which surely took the wind out of Sejanus' sails. A section of the letter may well be a verbatim passage from an imperial correspondence, since Tacitus as a highly placed Roman official (he had held numerous offices including the highly prized post of proconsul of Asia) will have had access to the imperial archives. It reads as follows:

> You are mistaken, Sejanus, if you think that you will remain in the same rank, and Livilla, who was married to Gaius Caesar and soon after to Drusus, will act with the same mind, so that she grows old with a Roman equestrian. Grant that I permit the marriage – do you believe that they would endure it, who saw her brother, who saw her father and our ancestors in the highest offices? You wish to maintain your present rank: but those magistrates and men of distinction who press you with business (although you don't desire it) and consult you on everything, openly say that already long since you've proceeded beyond the rank of an equestrian and the friendships of my father [Augustus], and through envy of you they also accuse me.[45]

In the remainder of the letter Tiberius added that he was not strictly opposed to Sejanus' and Livilla's marriage plans, and it is worth noting that at some point – when is uncertain – Claudius' son (named Drusus after Claudius' father) was betrothed to Sejanus' daughter (who was later brutally executed in the wake of her father's downfall, see p. 63); consequently, even though the marriage never took place, Sejanus' family was to be connected with the ruling family.[46] But Sejanus for now took the hint and, somewhat alarmed, started to urge the emperor, now in his late sixties and growing weary of the responsibilities of governance, to retire from Rome.[47] By so doing, Sejanus hoped to isolate Tiberius, control access to him (as well as control his correspondence), make himself more popular, and, in essence, govern Rome himself.[48] Tiberius was growing weary, too, of dealing with the Senate and its members. Departing from it one day he was heard to mutter in Greek, '*O homines ad servitutem paratos!*', 'O men ready for slavery!'[49] And as already noted, there may have been a multiplicity of reasons for Tiberius' final departure from Rome.[50]

Two important incidents in the conflict with Agrippina intervened, however, before Tiberius' retirement. In 26 a cousin of Agrippina's, Claudia Pulchra, was charged with adultery with a man named Firmius. She was also charged with an attempt to poison Tiberius and with using magic against him. Both Claudia and Firmius were found guilty and condemned.[51] The trial threw Agrippina into a rage, and one day she reportedly confronted Tiberius while he was sacrificing to her divinized grandfather Augustus. She upbraided him for paying homage to his godhead while persecuting his living descendants, and further attacked him for putting her friends, first Sosia Gallia, and now Claudia, on trial. Her barbs hit the mark, and in a rare outburst Tiberius wheeled on her and asked her – citing a Greek verse – if it was an injury that she herself was not queen?[52] Agrippina soon started to grow physically ill from the emotional stress. One day during her illness, when Tiberius came to call on her, she begged him to let her remarry. Tacitus, who tantalizingly reports that he read these deeply personal anecdotes in the now lost memoirs of Agrippina the Younger (Caligula's sister and the mother of the emperor Nero), tells us her request went ignored.[53]

Sejanus continued to exploit the breach that had been opened between Agrippina and Tiberius. He now suborned agents who, under pretence of concern for Agrippina, warned her that the emperor was trying to poison her. The next time she dined with Tiberius, he noticed that she had not touched her dinner. Praising the quality of a bowl of fruit brought in by a slave, he offered it to her, and she passed it off to her slaves, uneaten.[54] Rumours started to spread that Tiberius was, in fact, plotting her death. It was in the midst of this that Tiberius finally retired to Capri. As discussed, on the journey there, while at an imperial villa at Sperlonga whose dining room was an elaborate natural sea grotto, part of the grotto collapsed and Tiberius was only saved by Sejanus' quick action, something that further boosted Tiberius' confidence in his prefect.[55]

With Tiberius now in seclusion on Capri, Sejanus could further tighten the noose around Agrippina and her family. His first target was her son Nero, a young man of modest comportment according to Tacitus, who was the heir apparent to Tiberius.[56] According to Tacitus' account, Sejanus now suborned agents to play on the young man's ambitions and, above all, to lure him into indiscreet remarks and actions that could be interpreted nefariously or magnified to look more sinister than they were. In addition, Suetonius' account appears to imply that Tiberius carried some of the responsibility for their persecution by putting a curb on the honours and offices the Senate had conferred on them, something people viewed as a signal of imperial displeasure. Already in AD 24 he had rebuked members of the pontifical college for including Nero's and Drusus' names in the annual vows (usually made on 3 January) for the safety of the emperor, a privilege that Tiberius did not wish to share with the two princelings; he let his displeasure be known, stating that vows should not be made to those who were still of immature years and whose heads might be swollen by the premature bestowal of such honours.[57] He further asked the college if this had been done at the request of their mother, Agrippina. It was already then in 24, Tacitus asserts, that Sejanus saw his opening and began to work on the enmity between Tiberius and Agrippina's family – an arguably anachronistic assessment viewed in hindsight.[58] But two years later, in 26, Sejanus exploited an opportunity and started to make use of his agents to spy on Nero's conversations. Soon word spread that friendship with Nero was no longer a desirable commodity, and friends and acquaintances started to avoid his company. His wife, Livia Julia (daughter of Livilla and Drusus, and his cousin), was also suborned to report to her mother, Livilla, any remark that could be interpreted negatively, and she in turn reported it to Sejanus who then reported it to Tiberius. Sejanus was helped by Nero's indiscretion, since he had a tendency to make unguarded and impertinent utterances. While not climbing to the level of treasonable remarks, they were magnified and met with Tiberius' displeasure. Soon Nero was in a no-win situation according to Tacitus, where any word he spoke and any silence he maintained were both viewed suspiciously.

Sejanus, as the director and producer of this slow-motion family tragedy, was a master. He now started to work on Drusus, Nero's brother, in order to foment discord between the two.[59] Drusus was perhaps more temperamentally akin to his mother, Agrippina, and his brother, the future emperor Caligula: of savage nature, lusting for power, and envious of Nero (whom his mother preferred). Sejanus read Drusus' character and concluded rightly that he would likely do something foolish, his ferocious nature making him more opportune for indiscretion and subsequent elimination. By the end of 27, however, Sejanus, with Tiberius in splendid isolation on Capri, began to attack Agrippina and Nero more aggressively: Sejanus used soldiers from the praetorian guard to report on their correspondence, visitors, and actions both private and public. He even attempted entrapment, encouraging both to flee to the armies of Germany or to openly appeal to the people of Rome in the Forum itself to goad them to revolution.[60]

Sejanus loved nothing more than spinning a web to entrap his hapless victims, and in 27 he was quite busy indeed. In that year, Sejanus received help when Domitius Afer, a wealthy rhetorician and orator, attempted a prosecution against Claudia Pulchra's son, P. Quinctilius Varus (son of the former governor of Syria by the same name who perished in the Teutoberg Forest in AD 9). Domitius Afer had squandered the rich rewards he had received in his prosecution of Pulchra, and was hoping to turn a quick profit by prosecuting the case; P. Cornelius Dolabella, the recent victor over the rebel Tacfarinas in North Africa and a relative of Varus, was Afer's fellow prosecutor. We are unclear of the charge, but *maiestas* (treason) remains a possibility; in this instance though the outcome could not have pleased Sejanus, since the case was deferred and we hear nothing more.[61]

Towards the year's end, Sejanus proved more fortunate when he set his sights on yet another friend of Agrippina's, Titius Sabinus, who had been friends with Germanicus and maintained his close friendship with the family after Germanicus' death.[62] Sejanus suborned four ex-praetors, each of whom were desirous of Sejanus' patronage in order to win the consulship: Lucanius Latiaris, M. Porcius Cato, Petilius Rufus, and M. Opsius. Latiaris was an acquaintance of Sabinus'. He lured Sabinus into indiscreet conversations, feigning sympathy for Agrippina and extolling Sabinus' fidelity; soon Sabinus believed him no longer an acquaintance but a close friend and sought him out frequently to commiserate about the plight of Agrippina and her family. Latiaris then sprung the trap. Pretending to have some fresh news for Sabinus, he escorted Latiaris into the inner-sanctum of his house, a bedroom. He lured Sabinus into rehearsing a list of grievances, but unbeknownst to Sabinus, Latiaris' three fellow senators had been smuggled into the house and were taking notes as they listened in on the conversation while hiding in a crawl space between the ceiling and the roof. Tacitus expresses his disgust at all four, who proceeded to send their report to Tiberius.

Tiberius had a letter read in the Senate on New Year's Day of 28. The letter accused Sabinus of plotting against his life, and demanded summary punishment. Sabinus was dragged from the senatorial chamber with a noose around his neck and a cloak muffling his mouth, but that did not stop his fellow senators from hearing his cries that he was 'this year's sacrifice to Sejanus!' He was executed and his body displayed on the Gemonian Steps, where criminals' bodies were exposed for public mutilation; it was then cast into the Tiber. His faithful dog reportedly never left his body and leapt into the Tiber, following his master.[63] It was a stunning move, in part because the execution took place on a day normally set aside for solemn festivities, as the consuls assumed their office amidst sacrifice and feasting. Tiberius soon followed up with a letter of thanks to the Senate, in which he added that he was still deeply anxious and suspected that there were still people plotting against him.[64] He did not name Nero and Agrippina – but then again, he did not need to, since it was clear to all just who was meant. Nero's and Agrippina's survival was appearing increasingly tenuous.

In the interim, by late 28, Sejanus himself had retired to the mainland of Campania, where senators travelled to flatter and pay court to the prefect in an effort to gain anxiously awaited access to Tiberius, who was completely isolated on Capri since any approach to him was strictly controlled through Sejanus. In an effort to win favour with both, late in the year the Senate decreed altars of Mercy (*clementia*) and Friendship (*amicitia*) be set up in Rome flanked with statues of Sejanus and Tiberius, with Sejanus receiving prayers and sacrifices along with the emperor.[65] As Tacitus ominously hints, however, Sejanus' and Tiberius' friendship was destined to end in disaster, and is underscored in the final paragraph of Book IV of the *Annals*: it is no accident that Tacitus ends this book with the notice of an imperial marriage between Agrippina the Younger and a nobleman named Domitius Ahenobarbus. Their offspring was to become the imperial firebrand known to history as the emperor Nero, a reminder and a portent of Rome's impending future perils.[66]

First, however, there intervened the destruction of Nero and Agrippina in AD 29, with Drusus soon to follow. Events took a turn for the worse once Tiberius' mother, the former empress and empress mother, Livia Augusta, died. Tacitus tells us that she had been a moderating influence on Tiberius.[67] This influence now gone, Tiberius moved to destroy Agrippina and Nero, sending a letter to Rome denouncing both.[68] He first accused Nero of the vague charges of *amores iuvenum et inpudicitiam,* which translates literally 'the loves of young men and shamelessness', something we could more idiomatically yet accurately translate as 'homosexuality and immoral conduct'.[69] As for Agrippina, Tiberius attacked the disobedient and contumacious nature of her defiance. Tacitus notably remarks that neither were accused of revolution or taking up arms, though Suetonius – who says that the charges were false – states that Tiberius charged Agrippina with planning to take refuge at a statue of Augustus or with the armies in Germany.[70] Tacitus tells us that the words of Tiberius' letter were of studied harshness (*quaesita asperitate*). Crowds gathered outside the Senate with statues of both Agrippina and Nero, cheering the pair – as well as Tiberius, believing his denunciatory letter a forgery, refusing to accept that Tiberius intended the destruction of Germanicus' family. Anonymous attacks now started to circulate against Sejanus, some with the names of men of consular standing (falsely) penned on them. Sejanus accused the people of disloyalty and the Senate of disregarding Tiberius' sentiments in the matter, even though the senatorial and equestrian order did not lack for malfeasant careerists, their fingers in the wind, to carry out the wishes of Sejanus and Tiberius on whom their careers and advancement depended – or individuals who opposed them, though most senators, Tacitus states, were simply stupefied into a state of alarm.[71] Tiberius moved to make it clear that the denunciatory letter was indeed his, and he rebuked the Roman people for their riotous behaviour.

And that is where our manuscript of Tacitus abruptly and regrettably ends – at the beginning of AD 29 – the very year in which Jesus, according to *Luke* (3:1–23), was baptized by John and began his ministry. It resumes only with the end of 31 and thereby deprives us of the three most dramatic years of Tiberius' reign from the hand of a historian who was a master of his craft. From this point forward we are forced to cobble together sources for what happened next, including the Judeo-Grecian historian Josephus, the Roman biographer Suetonius, the Roman senator and historian Cassius Dio, and scattered fragments from various literary sources. It is from these that we are able to reconstruct a fair outline, schematic though it is, of events. Nero was soon declared a public enemy, while at the same time sentence was passed against Agrippina.[72] They were conveyed to their places of exile, for Agrippina, Pandateria (modern Ventotene, about 20 miles north-west of Ischia), where her mother Julia had also endured a long exile and where the remains of the villa where they spent their bitter exiles are still visible, and for Nero, Pontia (modern Ponza, another 20 miles north-west of Ventotene). Both Agrippina and Nero were held and transported in chains, under heavy guard, concealed in covered litters.[73] In her place of confinement Agrippina was beaten so severely that she reportedly lost an eye, and was force-fed when she attempted to starve herself to death. While Agrippina and Nero wasted away in exile, Sejanus continued to enjoy the successes of his rise to power and to plan his continued ascent.

Sejanus' Nemesis

By the end of 29, Cassius Dio reports that through a combination of senatorial fear, flattery, and careerism, the Senate, with support of the equestrians and the Roman people, voted to make Sejanus' birthday a public holiday, complete with prayers and sacrifices to the Fortune of both Sejanus and Tiberius, by whom they were to take their annual oaths.[74] Dio furthers states in the same passage that senators and equestrians set up more statues of Sejanus than were possible to count in individual efforts to curry favour. The heaping up of titles, the divine honours that were shared, the close public association between the two, all attest to Sejanus' power and the trust in which Tiberius held him. While we have almost no images of Sejanus as a result of a studied attempt to erase his

Fig. 3.1: A Tiberian *as* (bronze penny) reading on the reverse Tiberius Caesar Augustus, son of the Divine Augustus. The obverse is now damaged but would have read: From the Bibilis Mint in the Consulship of Tiberius Caesar and Lucius Aelius Sejanus. The damage was likely part of a *damnatio memoriae* directed against Sejanus. (Classical Numismatic Group via *Wikimedia Commons*)

memory after his fall (see fig. 3.1), it has been argued that the so-called Grand Cameo of France (*Le Grand Camée de France*, fig. 3.2) shows him standing quite prominently next to Tiberius. His image may well have been pervasive in Rome to the point of over-surfeit. By early 30 it appears his statues, now in gold – a material usually reserved for divinities and, only of late, members of the imperial household – were on view in the city.

It was now time for Sejanus to go after yet another target, Nero's brother and Agrippina's son, Drusus, who had recently been married to a woman of high standing, Aemilia Lepida.[75] If not a replay of 23 when Sejanus seduced Livilla and her husband Drusus conveniently died, it was to at least prove a rhyming echo: Sejanus seduced Drusus' wife, sought information against him, and, possibly with the help of one of the consuls, had him condemned (based on false accusations according to Dio, and according to Suetonius based on charges presented by Tiberius), and confined to a prison in the Palatine, where he eventually starved to death in 33.[76] The year 30 was Sejanus' own *annus mirabilis*: he was promised the consulship for 31, the highest honour one could enjoy in Rome; he was also finally pledged the hand of a member of the imperial family, something Tiberius had already held out before – although to whom precisely is uncertain – and Tiberius (who, according to our

Fig. 3.2: The Grand Cameo of France. The man standing before and facing a seated Tiberius has plausibly been identified as Sejanus. (GFDL / Marie-Lan Nguyen via *Wikimedia Commons*)

sources was already planning Sejanus' destruction) started to refer to him on intimate and affectionate terms publicly as 'My Sejanus', and 'Partner of my Cares'.[77]

Following Tiberius' deceptive cue, the Senate now decreed gilded chairs be set up in honour of Tiberius and Sejanus in the theatres, that they should hold the joint consulship every five years, be greeted by a select body of citizens when they entered the city, and that sacrifices be made to the images of both.[78] All of this Cassius Dio presents as a lethally shrewd move on the part of Tiberius, who, recognizing Sejanus' enormous power of patronage and his firm grip on the praetorian guards, understood that he had to move cautiously and dissemble his ultimate design of bringing down Sejanus, in part because he had so trusted Sejanus and isolated himself.[79] When Sejanus left Tiberius in Campania to return to Rome to assume the consulship in the autumn of 31, Tiberius reportedly wept false tears lamenting that half his soul was leaving him, and held out hope that he would soon follow.[80]

All of this begs the questions, when, why, and how did Tiberius turn against his prefect? One tradition, reported in Josephus, hinges on his sister-in-law, Antonia, daughter of Marc Antony and Octavia (Augustus' sister), mother to the emperor Claudius, grandmother of Caligula, great-grandmother of the emperor Nero. Josephus states that somehow Antonia got wind of Sejanus' plot against Tiberius – how we are not told, but possibly through a family member – and wrote a detailed letter to Tiberius, which she gave to her most trusted freedman, Pallas, to deliver.[81] Josephus asserts that she sent the letter once Sejanus was at the height of his powers, and he had most senators paying court to him along with the army, which he had bribed (though this is a vague term at best, possibly a simple reference to the praetorians), and 'once the plot had greatly progressed'.[82] Cassius Dio also reports about Antonia's letter, but asserts that the messenger was not Pallas but her freedwoman, Caenis, who was gifted with a photographic memory.[83] The letter, whoever delivered it, reportedly moved Tiberius to take action; although he had trusted and promoted Sejanus, he held the widow of his late brother Drusus, Antonia, in the highest regard. She was noted for her virtue and chastity, which was underscored by her refusal to remarry, even though still young, after Drusus had died in 9 BC, and despite imperial pressure to do so.[84] It has been suggested, and it may well be the case, that Sejanus' fall was engineered by a faction at court that supported Gaius Caligula to succeed Tiberius. If so, it could be that Antonia as his grandmother was lending her support, but this is conjectural.[85] Tacitus is in fact quite explicit that Sejanus had Gaius Caligula in the crosshairs, but was checked before he could make his move, and there are clear indications in Cassius Dio (see p. 59) that Gaius Caligula was set up as a rival against Sejanus.[86]

No matter who or what ultimately warned Tiberius of the danger he was now facing, once alerted he reportedly played the role of a master dissimulator, seemingly enjoying a game of cat and mouse with his prefect.

According to our sources, he was growing suspicious, and likely by now understood the heights to which Sejanus had aspired – and reached – and knew he had to play his cards closely. What specifically started to rouse his suspicions is not easy to guess; perhaps Sejanus' going for the jugular against Agrippina along with Nero and Drusus, perhaps one of the many prosecutions Sejanus helped arrange against perceived enemies in the Senate. Senators and others, Tiberius knew, viewed Sejanus as a virtual rival emperor, as capable as he, if not now more so, of bestowing favours and offices; the case was the same with the praetorians, on which Sejanus had a virtual lock; and, were that not enough, Sejanus had courted the favour of the plebs.[87] In his election for the consulship he had assiduously cultivated the people of Rome, despite the fact that consular elections under the emperors were a sham. The *princeps* put a name in nomination – who would oppose it? Indeed, so studiously did he court the people – who just over a year before had agitated against him – that he even went so far as to stand for election on the Aventine, a hill by tradition associated with the plebeians and technically outside the sacred boundaries of the city where – by law and religious sanction – elections ought to have taken place, and thereby elicited a rare reproach from Tiberius.[88] Be that as it may, when Sejanus stood in 30 for the consulship of 31, he was to share the office with Tiberius. Dio in a notice under late 30 or early 31 states that Sejanus, as a result of his arrogance and power, seemed to be emperor himself, with Tiberius a mere petty tyrant who ruled a small island: that may be Cassius Dio's opinion, but perhaps Sejanus and those around him genuinely felt that.[89] And so his election and this year brings us back to the beginning of the chapter, and the ill omens that attended Sejanus' assumption of office that New Year's Day.[90]

For much of the year, Dio portrays Tiberius as one who had decided to wage psychological warfare against his once beloved prefect, even as he planned his destruction.[91] Contradictory missives started coming from Capri from Tiberius stating now that he was in ill health and near death, now that he was well and would soon return to the city. One letter would praise Sejanus and the next would rebuke him. Some friends of Sejanus were exalted out of regard for him, others disgraced. Tiberius kept Sejanus off his balance, and those around Sejanus were equally kept in a constant state of doubt. Sejanus' anxiety was doubtless exacerbated by a series of ominous portents: smoke emerged from a hollow bronze statue of Sejanus and when the head was removed a snake jumped out; soon after the head was repaired, a noose was found coiled around the neck; and a favourite and ancient statue of the goddess Fortuna that had reportedly belonged to one of Rome's ancient kings (Servius Tullius) spontaneously turned its back on him during sacrifice.[92] In hindsight, astute observers noted that Sejanus perhaps never should have assumed the consulship with Tiberius, whose colleagues tended to meet very bad ends: one colleague, Quintilius Varus, had died in the disaster of the Teutoberg Forest in AD 9; another, his own nephew Germanicus, had died in the East; yet another, Germanicus' rival, Cn. Calpurnius Piso, committed suicide during his trial in the wake of Germanicus' death; and another, his own son Drusus, was (rumour had it) murdered. The history of Tiberius' former colleagues was not a record to inspire confidence.

More perplexing still for Sejanus, Gaius, known later to the world as Caligula, Agrippina's one remaining son who had not yet become a target, was now elevated to a priesthood, and Tiberius cryptically indicated that he was contemplating him as successor.[93] At about the same time Nero died in exile, and his death has been conjectured to have been an execution in the manner of an enforced suicide; in writing to the Senate about his death Tiberius omitted the normally honorific titles he gave Sejanus in his formal correspondence.[94] It is worth noting that a recent study on Sejanus sees this as a turning point, arguing that the death of Nero had been carried out without Tiberius' express order, and marks a break between Sejanus and Tiberius.[95] The effect of Gaius' elevation, in conjunction with Nero's death (for which Sejanus will have likely been blamed by popular sentiment) may have been to undercut Sejanus' popular support in Rome, which should perhaps not be underestimated.[96] Yet Germanicus' family and offspring were always popular, and the people of Rome were particularly pleased at Gaius' elevation. [97]

According to Dio, Sejanus started to regret not attempting rebellion when he had greater support, and was particularly depressed at the enthusiastic support for Caligula. When Sejanus next moved against an old enemy – a man who had governed Spain ten years earlier and was now brought to trial (possibly a despicable creature named Vibius Serenus the Elder), Tiberius moved to stop the indictment.[98] He next moved to curb any divine offerings to any living human, putting an end to offerings to both himself and Sejanus and curbed any honours to himself and, by implication, to Sejanus as well.[99] But just for good measure, to really take Sejanus off his guard, Tiberius then started a disinformation campaign by spreading the rumour that he was about to invest Sejanus with *tribunicia potestas*, the power of a tribune. This was an honour Augustus had bestowed on Tiberius to indicate that he would be in control of the government upon his death. It was at about the same time that Tiberius moved to put Quintus Naevius Sertorius (or, alternatively, Sutorius) Macro in power, a praetorian careerist who would prove an apt replacement for Sejanus and whose promotion and moves against Sejanus were maintained as a tightly kept secret.[100]

All the pieces in place, the trap was now sprung, while the emperor played an anxious waiting game on Capri, ready for alternative measures if his move to check Sejanus failed.[101] Tiberius sent a denunciatory letter to the Senate and waited for the signals to be raised down the coast that would either bring him news of success or send him scrambling for the fleet and the legions with his great-nephew Drusus, who was to be released from confinement and spirited to him if Sejanus' arrest failed. The missive was delivered by Sejanus' ultimate successor, Sertorius Macro, who had already been given command of the guards under secret orders.[102] Macro entered Rome at night, communicating the actions about to take place to Memmius Regulus, one of the consuls, and Graecinus Laco, commander of the night watch (*vigiles*). Early in the morning of 18 October, Macro ascended the Palatine. The Senate was to meet that day in the Temple of Apollo Palatinus, built next to the modest house of Augustus in commemoration of his victory over Antony and Cleopatra at Actium.[103] Macro met Sejanus outside. Sejanus was anxious because he had received no correspondence from Tiberius. Macro responded by telling him in confidence that he was carrying the official orders for his investiture with *tribunicia potestas*. He was to rule the Roman world upon Tiberius' death.

Sejanus was jubilant, and entered the chamber to await the senators. Meanwhile, the praetorians accompanying Sejanus were dismissed to camp after showing them a letter from Tiberius that indicated his authority and granted them a donative for their services. Laco and his night command now took over the watch around the temple, while Macro went back to the praetorian barracks to secure the camp in case of any disturbances or dissent on the part of the soldiery (they ultimately remained loyal to Tiberius and were rewarded with ten gold pieces each).

Then the notoriously 'wordy and long' letter (although Suetonius calls it a 'shameful and pitiable speech') was recited denouncing Sejanus, famously encapsulated in some wonderful lines by the Roman satirist, Juvenal:[104]

> '*quisnam delator quibus indicibus, quo teste probavit?*'
> '*nil horum; verbosa et grandis epistula venit a Capreis.*'
> '*bene habet, nil plus interrogo.*'

> 'But what informant, with what information, by what witness proof?'
> 'None of these things; a wordy and long letter came from Capri.'
> 'Ah, I see. No need to ask further!'

The letter, as was Tiberius' style, was a cryptically worded indictment – with nothing overt at first, so as not to alarm his intended target.[105] It was not a complete denunciation, but a slow burn, we may guess, of displeasure with his prefect: it started by discussing what might have been some unrelated business (Cassius Dio says *ta men prota allo ti*, 'first there was another matter'), then there was some minor criticism of Sejanus' conduct, then, Dio continues, *kai met' autēn heteron ti*, ('and after this some other thing'), then yet another criticism aimed at Sejanus, presumably placing Sejanus on an emotional roller-coaster. Towards the close of the letter Tiberius called for the punishment of two senators (we lack names) who were among Sejanus' intimate associates and for Sejanus to be kept under guard.

Cassius Dio asserts Tiberius avoided calling for his execution to prevent a disturbance, but his desire was clear enough. Then Tiberius alluded to concerns for his own safety, and summoned one of the consuls to him with a military force, giving indication of his intent to enter the city, but first requiring sufficient protection.[106] As the letter continued, some sitting near Sejanus left their seats, putting physical distance between themselves and the praetorian prefect. The reversal left many in the Senate stunned; expecting cheers of congratulations as Sejanus was named Tiberius' successor, their expectations had been cast like a hapless victim down from Tiberius' Leap on Capri, their hopes dashed against the rocks of false hopes below. The praetors and tribunes, meanwhile, surrounded Sejanus, ready to move against him if he attempted to flee and create a disturbance.

But Sejanus kept to his seat, thinking each of the individual criticisms of little account or ones to which he could easily respond.

The consul Regulus then summoned him forward while the letter was still being read aloud.[107] More accustomed to giving than taking orders, Sejanus at first was befuddled and uncomprehending. The consul raised his voice and called him a second, then a third time: 'Sejanus, come here!' 'Me?' Sejanus asked, 'Are you calling me?' He stood up, and Laco, now inside, stood next to him. After the letter had been read, the consul did not call for a vote or propose any penalty, fearing disturbances from supporters and friends, despite the fact that all had started to threaten Sejanus in unison, some out of fear due to their previous association with him who wanted to conceal their friendship, some out of genuine anger because he had wronged them in the past, some genuinely happy at his downfall. Regulus now simply asked a single senator if Sejanus should be imprisoned, and the senator replied in the affirmative.

Laco then led him to the Tullianum, what passed for Rome's prison. It was here that Roman state prisoners, including kings led in Roman triumphs, were kept until execution, including Jugurtha, the King of Numidia; Vercingetorix, the Gallic chieftain who led a massive rebellion against Julius Caesar in Gaul; and others who had cooled their heels in the Tullianum awaiting death. On the way, Sejanus was beaten, some blows landing on his face, while the populace jeered in derision and began to pull down his statues.[108] Earlier that morning, Sejanus had been accompanied to the meeting of the Senate by a large retinue of well-wishers: as Cassius Dio notes, the Senate and People of Rome had bestowed upon him the senator's toga with its purple border and worshipped him like a god, though now he languished as an example of the frailty of human fortune.[109] Later in the day, the Senate reconvened in the Temple of Concord, which was next to Sejanus' place of confinement. The Senate, seeing Sejanus' fate and realizing that the people had abandoned him, and further noting that the praetorians were nowhere to be seen (and presumably interpreting their absence as abandonment of their former prefect), voted for his execution.[110] Strangled in his cell, Sejanus' body was cast on to the Gemonian Steps where the people abused it for three days before casting it into the Tiber.[111]

'Mud Kneaded with Blood'

Within a month or two, many of Sejanus' family members, including his uncle, Junius Blaesus, had been executed, as likely had one of Sejanus' children, possibly the eldest of the three children he had had with Apicata.[112] It is with the continuing recriminations of those who were closely tied to Sejanus, and amidst the ongoing executions, that Tacitus' manuscript again resumes at the very end of 31 some two months after Sejanus' fall. In one of the more harrowingly intimate scenes from the ancient world that comes down to us, Sejanus' two younger children, neither yet of age, were brutally executed. Here the Latin is worth quoting for its horror and vividness, and requires little comment, the text and translation speaking for itself:

> *Placitum posthac ut in reliquos Seiani liberos adverteretur, vanescente quamquam plebis ira ac plerisque per priora supplicia lentis. Igitur portantur in carcerem, filius imminentium intellegens, puella adeo nescia, ut crebro interrogaret, quod ob delictum et quo traheretur; neque facturam ultra, et posse se puerile verbere moneri. Tradunt temporis eius auctores, quia triumvirali supplicio adfici virginem inauditum habebatur, a carnifice laqueum iuxta compressam; exim oblisis faucibus id aetatis corpora in Gemonias abiecta.*

> It was decided after this that punishment be visited on the rest of Sejanus' children, although the anger of the plebs and of many had softened as a result of the punishments already visited on them. His son and daughter were thus conveyed to prison, the son knowing full well what was coming, and his daughter so ignorant of her impending doom that she frequently asked on account of what wrong and where was she being dragged away; she would not do it again and she could be admonished with a beating suitable to a child. Authors of the period pass down that because it was considered unheard of that a virgin be put to death according to the customs of the *triumvirales*, she was raped then and there, next to the noose used to strangle her; and straightaway strangled at so young an age their bodies were immediately cast onto the Gemonian Steps.[113]

When Apicata learned of her children's deaths (and saw their bodies on the Gemonian Steps) she composed a letter to Tiberius revealing that eight years previously it had been Livilla who connived with Sejanus and implicated them both in the death of his son Drusus. She particularly singled out Livilla, blaming her for the divorce and subsequent separation from both her former husband and her children. Apicata then committed suicide.[114]

In the aftermath, Tiberius put to death his niece, Livilla, and any involved in the alleged murder of his son.[115] Dio states an alternative tradition that Tiberius was inclined to spare Livilla out of respect for her mother but that Antonia, the early empire's matriarchal version of Cato the Elder, would have none of it, and starved her daughter to death.[116] Nor did Tiberius mitigate his rage against Agrippina and Drusus: two years later both died, still in captivity. Drusus, as noted above, had reportedly been held in reserve as a possible propaganda instrument to be deployed against Sejanus in case his arrest resulted in armed conflict, as a means to rally the people and Senate around the family of Germanicus.[117] But after Sejanus' fall Tacitus says Tiberius preferred cruelty to penitence, seemingly fulfilling the prescient observation of a former teacher of his, the renowned rhetorician Theodorus of Gadara, that he was merely 'mud kneaded with blood'.[118] Drusus was starved to death in confinement on the Palatine, reportedly staving off death for eight days by eating the stuffing of his mattress, and was occasionally beaten by some slaves who stood watch. The guards at his door noted and wrote down any chance remark he uttered concerning his situation and that of his family. In his despair he uttered a formal and dying curse against Tiberius: 'As he has butchered his daughter-in-law, the son of his brother, and their progency, may he pay the penalty owed to the name and race of his ancestors and descendants!' Tiberius had the curse and Drusus' other chance remarks read to a mortified Senate. Directly afterwards, Drusus' mother, Agrippina, died in exile; either she committed suicide or was starved to death according to Tacitus.[119] Tiberius used the opportunity to attack her with scurrilous accusations, including adultery with Asinius Gallus, the man who married his much-loved Vipsania after he was forced to divorce her, and who had embarrassed him at one of the first senate meetings upon his succession.[120] Agrippina perished two years to the day on which Sejanus had been executed, 18 October AD 33. Tiberius boasted of his moderation in not having her body thrown on the Gemonian Steps, and the day was decreed a public holiday, with sacrifices to Jupiter.

In the years in which Jesus ministered in Judaea, during which we are told he was tempted by Satan to rule the kingdoms of the Earth only to reject it and minister to the sick, the destitute, and the sinner, Sejanus was seducing, networking, and bribing his way to worldly power. As John the Baptist and Jesus became matters of concern to Herod Antipas and Pontius Pilate, the praetorian prefect's growing power and popularity grew too as a matter of grave concern to a solitary emperor on a lonely island. While the drama of Jesus, his mature adulthood, his baptism, his ministry, and his death, caused schism in his community and among his people, as he proclaimed to set family members one against the other, the imperial house that ruled the empire, where he ministered, lived that schism to the most ruthless and bloody degree. The contrast cannot be more stark: both Sejanus and Jesus perished possibly in the same year, but almost certainly no more than two years apart, and both perished violently. One was a radical Jewish rabbi who was betrayed and forgave, the other a well-connected careerist of ancient Etruscan descent who provoked his emperor to a wrathful vengeance. It is worth noting as we leave Sejanus that as the early Christian community took hold in Judaea, Tiberius, after AD 31 until the end of his life in 37, did not cease to persecute and punish any and all connected with his ambitious praetorian prefect, once the most powerful man in Rome after the emperor. Sejanus perished in the pursuit of power and an earthly kingdom. In the same year Christ may have died due to his rejection of one.

Chapter 4

A Roman Governor: Pontius Pilate

> 'Everyone that is of the truth heareth my voice.' Pilate saith unto him, 'What is truth?'
>
> *John* 18:37–38

By AD 109 the emperor Trajan's patience stood at the breaking point. The cities of the province of Bithynia-Pontus, roughly equivalent to the northern region of Asia Minor in modern Turkey on the Hellespont and Bosporus, had been having difficulties with civil disorder, driven in part by what were known as *collegia* (*collegium* in the singular). These were the ancient equivalent of guilds but with a twist, since religious organizations also could constitute a *collegium*. Its board would often collect dues in order to help members cover the costs of funerals, wedding feasts, and sacrificial celebrations on public holidays. Shipwrights, undertakers, fullers, members of the ancient cult of the Great Mother from Asia Minor or Isis from Egypt, any of these could be recognized as a *collegium*. To manage the situation, the emperor Trajan sent a trusted senator of good standing and moderate temperament, Pliny the Younger, a friend of Tacitus' and, through the fortunate survival of ten books of correspondence, our most important eye-witness account of Vesuvius' eruption in AD 79 and our earliest surviving account of the encounter between the pagan and early Christian community.

One of his predecessors in the Roman administration, Pontius Pilate, was himself an unwitting instrument in the creation of the burgeoning early Christian community that Pliny encountered.

Nearly eight decades had passed since Pilate had executed a recalcitrant Jewish rabbi and heretic, who was intransigent in his refusal to answer Pilate's queries about accusations against him by the Jewish authorities. In the gospels, Pilate is one-dimensional, an actor who walks on the stage to fulfil his role as a befuddled sceptic who is tantalizing by nature of his brief appearance, his curious questioning of the accused, and his frustration with all sides in the dispute. Scholarly discussions of Pilate try to recover his origins, consider his relationship with Sejanus, or with Tiberius himself. However, to appreciate more fully the character of Pilate and his perspective both as a Roman and a governor, it is important for us to set him in a wider context that considers the personalities of Roman governors which covered a broad spectrum – from the benignly diligent to the callously rapacious and sadistic. It is equally important to bring into play a wide set of cultural dynamics, from the deference demanded by a Roman governor towards his dignity and status, to laws concerning magic, to some of the sensational events that shaped Pilate's character as he learned with other Romans how to navigate the often fraught dynamics of the still newly established and rapidly developing politics of the imperial court that pervaded Rome in the 10s, 20s, and 30s AD.

To that end this chapter will include a brief and selective survey of the nature of Roman governance, with a focus on Pliny's relatively careful response to the Christians in Bithynia-Pontus between AD 109 and 111 and contrast it with the malignancy of Verres' administration of Sicily in the 70s BC. This background is intended to set Pilate in his 'temperamental' context in the spectrum of Roman governors, before specifically focusing on Pilate himself. The current discussion seeks to put Pilate as much as possible in his uniquely Roman milieu. Of course, no one is ever alone in this task and there are numerous approaches. In 1999, Anne Wroe published a popular history about the prefect, in the nature of a sprawling literary biography that covered not just the historical Pilate but a substantial portion of the diverse apocryphal traditions about him as well in both the historical and literary record up until the twentieth century.[1] Warren Carter's 2003 study conveniently categorized the scholarly approaches to Pilate (and how we understand him) into five distinct categories since the Second World War: he is variously argued to be a cruel anti-Semite; a weak man without conviction; a typically insensitive and culturally unaware Roman official; a Christian himself (we might more properly say proto-Christian); or a saint.[2] Schiavone's (2016) hard-nosed legal and theological examination of Pilate stands out as perhaps the most interesting and provocative of studies, and is one to which we shall refer frequently in this chapter.

Pliny the Younger and the First Christians

Now the encounter with the Christians noted above comes in the last of the books (Book X) of Pliny's letters. Pliny had intended his correspondence to be a carefully constructed series of nine books, and these, taken in sum, give a picture of a man who is a dutiful, humane man of letters, a reputation Pliny studiously sought to cultivate. Court cases, literature, a day at the circus to see the chariot races, descriptions of villas, letters of commendation for promotion of friends, recollections of imperial ministers of dubious character now dead – these are the sorts of subjects that make up the collection. The tenth book was almost certainly not intended to be a part of the collection for publication, and is a chance appendix by a later editor, or by a contemporary who added it possibly as an afterthought. Whatever the reason, Book X is an invaluable series of 121 letters, the vast majority of which are Pliny's, although some are Trajan's replies to his governor.

Letter 96 is, in fact, our first pagan reference to Christians and begins with a peculiar remark: *Cognitionibus de Christianis interfui numquam: ideo nescio quid et quatenus aut puniri soleat aut quaeri*, 'I had never been present at the investigation of Christians: so I did not know how much or to what extent they are accustomed to be punished or investigated.' That should cause us no problem, were it not for the odd sense that his encounter sounds as though this was something new to Pliny, something that he himself was encountering for the first time; he had, perhaps, vaguely heard of them (the perfect plus the adverb, *interfui numquam,* can be taken to infer he had never been present at the interrogation of Christians but holds out that he had possibly heard about them from others, without giving too much mind to the reports). Why that is a problem we shall see shortly. He expressed some confusion though about whether distinctions should be made based on age, or if renunciation of faith should be grounds for a pardon. Is the mere name 'Christian' to be punished even if innocent of a crime, or is it necessary that an actual criminal action take place? Pliny sought some guidance.

For the moment though, Pliny reviewed for Trajan the procedure he followed: he asked in person those accused of practising Christianity if they were still a practising Christian. If they admitted it, he asked again, and then a third time, with a warning that they faced punishment.

If they persisted they were led away to execution; for Pliny, regardless of the nature of whatever it was they confessed, he believed, in a fit of pique, that their persistence and obstinacy in and of itself deserved punishment, a telltale sense of the arrogance and demand for obedience Roman governors expected. Pliny further reports to Trajan that others 'of a similar madness' (as Pliny phrases it), were sent to Rome if they were a Roman citizen. This was the difference between Jesus and Paul (the former persecutor of Jesus' disciples turned fervent apostle). Jesus as a non-citizen was subject, as were Pliny's less fortunate Christians, to summary execution (a slow crucifixion), while Paul as a citizen was entitled to be sent to Rome and given the privilege of a swift death by beheading with the sword were he found guilty.

Then local politics came into play. Once word spread of Pliny's actions against the Christians, other accusations came forward. Many were anonymous, perhaps to settle feuds of an ancient and personal nature, but still, many were brought before him who had been falsely accused of being Christian. Those who denied the charge were dismissed after they had repeated a formulaic invocation of the gods, made an offering of wine and incense upon the altar to the imperial godhead of Trajan, and reviled the name of Christ – none of which, to Pliny's understanding, a genuine Christian would do. Some apostates admitted the charge, but made clear they were no longer practising Christians; Pliny made them prove it, to his satisfaction, by the procedure noted above, giving offerings to the emperor's statue and to those of the gods. Some of the apostates gave Pliny details about their faith (which Pliny does not call faith, but *culpae suae vel erroris*, 'guilt or error'): they met regularly on a fixed day to sing a song to Christ as if to a god (Pliny uses the adverb *invicem* – 'in turn', which may indicate a type of meditative chant), and bound themselves by sacrament not to commit any crime, not to commit theft, not to commit adultery, not to betray a trust, or a deposit of money when it was called in. They then depart and later meet to share a common meal that Pliny says was ordinary and harmless (*promiscuam et innoxiam*). However, the Christians stopped practising this ritual, Pliny notes, after Pliny had issued the edict on Trajan's instructions that forbade *collegia* of a political nature. To ensure that this practice had ended he put two deaconesses to the torture. In a succinct summation Pliny tells Trajan what he discovered from these two women: *Nihil aliud inveni quam superstitionem pravam et immodicam* – 'I found nothing other than a depraved and excessive superstition.' It is important to keep in mind that Pliny, at least to judge from his own words (and we should of course retain a healthy scepticism on this score), appears a relatively humane individual, yet was perfectly at home with the roughest of summary justice.

However, Pliny had temporarily put a moratorium on examination since the number of individuals in peril had ballooned, with a great number of people of every age, men and women included, now brought to trial – something Pliny warned was likely to continue, since it was not only in the cities where Christians were active, but in the rural towns and villages as well. If Pliny's words are any indication, the cult had become so widespread and popular that the temples were substantially less frequented, and sacrificial meat had grown scarce – that is until he took some action and could happily report to Trajan that the temples were once again full, and meat, the product of sacrifice, plentiful. Trajan's response was to praise Pliny's prudence and moderation, but admonished that the Christians were by no means to be hunted down.[3] 'Instead,' wrote Trajan, 'follow the same procedure as you have: anyone who denies being a Christian must make it clear that this is indeed the case by offering prayers to the gods, and then receive a pardon regardless of past conduct.' Trajan ordered Pliny to reject outright anonymous denunciations circulated via pamphlets.

There are several striking things we find out in these letters. First, we may adduce from one of Pliny's opening phrases that he had certainly heard of the Christians and of investigations into their activities, otherwise the use of the perfect in conjunction with the adverb ('I had never been present at investigations concerning Christians before') would seem to make little sense. We also find out that women have a role, although possibly a limited one, in the hierarchy of the early Christian community (hence the reference to deaconesses). Finally, we note that although by this date there were persecutions on a local level, and a short but savage one in Rome under Nero in AD 64, Trajan is quite explicit here that there is to be no 'search and destroy mission' to root out the cult. But perhaps the most perplexing aspect of the letter is that it appears Pliny was quite unfamiliar with Christian practices, and also seems to assume that Trajan was as well. He consequently expounds, albeit briefly, on Christian practice and liturgy, before dismissing it as a mere superstition.

And yet Pliny's ignorance may not be so strange after all. There is little indication that even Roman intellectuals had a deep interest in trying to approach anything remotely close to an accurate understanding of cultures and customs of which they were suspicious or that stood outside customary Roman religious practices. His contemporary, Tacitus, is one of the better examples of this, and his understanding of Judaism and the origin of the Jews are exotic to say the least.[4] Among the theories of Jewish origins that he reports are that they were descendants of the inhabitants of ancient Crete, deriving their name from Mount Ida, or alternatively that they were from Ethiopia, or from a group of people in Homer known as the Solymi, hence the derivative name of their chief city, Jerusalem. In addition, Tacitus' narrative concerning Moses is hopelessly muddled, although he concedes his importance when he credits him with establishing a novel religion. Some historians might argue, rightly so, that we cannot apply modern standards of accuracy and understanding to ancient historians, especially in the context of attempting to understand cultures that were alien to them or to which they were actively hostile (Tacitus excoriates what he views as Jewish exclusivity and misanthropy, as well as their peculiar monotheism and their religion's aniconic nature).[5] While it is true that we must be careful when applying modern standards, weighed against Tacitus in this instance is that Judaism had been around longer than the Romans had, that there was, at the very least, interest in the religion on the part of the Greek community (who were if anything more prejudiced against non-Greeks than Romans were against non-Romans), and that there had been a Jewish community in Rome for at least two centuries, if not longer, when Tacitus is writing. One would think someone as experienced and intelligent as Tacitus would have had a deeper familiarity with Judaism. To Pliny's credit, however, what he depicts as Christian practice – unlike his contemporary Tacitus' portrayal of the Jews – is quite plausible, despite his prejudice against them as practising a 'depraved superstition'.

Two other aspects of Pliny's letter concerning the Christians are of note. First, it implies that historic memory and knowledge of the Christians was still something very much on the margins. Pliny and Tacitus will have been young boys, probably not much older than 10 if that, when the Great Fire of AD 64 broke out under Nero. One would have thought that the brutal persecution of Christians in its wake would have held a place in Roman memory, and we may wonder if Trajan, who was roughly the same age as Pliny and Tacitus, will have had a memory of it too – certainly Trajan, with his vast workload of correspondence and imperial secretaries, will have heard from more officials than just Pliny (although Christians will have had an especially heavy presence in the East) about this eccentric and idiosyncratic group. Second, the language of Pliny, with his reference to the Christians as a *pravam superstitionem* ('depraved superstition') is language that also recalls Tacitus – or rather, Tacitus echoes Pliny, since he likely wrote the vast majority of his *Annals* in the years after his friend's death (Tacitus appears to have started the *Annals* in AD 110, and Pliny died in his province in AD 111).

In what is only our second pagan author to mention the Christians, Tacitus also refers to their religion as a *superstitio* in his discussion of their persecution in the wake of the fire in 64, but goes one better. It is not depraved, it is destructive (*exitiabilis*). The passage is worth citing in full:

> *Sed non ope humana, non largitionibus principis aut deum placamentis decedebat infamia, quin iussum incendium crederetur. ergo abolendo rumori Nero subdidit reos et quaesitissimis poenis adfecit, quos per flagitia invisos vulgus Christianos appellabat. auctor nominis eius Christus Tiberio imperitante per procuratorem Pontium Pilatum supplicio adfectus erat; repressaque in praesens exitiabilis superstitio rursum erumpebat, non modo per Iudaeam, originem eius mali, sed per urbem etiam, quo cuncta undique atrocia aut pudenda confluent celebranturque. igitur primum correpti qui fatebantur, deinde indicio eorum multitudo ingens haud proinde in crimine incendii quam odio humani generis convicti sunt. et pereuntibus addita ludibria, ut ferarum tergis contecti laniatu canum interirent aut crucibus adfixi aut flammandi atque, ubi defecisset dies, in usum nocturni luminis urerentur. hortos suos ei spectaculo Nero obtulerat, et circense ludicrum edebat, habitu aurigae permixtus plebe vel curriculo insistens. Unde quamquam adversus sontes et novissima exempla meritos miseratio oriebatur, tamquam non utilitate publica, sed in saevitiam unius absumerentur.*

> But Nero's infamy did not subside either by human aid, by his largess, or by the appeasements of the gods, and consequently it was believed he ordered the fire. And so to end the rumour Nero put up

> defendants and treated with the most exquisite punishments those whom the mob called Christians, who were hated for their disgraces. The author of this name, Christ, had been put to death by Pontius Pilate, the procurator when Tiberius was emperor; and the destructive superstition although having been repressed for the moment broke out afresh, not only throughout Judaea, the place of this evil's origin, but even throughout the city, where everything from everywhere that is atrocious or shameful flows as in a confluence together and is made popular. First, therefore, those who confessed were arrested; next, upon their information, a huge multitude was convicted not on the charge of arson so much as because of the hatred of the human race against them. Sport was added to their deaths so that covered in the skins of wild animals they perished when dogs tore them to pieces, or they were crucified or condemned to be burnt alive, and at night they were set alight as human torches. Nero provided his own gardens for this spectacle and presented a circus game, having mingled with the crowd in the dress of a charioteer or wheeling his chariot in a circle. Consequently there was pity for them, although it was directed towards those who were guilty and deserving of the ultimate penalty, on the grounds that they had not been punished for the public's welfare, but to satisfy the cruelty of one man.

Tacitus likely wrote this passage some years after Pliny's death, perhaps as long as a decade if not longer, but there is no need to think he was influenced by the letter or ever saw it even. *Superstitio* was a coded but common word that set apart religious practices that were deemed outside the mainstream of Roman life. These included at various times not just Judaism and Christianity but the cult of the Magna Mater (the Great Mother) from Asia Minor (whose initiates of a certain grade practised self-castration), Isis from Egypt, and Bacchus (the priestly administrators of the cult were brutally suppressed, and many were in fact executed, in 186 BC).[6]

A Bad Roman Governor: The Case of Lucius Verres

Though it might not seem so to us, the accused brought before Pliny were lucky. As already noted, Pliny at least appears to have been an even-tempered man with a studious concern for the details of government (as his stream of anxious letters to Trajan appear to indicate). Indeed, one can detect a tone of exasperation and impatience in Trajan's replies to his overly solicitous procurator (as in letter 117, in which he reminds Pliny that he chose him for his prudence and 'that you might govern by shaping their behaviour and decide what things might profit for the permanent peace of the province' – to which we might add when read between the lines, 'so stop bothering me'). Roman provincial administration ran a spectrum in terms of its efficiency and benevolence, from the benign to the hair-raising, and Roman governors had three essential tasks: maintaining public order; military defence of the province; and collecting revenues – as the jurist Ulpian observed, a good governor takes his duties seriously and keeps his province peaceful and quiet. But Roman governors are a spectrum from the energetic and efficient to the horrific. Caesar's administration of Gaul and its conquest was by degrees vigorous and meticulous, ruthless and cunning – and diligently recorded in annual reports that later became his *Gallic War Commentaries*, all set down in limpid, well-balanced, unadorned, periodical Latin sentences. Cicero was a careful and diligent, albeit a grumpy and somewhat pouting, administrator of Cilicia who sent dry reports of local tribes and feuds to the Senate.[7] Over two decades prior to his own governorship, Cicero had prosecuted a governor, Lucius Verres, who was not merely lax, but studiously malicious in his governance of his province. Cicero's prosecution survives in its entirety, and gives an account of the sort of atrocities a Roman governor in the republic could commit, often with impunity.

Verres' career as governor of Sicily in the 70s was one of savage and ferocious rapine, even granting some scope to Cicero's brutally polemic depiction, on which we rely as the sole source, although given that Verres' abandoned his defence despite powerful legal protection, which included the help of Cicero's famous rhetorical rival Hortensius, much of Cicero's depiction is almost certainly true. Verres was most notorious for his virtually systematic pillaging of Sicily's artistic patrimony.[8] For centuries, starting in the eighth century BC, Sicily had been colonized by Greeks whose cities had been adorned with some of the greatest artworks of antiquity. During his governorship, Verres hired two brothers to his staff, artists named Tlepolemus and Hiero from a town called Cibyra, in order to scout out particularly fine pieces of art, Verres believing no doubt that as artists they would have connoisseurs' eyes for fine collections to appropriate for his own use.[9] Armed with his agents, Verres undertook a devastating programme of pillaging the island of its cultural treasures. In Syracuse, Verres took a statue of Paean and of Aristeus from the Temple of Liber (i.e., Bacchus), and a statue of Jupiter *Imperator* ('Who Commands') from Jupiter's temple; the last of these was particularly egregious, if Cicero's claim that it ranked among the top three statues of Jupiter in the world is credible.[10] He also removed from Syracuse, for his own use, a series of paintings in Minerva's temple that depicted a cavalry engagement of King Agothocles.[11] We could continue going town by town, as Verres divested Sicily of its artistic and cultural patrimony, but renowned artworks on public display were not his only target.

In addition to looting Sicily's cities and towns of their artistic treasures wholesale, Verres had a practised nose for sniffing out fine pieces in private collections as well. One of those to suffer at the hands of Verres was Pamphilus of Lilybaeum (modern Marsala), who owned a jug made by a famous artist named Boëthius, a large and lovely work according to Cicero.[12] Indeed, Cicero asserts that, in the end, no statue, painting, or image remained in the province.[13] In some instances Verres used false accounting to make a pretence of legality. Hence Cicero produced in court the account books for purchase from a prominent and wealthy provincial named Heius: Cicero introduced these accounts into evidence and ridiculed them, since Verres had bought pieces by renowned artists, including Praxiteles, Polyclitus, and Myron – a virtual who's who of what are still household names for art historians of any stripe – for a very small sum through intimidation.[14] In this instance, and in many others, since artwork often was displayed in a sacred context, such as a religious offering or cult statue in a temple, there was also an element of sacrilege on the grounds that Verres had plundered statues consecrated in Heius' family chapel.[15] Silver dinnerware, fine textiles, prize horses, young women – nothing was protected from his avarice, which he also employed to further corrupt his staff, and used not infrequently to co-opt the local population of a given community into compliance.

But there were far more fearsome ways that Verres had abused his power, and one example will suffice from an incident that took place early in his career, when he was a legate on the staff of Cn. Dolabella, governor of Cilicia between 80 and 79 BC. At one point Verres was sent (at his own request) to the court of a local king, Nicomedes of Bithynia (with whom

Julius Caesar had a notorious affair as a young man). Cicero says it was a mere pretext for Verres to profit off provincials. On his way he arrived at the town of Lampsacus.[16] Now it was customary when Roman officials travelled a province for the most prominent men of the community to house and entertain them. Lampsacus was an ancient Greek community, perhaps best known for its importation to Rome of the god Priapus, a deity with an absurdly large penis that was intended to ward off evil spirits and protect, among other things, one's home and gardens.

Verres' first priority was to send out agents to see if there was any woman or girl that would make a prolonged stay worthwhile, and his agent, Rubrius, reported that there was a man named Philodamus, who by virtue of birth, rank, and wealth, was the foremost member of the community, and whose daughter was of exceptional beauty. Verres had Rubrius installed in the house (Philodamus' reluctance not withstanding), and Philodamus, trying to be a good host, threw a dinner party for his Roman guest with an open invitation to Rubrius to invite any friend he wished. He invited Verres and his staff. Once the first round of wine had been imbibed and the room began to hum with conviviality, Rubrius posed a question to his host: 'Philodamus, why don't you order your daughter to be summoned here to us?' Philodamus demurred, and explained that it was contrary to Greek custom for women to join men at such a gathering, but some creature on Verres' staff shut him down: 'This really is intolerable – let the woman be summoned!' Slaves on the general staff were immediately posted as guards at Philodamus' front door. Philodamus managed to meet with his own slaves, urged them not to worry about him but to preserve his daughter, and to send word to his son who was at the house of a friend that night to come and help save his daughter's honour. Meanwhile, a general melee ensued between Philodamus' and Verres' men, in the course of which Rubrius even scalded Philodamus with a jug of boiling water. His son, rushing home, alerted the townspeople, and enraged they rallied to Philodamus' house; Cornelius, a lictor of Verres, and several of his slaves were killed in the ensuing fight.

Verres escaped, but the next morning angry townspeople gathered at the house where he was staying, surrounded it with brushwood, and tried to burn Verres alive. He escaped badly scorched. Verres' next move was to press for the trial of Philodamus and his son for the death of a Roman lictor. Even though the deck was heavily stacked against them since the

Romans had packed the courts, the verdict was that further evidence was needed to condemn Philodamus and his son. This enraged both Verres and his superior, the corrupt Cn. Dolabella, who very openly fumed; they demanded and got a second hearing. Even though the officials knew it was a sham, Philodamus and his son were both condemned and then swiftly beheaded in the forum in the city of Laodocea (later one of the seven churches of Asia mentioned in *Revelation*). It is a scene whose justice – or gross lack of it – is evocative of a scene right out of Dostoyevsky.

Verres' trial took place in 70 BC, and he was, rather miraculously, condemned. Miraculously, because the old boys' network was so entrenched in Rome – much as it still is in governing systems today – that justice was almost impossible to obtain against the well placed and privileged. Provincials rarely received any real restitution or satisfaction. The network even rallied around Ser. Sulpicius Galba, a governor of Lusitania who in 153 BC committed what today we would recognize as a crime against humanity when he treacherously attempted to exterminate the Lusitani (a Celtiberian tribe living in modern Portugal) through ethnic cleansing, reportedly massacring over 150,000 of them according to our sources, despite pledges and assurances of their safety upon surrendering to him. Cato the Elder, the ancient stalwart and symbol of republican dignity, tradition, and probity, tried to prosecute him, but Galba entered the Senate in black garb of mourning, hair long and dishevelled, beard unshaven, with his wife and children in an equally humble state, and his fellow senators, showing a pity that was utterly undeserved, became instruments in the miscarriage of justice and protected Galba.[17] As the great Roman satirist Juvenal was to put it over 250 years later: 'What does infamy matter so long as one's cash is safe?/ Marius drinks in exile from the eighth hour of the day and enjoys his angry gods,/ but you, a province victorious in your trial, weep' (*quid enim salvis infamia nummis?/ exul ab octava Marius bibit et fruitur dis/ iratis, at tu victrix provincia ploras*).[18] Marius Priscus was a corrupt governor of Africa in AD 98 who was prosecuted for provincial maladministration in 100 by no less than Pliny the Younger and his colleague, Tacitus.[19] They won their case, but as was typical, while Marius was driven from political life into a more than comfortable retirement, his victims went without restitution.

However, Priscus and other corrupt governors notwithstanding, provincial administration in the Rome of the emperors was generally better than during the republic. During the republic, senatorial cliques, factions, and old allegiances protected the deleterious senator-turned-governor. Under the emperors, the empire turned into the property of one family, and it was a governor's duty to be steward of the *princeps*' interests when in the provinces. But there were still problems, and our sources relate cases in which abuse took place on a horrific scale. To cite but one example, the future emperor Galba who governed Spain under Nero (emperor AD 54–68), cut off the hands of a dishonest moneylender and had them nailed to the table where he conducted business. He later had a man crucified for allegedly poisoning his ward to gain his inheritance; when the man invoked his Roman citizenship, meaning right of appeal to Caesar, he merely ordered that his cross be white-washed and raised much higher than the rest.[20]

Reasonable Roman governors on the other hand respected a Roman citizen's appeal to be heard before Caesar, as was the case with Pliny and the Christians, and sent them packing off to Rome. It was a similar appeal to Festus, the Roman governor of Judaea under Nero from ca. AD 60–62, which saved Paul: 'Then Festus, when he had conferred with the council, answered, Hast thou appealed unto Caesar? unto Caesar shalt thou go.'[21] Systemic abuses rarely are wholly eradicated. The stunning cruelty and bad faith of governors during the republic by no means vanished but, on the whole, governance of the provinces improved with the advent of greater accountability to an emperor. Grinding the provinces down to the point of rebellion, one suspects was an expensive business, and sucked down like Charybdis the profits extracted by avaricious equestrian businessmen, co-opted local nobility, and nefarious imperial operatives. One can only wonder how much return was lost when Seneca's collection of a 62 million sesterces state loan was called in at higher rates of interest in the recently conquered and newly incorporated province of Britannia. The province exploded (see pp. 142–8). Containing and ultimately crushing it could not have been cheap, and took three years, from AD 60 to 62.

Pilate in the Ancient Historical Record

Roman provincial governance had a spectrum from the competent but stern Pliny, to the rapacious and murderous Verres. It is now for us to consider where the prefect of Judaea, Pontius Pilate, stood within that range. Of his predecessors in his prefecture we know little or nothing: not much is known about Coponius (prefect from AD 6–9), Marcus Ambibulus (AD 9–12), Annius Rufus (AD 12–15), and finally Valerius Gratus (AD 15–26).[22] In our pagan sources Pilate is only mentioned once, in Tacitus' account of the Great Fire of AD 64 already cited above. And in fact, Tacitus tells us virtually nothing, except that he was *procurator* of Judaea, one of the smallest provinces of the empire, under Tiberius, and an anachronism, since it was only from the time of the emperor Claudius in the 40s that the governor of Judaea was called a *procurator*, with the post previously held by a prefect. Our one surviving inscription concerning Pilate (see fig. 4.1) refers to him as [PRAEF]ECTVS IVDA[EA]A, with the inscription accepted as the correct title, and it is all but certain that he was of the equestrian class, as was his ambitious contemporary, Sejanus, since it was equestrians who always governed Judaea.[23] It probably came from a tower in Caesarea (the *Tibereium*, named possibly after Tiberius himself) and such dedicatory homages were not unusual in the empire. Unfortunately, the inscription does not include Pilate's *praenomen* (i.e., first name), and his origins remain equally obscure, though the inscriptional and literary records indicate an origin of the Pontii (his family or clan name, known

Fig. 4.1: The inscription recording Pilate as prefect of Judaea is a part of a dedicatory inscription that was found reused in the staircase of the theatre at Caesarea and is now in the Israel Museum in Jerusalem; it is the first and only mention of Pontius Pilate's name outside of the literary record. (Carole Raddato via *Wikimedia Commons*)

as a *gentilicium*) from somewhere between Latium and Campania, and the Pontii were a prominent clan among the Oscan-speaking Samnites with whom the Romans fought a fierce series of wars in central Italy from the mid-fourth to the early third century BC.[24]

The name Pilate, his last name or *cognomen* (often derived from a profession or characteristic) means literally 'armed with a javelin' and may indicate an ancestor known for his skill with this weapon. We can state with a reasonable degree of certainty that as an equestrian Pilate would have started his career as a military man, very likely will have been personally known to Tiberius, and very probably will have been stationed outside of Italy for his service.[25] Perhaps he became acquainted with Tiberius while under his command in a province such as Germania or Pannonia. Beyond the New Testament and these conjectures, we must turn to Josephus and Philo for our knowledge of how Pilate governed – a matter of some controversy among scholars, although he does not appear at first glance to make a good impression.[26] First, early in his tenure, while he settled his army into their winter quarters in Jerusalem, in secret and under cover of night he moved the Roman standards into Jerusalem. The artistic record gives us outstanding evidence for the appearance of Roman war standards: a *signifer* (literally, 'a bearer of the standard'), carried a *vexillum* ('standard'), topped with various symbols, such as hands or eagles or other animal totems, followed by a series of medallions with the portraits of gods and emperors lining the banner's staff (see fig. 4.2).[27] It was a symbol sacred to the Roman legions, and if a *signifer* found his maniple (a sub-division of a Roman legion) in a tight spot in battle, he was known to throw the sacred symbol into the enemy throng, which the Roman troop of young soldiers, driven by shame and testosterone, were bound to retrieve.

Pilate's move was bound to be offensive to Jewish sentiment. In fact, it might have been a deliberately provocative move on his part if we can believe Josephus who remarks that previously Roman magistrates ensured medallions on the standards were aniconic out of respect for Jewish sensibilities.[28] When the city's inhabitants awoke the next morning and saw them, an angry crowd gathered, including many from the surrounding countryside who had quickly heard the news.[29] They marched to Caesarea, the administrative capital for Roman governors in Judaea built by Herod the Great, where Pilate was staying, and surrounded

Fig. 4.2: A detail from Trajan's Column: troops arrive at a sacrifice; on the left Roman soldiers bear Roman standards adorned with a variety of decorations and symbols, including what are likely images of deities and emperors. (Public Domain via *Wikimedia Commons*)

his house, besieging it for five days and nights. On the sixth day, Pilate summoned the crowd to Caesarea's stadium (whose magnificent ruins today run parallel to the Mediterranean, see fig. 4.3), leading them to believe he was ready to give a response to their complaints. Then, upon a pre-arranged signal, he surrounded the Jewish petitioners with a troop of armed men, three men deep, and threatened a massacre if they refused to accept Caesar's image in the city, commanding the soldiers to bare their swords for good measure. En masse, the Jews knelt down, bent their necks, and began to shout that it was better to perish by the sword than to transgress the law – a form of peaceful civil disobedience that reflected that of John the Baptist and Jesus as well.[30]

Stunned by what he surely perceived as their dangerous fanaticism, Pilate relented, and the standards with their images of Tiberius were immediately removed. One scholar, Schiavone, here sees Pilate not as provocative but as cautiously testing the limits of Roman imperial force and trying to avoid deliberate confrontation by moving the standards into Jerusalem at night. He further notes that Pilate ultimately backed off from confrontation and argues that Pilate was a moderate man of intelligence who was flexible during 'an evolving situation'.[31] But Pilate

Fig. 4.3: A general view of the ruins of ancient Caesarea, the administrative capital of Roman Judaea, with a view of the hippodrome where the Jews congregated to protest Pilate's offensive actions. (Abraham Gracier via *Wikimedia Commons*).

did not need to drive his province to the brink, and not all Roman officials were so wilfully insensitive towards Jewish beliefs and practices: Vitellius, subsequently the governor of Syria, when planning to campaign against King Aretas (a Nabataean king ruling from Petra) in AD 37, was asked by the Jews not to pass through Judaea, again, because Roman standards displayed graven images; he complied with the request, went by a different route, and even left his army to join Herod Antipas in Passover celebrations in Jerusalem that year where a crowd warmly greeted him in gratitude.[32] Pilate's actions are praiseworthy only in the hindsight that a situation that could have turned much worse and spiralled out of control, by a fortunate accident did not.

This was not the end of Pilate's inept cultural insensitivity. Some time after that incident, he appropriated a part of the sacred Temple treasure known as the Corban.[33] This was a fund raised by the Temple through an annual tax of half a shekel – roughly equal to 2 Greek drachmas; all adult males throughout the Jewish diaspora paid it annually. Once upkeep obligations for the Temple were met, it could be expended on other projects for civic maintenance, and Pilate's intended project was an aqueduct some 50 miles long. As some have noted, this was in fact the act of a good governor who was responsible for the upkeep of a province's infrastructure, and it was by no means unprecedented to appropriate funds from the Temple to do so.[34] That is a fair enough assessment, but then something, and we have no idea what, went awry, and the people protested. The next time Pilate was in Jerusalem, the people surrounded his tribunal and quite obstreperously expressed their rage. But Pilate had learned from his experience with their religious zealotry at Caesarea and was ready. He had soldiers dressed in plain clothes over their armour who were ordered not to draw their swords, but to use cudgels on the most vocal. At a given signal, the soldiers drew their cudgels and beat many to death, causing a panic, with numerous protestors trampled to death as they attempted to flee. The crowd was horrified and silenced its objections. Some have defended the prefect's actions, arguing that Pilate was not provocative but cautious and ready, hence the men deployed in the crowd to silence it, and have further argued that while some of Pilate's men might have gone overboard, that Pilate was obligated as governor to maintain order and to keep violence at a minimum in his province. We should perhaps only accept this with reservations. Although we do hear of wilful disregard for human life on the part of governors, sometimes on a large scale, we do not often hear of them killing 300 people to 'test the waters', and it is a scenario that must remain conjectural.

The Jewish author Philo of Alexandria gives us further information about Pilate, and he is relentlessly hostile, again a perspective that has been challenged more than once.[35] Yet Philo had lived during Pilate's tenure as governor and likely will have had friends from the province who knew whereof they spoke. Scholars criticize Philo for his vague and schematic outline – some would say caricature – of Pilate, but while we should be cautious of an enthusiastic embrace of Philo, we should be equally sceptical of wholesale dismissal, given the larger context of how Roman governors tended to behave. Philo in fact construes Pilate as wilfully antagonistic, telling us that in an act of deliberate provocation he dedicated some golden shields in the Palace of Herod in the holy city with a view to honouring Tiberius; the shields contained honorific inscriptions to Tiberius and the name of Pilate who had dedicated them, but no iconography.[36]

Philo says the move was intended quite deliberately to antagonize the Jews of Jerusalem. They sent a delegation of their highest authorities to

Pilate, including four sons of Herod the Great, and begged him to remove the shields that had been put up contrary to custom.[37] According to Philo, who noted his inflexible obstinacy and cruelty, he refused. The delegation made clear that the action was an insult and demanded to see an imperial missive or order mandating the action, which Pilate saw as a veiled threat to take their case to Tiberius. This alarmed Pilate, who was fully aware that the administration of his province had been corrupt, with his open contempt, rapine, insult, and cruelty well known; a cruelty that included the deaths of men who had been untried and uncondemned. Pilate was in a state of enraged perplexity, and appears to have waivered concerning whether or not to remove the shields, when the Jewish authorities made good on their threats, and sent a supplicatory missive to Tiberius.

The letter elicited a harsh, reproachful reply from Tiberius, chastening his prefect. It commanded Pilate to remove the shields immediately, and to rededicate them in the Temple of the Divine Augustus at Caesarea, a looming and beautiful structure that overlooked Caesarea's harbour and stood on an elevated platform, making it one of if not the most prominent building in the city. The episode, as related in Philo, is important for another reason, since it supports the harsher depiction of Josephus, belying and undercutting in the starkest terms the more benign depiction of Pilate in the New Testament. Pilate, according to Philo, had far more to fear than an embassy of royalty denouncing him about the shields fearful that, in Philo's words:

> [the embassy] might impeach him with respect to other particulars of his government, in respect of his corruption, and his acts of insolence, and his rapine, and his habit of insulting people, and his cruelty, and his continual murders of people untried and uncondemned, and his never ending, and gratuitous, and most grievous inhumanity.[38]

Tiberius, Pilate knew, was not one to countenance mismanagement of his provinces lightly, and his record was far from above reproach.

Some of Pilate's policy may have issued from Sejanus, who as a powerful prefect of equestrian status may have been the patron of Pilate and helped him in his career, though just how closely tied Pilate was to Sejanus remains a matter of controversy, and a cautious interpretation might lead us away from such a conclusion.[39] Sejanus, Eusebius writes, was a murderous anti-Semite, who desired to exterminate the race entirely (genocidal fantasies are not limited to modern totalitarian states), and his remark receives support again from Philo, who says that Sejanus by virtue of his power was able to inflict open and immediate harm against the Jews.[40] We cannot be certain, but in AD 19 Jews were expelled from Rome and Sejanus could possibly have been behind the policy, although Suetonius tells us that the emperor Tiberius might have well been its driving force.[41] Whether it was a direct product of a generally anti-Semitic attitude is problematic, since the expulsion appears connected with a specific crime committed by some Jews in Rome against an aristocratic woman whose husband was a friend of Tiberius, and so is probably case specific rather than the direct product of Roman anti-Semitism.[42]

The expulsion, mentioned in Josephus, Suetonius, Tacitus, and Cassius Dio, is also connected with repression of the cult of Isis and may have been part of a general and periodic purging of foreign religious elements in Rome. While it is almost certainly a late interpolation that most scholars reject as authentically belonging to Josephus, the passage also focuses laser-like on a specific victim of Pilate's: at the behest of the Jewish authorities ('the foremost men among us' is the precise term he uses), Pilate executed Jesus.[43] The passage introduces Jesus as 'a wise man', refers to him as one who performed 'wondrous works', a teacher of truth who attracted Jews and Gentiles alike. He appeared to his followers alive on the third day after Pilate had condemned him to crucifixion, a significant remark that appears to lay the blame for his death heavily, though by no means exclusively, on Pilate. Josephus' interpolator sets Jesus among the most respected prophets, and remarks that he still had a vigorous following down to his own day, when Josephus was writing between AD 70 and 100. In addition, Eusebius recounts an apocryphal tradition that Pilate sent a report of Jesus' death and resurrection to Tiberius.[44] According to Eusebius, Pilate was familiar with Christ's deeds, the reports that he had risen from the dead, and was aware that he was now believed a god. Tiberius referred the report to the Senate, but the Senate rejected it and refused to recognize Christ as divine. Tiberius reportedly undertook no actions against Christ's teachings; what is more, Tertullian, cited in Eusebius, notes that Tiberius stipulated that the Senate make no moves against the Christians themselves and even showed favour towards Christian teachings, threatening anyone who took steps towards their persecution.

The execution of Jesus was, however, some years before what would be the final straw in Pilate's tenure as prefect of Judaea, which came in 36. In that year, a Samaritan rabble-rouser claimed to know the location of sacred implements deposited by Moses and gathered a large – and armed – following with the intent that they would encamp on Mount Gezzirim, a place Josephus says was sacred to the locals.[45] Today it is located in the West Bank, barely a mile from Nablus as the crow flies and even closer to Jacob's Well (the site of Jesus' encounter with the Samaritan woman in *John* 4:5–15). First, though, they gathered at a village called Tiranthana (possibly modern Tire) not far from Gezzirim.[46] When Pilate got the news, he could not tolerate a troop of armed men outside of his authority – and we may wonder the intent of being armed if it was simply to treasure hunt after sacred relics – and was suspicious of their motives, likely recalling that his charge was, after all, to maintain peace and public order. He occupied the approaches to Gezzirim with a combination of infantry and cavalry and engaged them. Some were slain, many were put to flight, and the leaders rounded up and executed. The inhabitants of Samaria, outraged at Pilate's actions, sent a delegation to L. Vitellius, governor of Syria, consul in AD 34, father of the future emperor Aulus Vitellius (one of the worst of our early emperors), and a sycophantic courtier of Caligula and later his uncle, Claudius. Of Vitellius, Tacitus says that he is not unaware that he was of adverse reputation in Rome, but he ruled his provinces with ancient virtue.[47]

It was before this man, Vitellius, that the Samaritans made their case against Pilate: they accused Pilate of judicial murder, for the Samaritans had not gone to Tirathana to revolt from Rome but to escape the cruelties of Pilate. Vitellius heard their case with sympathy, and sent his legate, Marcellus, who is otherwise unknown, to relieve Pilate of his command, send him back to Rome, and take over as prefect of Judaea. Marcellus was prefect for only a short time – until AD 37. According to Josephus, Tiberius was dead before Pilate made it back to the city, though we might wonder whether Vitellius himself did not have some further orders concerning looking for an opportunity to replace Pilate who had been at his post now for ten years. Schiavone is perhaps right to note that the incident that resulted finally in Pilate's removal was not the incident at Gezzirim but rather the cumulative ten years of relatively minor incidents that had had a collective effect resulting in complaints against the prefect and his ultimate removal.[48] Tiberius was famous for keeping governors in their provinces for an extended period, as Josephus and Tacitus both noted, and Josephus used a macabre metaphor to explain why. A man once fell along the road with a grievous open wound.[49] The wound bled and flies gathered around it, yet when a passer-by came to help and was about to wave the flies away from his wound, the injured man stopped him; the flies were full having sucked all his blood and now lethargic, were no longer consuming it. Drive them away and more would simply come and drink more of his blood. A province was like a man with an open wound – a new governor would simply suck more blood out of it. Remove the old governor and another will do the same. Keep him in place and his appetite will be less keen. After ten years it was time to drive Pilate from the wound. Vitellius' removal of Jesus' executioner is the last that we can recover from our proximately contemporary sources of the historical Pilate beyond the gospel accounts. All else, afterwards, is hearsay or apocryphal tradition.

The Pilate of the Gospels

The Pilate of the gospels is a distinctly different character from the one of Josephus. Although the gospels are not intended to be read as historical texts, looked at with the dispassionate eye of a deconstructionist or revisionist, there is little to give confidence that Pilate was the indifferent or disinterested administrator who in the gospels, on the whole, seems rather bored and world-weary.[50] Given potential animus against Judaism, his fears about religious fervour that reached their apex in the massacre at Gezzirim, and above all considering that Roman governors potentially had plenty of agents to give them intelligence concerning their province, it is hard not to imagine that Pilate might have had some knowledge about Jesus before he was brought in for interrogation and execution. The reasons for this are grounded in Pilate's social and political environment, and are closely connected with his likely career path and the period, culture, and legal system of which he was a part. Now we know for certain that Pilate governed his province between AD 26 and 36. That we have these dates is significant, because by working backwards we can guess his age and know something of his career and experience under Rome's early, still consolidating, Principate. Almost any man in Rome given the responsibility of governing a province will have been at least 40, if not older. If we put Pilate at 45 years of age when he started to govern then we can put his birth at around 20 BC. Augustus was well entrenched by the time he was born, and Tiberius already a young general serving as commander in his stepfather's legions and involved with administrative duties.

Pilate will have been a teenager in Rome and possibly undergone his military training, as many good elite Romans appear to have done in their late teens, when a series of scandals and deaths occurred that rocked Augustus' household between 6 BC and AD 2. In that period, Tiberius went into self-imposed exile on Rhodes (see p. 15), and his wife, Julia, was exiled after revelations of a scandal of a sexual nature. Also in that period came the deaths of Augustus' beloved grandsons, Gaius (in Armenia) and Lucius (in Spain). We have no idea whether Pilate was in Rome during the scandal that further rocked the imperial house in AD 8, resulting in the exile of Augustus' granddaughter, Julia, and the banishment of Rome's popular poet, the charming and playful Ovid (whose work proved offensive to Augustus' taste according to the poet).[51] In the next year, AD 9, came the disaster in Germania in the Teutoberg Forest whose dead included the commander, Quinctilius Varus, once himself a governor of Syria.[52] Five years later, in AD 14, Augustus died, entered the pantheon of Roman demi-gods, and Tiberius secured his place at the head of the government. Where Pilate was during these events is anyone's guess. Equally obscure is how Pilate initially came to Tiberius' attention. Was he an acquaintance in the army? Was he introduced through a letter of commendation from a friend? A shared interest (perhaps even, given the rumours swirling around Tiberius, a shared perversion)? Or did his praetorian prefect, Sejanus, have a soft spot for a fellow equestrian and bring him to Tiberius' attention? We remain very much in the dark.

One important point to bear in mind, however, is that the reign of Tiberius, from an early date, had a number of ominous prosecutions against conspirators who dared to use magic – to discern their future political prospects, to curse the *princeps*, or to cut a path to power. The ancients were surrounded by the supernatural, well beyond what a Roman might consider 'normal' or 'mainstream' state religion, with its religious holidays and festivals, and its steady stream of sacrifices and observances. There was as well an abiding reliance on astrology and as noted (p. 17) even Tiberius had a proper court astrologer, while beliefs concerning ghosts, witches, and werewolves appear throughout the literary record in authors such as Petronius, Horace, and Lucan. There was, in addition, a robust trade in magic that was divided into two distinct categories of one that could have beneficial ends, and another that could curse and consign one's life and spirit to the realm of the dead. Tacitus and Pliny, two very sophisticated and intelligent men, never question any of this. Apuleius, the great Roman novelist from North Africa, was compelled to defend himself against a charge of using a charm on a rich widow to seduce her and win her fortune. More to the point: there were laws on the books concerning magic and astrology, and the body count of highly placed Romans in the first century AD who were charged with magic, consulting astrologers, or employing necromancy (i.e., consulting the dead to divine the future), is not inconsequential. Legal codes had regulated and delimited magic since Rome's earliest laws, the Twelve Tables, and abided into the Justinianic Digest, the most significant body of Roman law, compiled in the sixth century AD, in a now Christian rather than pagan empire. Not that magic was inherently bad; it merely needed some fairly strict regulation, and we know that it was widely practised throughout the empire. Indeed, in early Christian art we occasionally encounter a beardless Jesus wielding a magician's staff, using it to divide loaves and fishes, turn water into wine, and to raise Lazarus from the dead (see fig. 4.4).

In the first twelve years of Tiberius' rule leading up to Pilate's appointment, there were a number of spectacular cases that could not help but impress on any Roman official the subversive dangers that lurked behind magic practices. One of the earlier and more sensational cases occurred in AD 16. In that year, a notorious prosecution took place in Rome when a rival claimant to the throne, M. Scribonius Libo Drusus, was arrested and condemned for pulling out all stops against the emperor, the recently installed Tiberius. He had used magic, astrology, and necromancy in an effort to ascertain his chances in usurping the emperor.[53] Betrayed by a treacherous friend and forced to suicide, over the next ten years this was but one of several cases in which magic and sorcery had a significant place.

Three years later, in AD 19, a member of the ruling family, Tiberius' popular nephew Germanicus Caesar, died in Antioch. While there were

Fig. 4.4: An early Christian sarcophagus, now in the Palazzo Massimo Museum in Rome, depicts a beardless Jesus with a magician's staff as he changes water into wine, performs the miracle of the loaves and fishes, and raises Lazarus from the dead. (Jean-Pol Grandmont via *Wikimedia Commons*)

only rumours of poison, there was hard evidence of the use of black magic and curses. Upon inspection it was found human remains had been buried beneath the floors and in the walls, with spells, curses, and lead tablets containing Germanicus' name used to communicate with the dark powers of the underworld, while ashes smeared with blood were also discovered – all used to consign a person's soul to the realm of the dead. In the end the alleged murderer, a Roman aristocrat by the name of Cn. Calpurnius Piso, was condemned, but on another charge for a very different reason.[54] Then there was the trial of Clutorius Priscus in AD 21, for attempted murder of Tiberius' son, Drusus. Priscus indiscreetly wrote a poem lamenting Drusus' death during an illness in which recovery was not expected. But Drusus lived until AD 23 (see p. 45), and Clutorius was condemned and swiftly executed by an over-zealous decree of the Senate, something that incurred Tiberius' displeasure.[55] There may well have been a charge of magic involved, since poems could potentially also be construed as incantations of nefarious intent, and in fact, the word in Latin for poem, *carmen*, can also have the sense of a song or incantation with magical properties. Magic and the supernatural were not light matters but perilous both for the individual and state. In Philostratus' historical fiction about the life of Apollonius of Tyana, when Apollonius is accused of wizardry and brought into the emperor's presence he is forbidden to have any amulet, book, or paper of any kind, presumably to deprive him of any magical powers he might employ to elude punishment.[56] We could cite other cases from the period in which magic played a part in the accusations, such as the one against Agrippina's cousin, Claudia Pulchra, who was accused of adultery, the attempted poisoning of Tiberius, and *devotiones* (which we can generally translate as 'formal curses') in AD 26, the year Pilate left for his province.[57] Numerous additional cases arose of a similar nature well after Tiberius, particularly under Claudius (AD 41–54) and Nero (AD 54–68) in which magic practices played a significant role.

It is difficult to imagine that Pilate was somehow unmoored from the culture and political atmosphere of the first twelve years of Tiberius' tenure between AD 14 and 26. We might then fairly ask, how would such a man, from such an environment, be expected to respond to a man in a distant province who, rumour had it, had the power to change water to wine? Who could, more ominously, raise people from the dead? Perhaps most alarming of all would be a miracle such as that of the loaves and fishes: yet it would not have been the astonishing feat of feeding 5,000 from three loaves and fishes that mattered. It was the 5,000 itself, and the charismatic personality that could attract them. What business had this magnetic rabbi of gathering 5,000, nearly the equivalent in size to a Roman legion? Even a lackadaisical Roman governor would begin to have concerns about the order and stability of his province. Magic, crowds, Pilate's cultural milieu and personality, and the behaviour, in general of Roman officials in the provinces: none of this bodes well for the prefect's reaction to someone such as Jesus. We have already noted how Pilate reacted to a large gathering at Gezzirim, albeit armed, and how ruthlessly he had already treated crowds in Jerusalem.

The role of Pilate in the arrest and execution of Jesus raises a number of problems, however: how much had Pilate cooperated with the Jewish authorities in Jerusalem? To what extent had the Jewish authorities consulted Pilate and deferred to him? And what was the nature of the charge that led not to a trial, but to a swift and summary interrogation, torture, and execution?[58] To consider the question we will first consider the execution of Jesus and Pilate's involvement as presented in the synoptic gospels of *Matthew*, *Mark*, and *Luke*, (with some forays into *John*) before turning exclusively to the gospel of *John* which merits independent treatment by virtue of how divergent it is from the other three.

Now in all four of the gospels Jesus enters Jerusalem to the great enthusiasm of the people.[59] Even before he arrived in the city, it is likely that the Jewish authorities were committed to punishing Jesus for his teachings, and once he entered the city they became quite intent on his death but, given his apparent popularity and charisma, were fearful about how to bring it about. Indeed, *Mark* and other gospel passages indicate to us more than once that the chief priests and scribes 'sought how they might destroy him: for they feared him, because all the people was astonished at his doctrine'.[60] For the sake of argument and convenience, we should perhaps follow Schiavone and refer to the scribes, priests, and elders collectively meeting as a body as the Sanhedrin.[61] It has been conjectured that the elders' interests in destroying Jesus were grounded in what one could call a matter of national security: Caiaphas, who was the Temple's high priest, and others presumably saw Jesus' teachings as a threat to the Jewish people.[62] Jesus was, furthermore, stirring up potential disorder that by this point had a tradition of volatile outcomes in Judaea; that effectively made it a Roman problem as well, taking it out of the realm of the religious and setting it squarely in the civic sphere.[63] The council's fear of the people is perhaps nowhere better expressed than at *Luke* 22:6 where Judas 'sought opportunity to betray him unto them [i.e. the Jewish authorities] in the absence of the multitude'. When the time comes, it is not the Romans but hired men who were agents of the chief priests and elders (*Matthew* 26:47; *Mark* 14:43; *Luke* 22:54; *John* 18:3, 18:12) who seize Jesus and take him to Caiaphas' house for questioning and a rather brutal interrogation, including physical violence (*Matthew* 26:57–68; *Mark* 14:63–66), although *Mark* (14:53) does not specify the location but simply states 'And they led Jesus away to the high priest: and with him were assembled all the chief priests and the elders and the scribes.' *Luke* (22:63–65) has Jesus first tortured after he is blindfolded, beaten, and mocked, before the chief priests, elders, and scribes gather first thing in the morning to question Jesus who then hand him over to Pilate (*Luke* 22:66–71) for interrogation and execution.[64]

Of the three synoptic gospels, *Luke* is the only one in which the council launches into accusations before Pilate can question him (almost certainly with the help of an interpreter), accusing him vaguely of 'perverting' or 'overthrowing' the nation, forbidding tribute to Caesar, and declaring himself as Christ the King, a grave accusation to Roman ears if ever there was one.[65] Upon interrogation Pilate first asks Jesus, 'Art thou the King of the Jews?'[66] Jesus in turn gives his famous non-response: 'Thou sayest'.[67] In *Matthew* and *Mark* Pilate asked him again, 'Hearest thou not how many things they witness against thee?', and Jesus refused to respond.[68] *Luke* here (23:5–12) is different, diverging from *Matthew* and *Mark* after Jesus' non-response response. Reacting to Jesus' 'Thou sayest', Pilate tells the Jewish council that he finds him without fault, inflaming the council: 'And they were more fierce, saying, He stirreth up the people, teaching throughout all Jewry, beginning from Galilee to this place' (*Luke* 23:5). Hearing he was from Galilee, Pilate sent him to Herod Antipas, who, disappointed in what he saw, sent him back to Pilate.[69]

Luke (23:13–16) then relates that Pilate called together the people and chief priests, and Pilate tells them that despite open interrogation before all he finds no fault with Jesus, and reports that neither did Herod Antipas whose sphere was Jesus' native Galilee. He therefore states his intention to chastise and release him, perhaps by way of compromise, perhaps by way of testing the council, perhaps sincerely thinking Jesus unworthy of any further penalty. It is at this juncture that *Luke*'s text (23:17–19) once again converges with *Matthew* and *Mark*, and that all three gospels state that it was a custom of the governor to release a notable prisoner, who in this instance was Barabbas, a man both the gospels of *Mark* and *Luke* state was in custody for sedition and murder.[70] Pilate, however, gives those gathered a choice – should he release Barabbas or Jesus?[71]

It should be noted that in the course of the Barabbas episode that *Matthew* states at 27:17 'when they were gathered together', presumably referring back to a reference in 27:15 to 'the people' – though it could easily be simply the elders, chief priests, and assorted officials and attendants, while *Mark* refers at 15:8 to 'the multitude' without any clue concerning from where, how, or why they had gathered and turned against Jesus whom they had so warmly welcomed several days before.[72] The term 'multitude', variously *to plethos* or *ho ochlos* in Greek, is a loose one. For example, at *Luke* 23:1 the passage states that leaving the house of the high priest 'the whole multitude of them arose' and it is difficult to understand what is meant by this.[73] Some have seen this as an attempt to shift blame away from the guilt of the Jewish authorities and to inculpate the entirety of the Jewish people in Jesus' death, and as we shall see, the presence of 'the multitude' is markedly absent in *John*. In addition, in the course of the Barabbas episode *Matthew* and *Mark* appear to stack the deck against the Jews, stating Pilate gave them the choice 'For he knew they had handed him over on account of envy.'[74]

Such accounts would appear to try to exculpate Pilate who seems to be struggling to find a graceful exit for someone he sees as undeserving of punishment and who himself sees through the malice of Jesus' accusers. Further making the episode and the presence of crowds problematic are the passages in *Matthew* (27:20) and *Mark* (15:11): *Matthew* states that 'the chief priests and elders persuaded the multitude that they should ask Barabbas, and destroy Jesus', while *Mark* similarly states 'the chief priests moved the people, that he should rather release Barabbas', indicating an attempt to manipulate opinion. Scholars have noted a number of difficulties in accepting this as a credible representation. One is simply a matter of time constraints, getting word out to enough people to traverse the city and gather before noon at the site of the hearing when everything had been done under secret cover of darkness. Another difficulty is the apparent enthusiasm with which Jesus was met during his entrance to Jerusalem and the following he attracted as a popular figure, the secrecy with which he was arrested, and the hearing taking place at night at the house of Caiaphas – none of this is promising of a 'multitude' that has changed its mind and suddenly and inexplicably turned against Jesus, and any popular animus against Jesus would appear to be undercut by the authorities' anxiety over his arrest and his interrogation taking place in the dead of night. For all we know the multitude, if such a one existed, was a gang of hired thugs, just as were potentially the false witnesses mentioned in *Matthew* (26:60) and *Mark* (14:55–57), something we will return to below in our discussion of *John*.[75] That the elders could find no one to testify against Jesus legitimately hardly speaks to a large multitude suddenly turning against him. However, *Luke* does mention agents, presumably hired by the religious authorities, used to attempt to entrap Jesus, clearly indicating a staff of men at work who could potentially drum up 'a multitude' in a pinch – though many clearly had limits, since as noted it was no easy task finding those who would bear false witness. The 'multitude in a pinch' scenario appears supported at *Luke* 22:47 where it states of Jesus' arrest: 'behold a multitude, and he that was called Judas, one of the twelve, went before them'.

Yet again, a 'multitude' to take action against Jesus is a vague term, as is admittedly the multitude that greeted him upon his entrance to Jerusalem – although again we must remember that the authorities appeared to fear the multitude, while the multitude attending Jesus upon entrance does not appear to fear the presence of Jewish authorities who apparently intermingled, some perhaps out of curiosity, but some likely genuinely disturbed at Jesus' presence in the city, particularly during Passover celebrations when there had been civil disturbances in the recent past (see p. 111), as we find for example in *Mark*. Moreover, as Schiavone notes, we would need to accept that the Romans allowed a crowd to gather in support of two arrested men – Barabbas and Jesus – who were like matches near a powder keg, a scenario that appears implausible given Roman treatment of crowds.[76]

In the midst of the Barabbas episode in *Matthew* we get a strange interlude, when Pilate's wife interrupts the proceedings: 'When he was sat down on the judgement seat, his wife sent unto him saying, Have thou nothing to do with that just man: for I have suffered many things this day in a dream because of him.'[77] Such an admonition, if one did indeed occur, will have conceivably given Pilate pause: dreams were genuinely portentous and significant in antiquity, and taken quite seriously. Suetonius therefore notes, that the night before his murder Caesar dreamed that he was flying above the clouds and shaking hands with Jupiter, while his wife, Calpurnia, dreamed that he lay in her arms stabbed and bleeding.[78] Pliny the Younger in a letter about the recent death of a friend, C. Fannius, relates that Fannius was writing a history of those executed or banished under the emperor Nero.[79] One night Fannius dreamed that Nero visited him: sitting on the edge of the bed, the spectral figure of Nero read through the first three books of his work, then left. Fannius took it as a premonition that he would live only to complete three volumes of his work, as was indeed the case. And the great hypochondriac, Aelius Aristides, spent twenty years sleeping in the temple precinct of Aesclepius at Pergamum in the province of Asia, receiving the god's advice in dreams about how to cure his various ailments. The understanding of dreams as prophetic indications of future events was not limited to Greek and Roman society, but a common phenomenon in Near Eastern culture in general, with Joseph's interpretation of dreams at the court of Pharaoh in Egypt perhaps the best known among these. The strange interlude would be understood as a further and perhaps powerful obstacle in Pilate's willingness to carry out the wishes of the Jewish authorities.

When the narrative of the synoptic gospels once again converges, at *Luke* 23:22, *Mark* 15:12–14 and *Matthew* 27:21–23, Pilate asks yet again what is to be done with Jesus, expressing a willingness to release him, and the response of the crowd was to crucify him, leaving Pilate befuddled at Jesus' wrong – 'Why, what evil hath he done?' Giving no reason, the crowd simply kept calling for crucifixion.[80] In *Matthew* (27:24) the crowd appears to intimidate Pilate and verge on riot: 'When Pilate saw that he could prevail nothing, but rather that a tumult was made, he took water, and washed his hands before the multitude, saying, I am innocent of the blood of this person: see ye to it.' In *Mark* (15:15) and *Luke* (23:22–24) the situation is a bit less dire, the passage in *Mark* simply stating 'And so Pilate, willing to content the people, released Barabbas unto them, and delivered Jesus, when he had scourged him, to be crucified.' The purpose of referring to the multitude is very likely intended to implicate once again the Jewish community at large, rather than simply a faction of rich, privileged old men who were disgruntled at being intellectually out-punched by a lowly parvenu such as Jesus. It is also the final appearance of Pilate in the episode of Jesus' ordeal until after Jesus is dead, when Joseph of Arimathaea requests from Pilate that he be allowed to bury Jesus. In *Matthew* (27:58) Pilate's reaction is not recorded, while in *Mark* (15:44) Pilate reportedly marvelled that he was already dead, a plausible enough reaction given it could take two or three days to die from crucifixion.

Now *John* deviates substantially from the narrative of the synoptic gospels after Jesus' initial arrest. In *John* Jesus is first taken to Annas' house (*John* 18:13) and at some point, we are not told when, Caiaphas the high priest (and Annas' son-in-law) joined the council for Jesus' interrogation, since in 18:19 we are told Caiaphas interrogated Jesus without success, and in his irritation an officer struck Jesus for his perceived insolence (*John* 18:19–23).[81] At some point he was taken to Caiaphas' house before they transferred him to Pilate (*John* 18:24–28) in the *Praetorium* (the term for a governor's official residence), where Pilate first encounters him. Pilate may have initially seen the case not as a criminal one but as one pertaining to local Jewish law, since he asked the Jewish authorities to judge Jesus according to their own law (*John* 18:29–31). They responded that they could not, since they were seeking a capital charge against him and were not allowed to execute him (while provincial governors were in charge of criminal law and capital cases, civil law was a matter for local municipalities, and Pilate may have seen Jesus' case as civil in nature). *John* leaves out the Sanhedrin's discussions with Pilate concerning Jesus' offence, since when Pilate next appears in *John* (18:33) he asks Jesus, 'Art thou the King of the Jews?' Jesus responds, 'Sayest thou this thing of thyself, or did others tell it thee of me?' to which Pilate responds, 'Am I a Jew? Thine own nation and the chief priests have delivered thee unto me: what hast thou done?' (*John* 18:34–35). Jesus famously responds that 'My kingdom is not of this world,' and Pilate demands clarification: 'Art thou king then?' (*John* 18:36–37). Jesus answers, 'Thou sayest that I am a king. To this end was I born, and for this cause came into the world, that I should bear witness unto the truth. Every one that is of the truth heareth my voice.'

Pilate next delivered his famous repartee, 'What is truth?' before going back to the Sanhedrin to announce 'I find in him no fault at all,' (*John* 18:38) upon which he offers the Sanhedrin a choice, as in the synoptic gospels, between releasing Jesus or Barabbas (*John* 18:39–40). Pilate then has Jesus scourged, the soldiers placing a crown of thorns on his head and dressing him in a purple robe, mocking his regal pretensions and beating him (*John* 19:1–3). Next, Pilate leads him to the Sanhedrin, probably hoping that that was enough punishment for them, since Pilate now states, 'Behold, I bring him forth to you, that you may know that I find no fault in him' (*John* 19:4).[82] The council, unmoved, calls for his crucifixion, and Pilate wheels on them and tells them to do it themselves, to which the council rejoins (*John* 19:6–7): 'We have a law, and by our law he ought to die, because he made himself the Son of God.' This apparently alarmed Pilate ('When Pilate therefore heard that saying, he was the more afraid') and he went back to Jesus who had been taken to the *Praetorium* and asked (*John* 19:8–9), 'Whence art thou?' Jesus gave no reply, so Pilate again urged him (*John* 19:10), 'Speakest thou not unto me? knowest thou not that I have power to crucify thee, and have power to release thee?' Jesus then does reply (*John* 19:11): 'Thou couldst have no power at all against me, except it were given thee from above: therefore he that delivered me unto thee hath the greater sin.'

From then on Pilate reportedly strived to release him, but the Sanhedrin would have none of it and replied (*John* 19:12), 'If thou let this man go, thou art not Caesar's friend: whoever maketh himself a king speaketh against Caesar.' The remarks would have doubtless raised memories of Herod the Great's successor, Archelaus, whom Augustus ultimately denied the title of king and forced into retirement for the abuse of his position as a client king. Augustus kept his client kings on a short leash, the memory of Archelaus' fall would have been relatively recent (it was doubtless still a searing memory for his brother, Herod Antipas, who was reportedly in Jerusalem), and as noted, Romans did not suffer claims to kingship lightly. On top of that, as Schiavone observes, the council's exclamation 'thou art not Caesar's friend' could be interpreted as a veiled threat against Pilate.[83] Would they report him to the governor of Syria, or even send a delegation to Tiberius to lodge a complaint? Pilate now placed him in the 'judgement seat', stating to the council, 'Behold your King!' and once again the council called for his death (*John* 19:13–15). Pilate asked one final time: 'Shall I crucify your King?' and the chief priests responded, 'We have no king but Caesar.' It was now noon. Pilate at last relented, and handed him over for crucifixion (*John* 19:16). In composing the sign to go on his cross, Pilate wrote JESUS OF NAZARETH THE KING OF THE JEWS in Hebrew, Greek, and Latin (*John* 19:19–20). However, Caiaphas, the high priest, objected: 'Write not, The King of the Jews; but that he said, I am King of the Jews,' to which Pilate brusquely replied, 'What I have written I have written' (*John* 19:21–22). Then Pilate vanishes from John's text and from our view forever, except for the one detail shared by all the gospels, that Joseph of Arimathaea asked Pilate's permission to bury Jesus' body, which Pilate granted (*John* 19:38).

Can We Make Sense of It?

What are we finally to make of the enigma that was Pilate? There are numerous responses to that question, though one of the difficulties with the interpretation of Schiavone and Carter is that while both very admirably analyse Pilate's actions in their legal or political context, their analyses appear also firmly grounded in post-Enlightenment values of rationality and efficiency. The world Pilate inhabited was far from either: it is, rather, a world permeated by the irrational and the miraculous, a place in which this world and the world of the supernatural are separated not by a wall but by a sieve with the two melding into one another. We cannot retrieve the religious attitudes of specific individuals, but we can tell a great deal about a society by its priorities. Romans produced literature that bore witness to the miracles that gods could produce, as in Apuleius' *Golden Ass*, a peculiar work bearing witness to the power of the Greco-Egyptian deity Isis. They believed that Roman success was attributable to divine favour and their own particular *pietas*, a word very difficult to translate, but one that implies a sense of religious reverence and duty, as starkly spelt out in Livy's preface. Episodes abound in their most sophisticated authors about Roman soldiers morphing into werewolves, and witches raising soldiers from the dead to practise necromancy, while their legal codes addressed matters pertaining to magic and astrology. Pliny believed firmly in ghosts, while Tacitus tells us that black magic was practised against Tiberius' nephew Germanicus. The state itself made substantial expenditures on temples and religious buildings, as did private individuals, such as we find in Pompeii with its beautifully decorated Temple of Isis.

If we accept the punishment of Jesus as historical and assume, as I believe we should if taken as such, that Pilate would have been well aware of Jesus' activities before his encounter with him in the New Testament, we should be cautious in accepting Pilate as excessively reluctant to reject Jesus' divinity and perhaps even as a reluctant executioner. And while some scholars are hesitant to accept that Pilate knew who Jesus was already, governors for the most part (but admittedly not always) had a staff that often included those who would gather intelligence, while a good governor would also tour his province. When we add to that the small size of the province, an abiding Roman hunger for news and rumour, and perhaps a heightened alertness for trouble in the wake of John the Baptist's recent execution and Herod Antipas' excited anticipation to meet the charismatic rabbi (which Jesus was according to *John* 6:25), it seems improbable that Pilate would not have some idea about him well before his encounter on Passover. Moreover, Pilate's reluctance to take action in Jesus' case could well have been driven by similar concerns Herod Antipas had had about John the Baptist (see p. 120), which was the people's response. Pilate's mandate was to keep order in his province, and Jesus and the Jewish council had put him between a rock and a hard place in which considerations of Jesus' popularity had to be weighed against the political consideration of Rome's thus far relatively good relations with the Jewish ruling elite. It is hard to believe, from that perspective, that Pilate's relationship with, or awareness of, Jesus was compactly and neatly isolated to within a few hours in a single morning.

However, that Pilate receives a sympathetic treatment in the gospels, one at variance with other historical sources, should perhaps not surprise us for a variety of reasons. The prophet is always variously ignored, derided, and persecuted not by the befuddled outsider, but by his own people, in his own land. The disobedience of the Hebrews towards Moses, the cries of Jeremiah that go unheeded, the beheading of John the Baptist, and the horrific civil strife that occurred during the Jewish rebellion of AD 66–70 which casts an enormously long shadow over the gospels – these are not inter-communal quarrels but ones that take place within a given community. Hence we may set the gospel's emphasis on the consistent persecution of Jesus by the Pharisees and elders against the faith of a Roman centurion or Pilate's befuddled indifference mingled with occasional glimpses of curiosity. The gospels were written by Jewish heretics, who eventually took on the name Christian, hence the fight was inter-familial, and there are few things more bitter. Moreover, a historical deconstructionist – we could even say revisionist or reductive – reading as the one undertaken here is to read the gospel accounts as a proper historical text. We can rail against the historical inaccuracies, the contradictions, the inconsistencies that abound in the New Testament. The weight of Roman culture and history, taken together with the accounts of Josephus and Philo, must be set against the New Testament's depiction of Pilate as relatively benign. Yet the writers of the gospels were not writing history.[84] In broad terms they were trying to create a distinctive community identity and to break off from their Jewish origins.

That is another piece to Pilate's puzzling characterization in the gospels. Pilate is integrated into the Christian sphere, made at one not with the pagan Romans or even Jews, but rather is adopted as one of Christianity's own. It is for that reason that Tertullian says that Pilate was a Christian 'in accordance with his conscience' (*pro sua conscientia*).[85] The result is a shift of maximum blame on the Jewish community for Jesus' death. As Schiavone points out, Pilate's hand washing while possibly fiction, is also 'the origins of a western tragedy' that effectively lays blame on the

Jews for Jesus' death: 'The Jews had to be isolated in their guilt; it was necessary for Pilate to remain out of it.'[86] In fact, the Jewish authorities themselves establish they had no power to execute him and that it was ultimately a Roman decision.[87] The writers of the gospels would not have it, and there is in the final analysis perhaps no clearer statement of this than the final response to Pilate in the gospel of *Matthew* (27:25), which pointedly states was shouted not by the Pharisees, scribes, and officials, but 'all the people' (*ho pas laos*): 'His blood be on us and on our children!' The origins of a western tragedy indeed.

Chapter 5

The Tetrarch: Herod Antipas

> 'Ah! Du wolltest mich nicht deinen Mund küssen lassen, Jochanaan. Wohl, ich werde ihn jetz küssen!'
>
> 'Ah! You would not let me kiss your mouth, Johnathan. Well, now I will kiss it!'
>
> Salome in Richard Strauss' opera, *Salome*

It is hard to communicate the experience of Richard Strauss' *Salome*, a violently jarring opera about the beheading of John the Baptist, to one who has never seen it. The intensely dramatic, stunning music, often riveting although sometimes atonal in nature, can leave one exhausted. The Dance of the Seven Veils (when Salome dances for King Herod Antipas), the long wait for John the Baptist's execution (some sixty-six bars of music), and, most hair-raising of all, the final seventeen minutes of Salome's macabre toying with the Baptist's head as she caresses, kisses, and dances with it, is not for the faint of heart – or stomach. Nor is its final conclusion, in which Herod Antipas, looking on in horror and grief says of Salome, 'Sie ist ein Ungeheuer!' ('She is a monster!'), before he orders his soldiers to crush her under the weight of their shields. Historically, there is no evidence that Herod took this drastic measure, although he may have desired to: he was concerned to maintain order in his province, and he feared that the execution of John the Baptist might lead to public demonstrations and rebellion. As it was, the subsequent military defeat Herod Antipas suffered at the hands of the neighbouring king of Nabataea, Aretas IV, was attributed to what some viewed as an unjust action against one who, many believed, was a righteous man.

Yet Herod Antipas must have done something right in his life: he managed to survive to at least 60 years of age, and when he finally fell from grace, denounced to no less than Gaius Caligula, he managed to keep his head.[1] He was the tetrarch of what was known as the tetrarchy (as opposed to province) of Peraea and Galilee, where Jesus and his family lived.[2] Thanks in small part to Tacitus, and in much larger part to Josephus, we know a good deal about the region of the empire where Jesus lived and died and about the history of the province. Tacitus gives us a big picture survey of the empire during Jesus' life, as well as a more detailed if still very bare and schematic outline of Judaea's history itself (and its surrounding regions), while Josephus gives us a very in-depth history of the province. Indeed, it is worth noting that while we cobble together from various Roman sources our general knowledge of their provinces, Josephus is the only detailed native source we have for any history of a province or region of the empire with the exception of Greek authors, who by Jesus' day had a centuries-long tradition of composing histories of their own regions (such as the historians of Athens and its surrounding territory of Attica, known as Atthidographers), universal geographies (such as Strabo), and tourist guides of Greece and Asia Minor (such as Pausanias).[3] But no Germans write on Germany or Britons on Britannia (although Tacitus has monographs dedicated to both), and there is no surviving source from the high empire that gives us a specific history of the Balkan provinces, Africa (with some Punic exceptions that are no longer extant), or Spain.

Under Tiberius All Was Quiet

The two general surveys of the empire from a Roman author we do have are found in the *Annals* and the *Histories*, both by Tacitus. In addition, we find in Tacitus our only extended discussion in a classical Latin author of a history of the Jews and Judaea, but 'extended' is a relative term: it consists of the first thirteen chapters (i.e., paragraphs) of Book V of his *Histories*, of which only the first part is extant. There is, to be sure, the detailed geography of Strabo, which includes the occasional historical detail, but little in the way of ethnographic information. Tacitus, nonetheless, is in some respects a better starting point for the context of Judaea within the Roman Empire, both because of what Tacitus does and does not tell us. If scholars – and ancient writers such as Josephus – viewed Judaea in AD 31 as in any way proto-revolutionary or destabilized, then Tacitus decidedly did not. Writing Book IV of his *Annals*, likely after the death of Trajan, Tacitus there interrupts his narrative to survey the Roman world of AD 23, a date he chose because he viewed this as the year in which Tiberius' reign started to go sour; his overview is the closest we come to any general survey of the empire at the date of Jesus' ministry and can be paraphrased (with some minor omissions) as follows:

> Fleets stationed at Misenum and Ravenna patrolled the seas; eight legions on the Rhine maintained order in Gaul and were prepared for any contingency with the fierce tribes of Germany; the recently subdued Spanish provinces were controlled by three legions; Mauritania was governed by Rome's client king, Juba, while the provinces of Africa and Egypt were controlled by two legions each; from the broad sweep of territory that stretched from Gaza to the Euphrates, encompassing all of Syria and bordering Parthia, were four legions; in what were known as Iberia and Albania (roughly the Caucasus and part of northern Armenia between the Black and Caspian Seas), client kings acted as protectors of Rome's interests; Thrace enjoyed the rule, too, of client kings, while the eastern Danube had stationed on it four legions, two in Pannonia and two in Moesia; inside Rome itself were three urban and nine praetorian cohorts for a total of over 7,000 men, about a quarter larger than the standard legion, with most of the recruits coming from inside Italy, especially Umbria and Etruria [modern Tuscany]. Provincials contributed all manner of naval crews and auxiliaries as well.[4]

Of Judaea, Tacitus has nothing to say. Presumably he discussed the history of the province later in his *Annals*, where he would have doubtless discussed the outbreak of rebellion in Judaea in 66, the year when the manuscript breaks off; however, we cannot be certain that he in fact did so, and any such discussion may well have been substantially less detailed, since he could refer his readers to his earlier work, the *Histories*, which he wrote between AD 100 and 110. It was in the first thirteen chapters of Book V, as he proceeds to recount the end of the Jewish rebellion of AD 66–70, where he gives a detailed albeit error-ridden history of the Jewish people and a more reliable but brief account of Judaea's history under the Romans:

> Cn. Pompey was the first of the Romans to conquer Judaea and to enter the Temple by right of his victory; it was divulged that inside

> was a god with no effigy, that his seat was empty, his secrets of no account. Jerusalem's walls were torn down; the Temple remained. Soon in the midst of our civil war, after the provinces had come into Marc Antony's power, the King of the Parthians, Pacorus, gained control of Judaea, only to be killed by P. Ventidius and the Parthians driven back across the Euphrates; C. Sosius subdued the Judaeans. Once Augustus was victorious he increased the size of the kingdom given to Herod by Marc Antony. After Herod's death, a certain Simon usurped the royal title without awaiting Caesar's decision. Quintilius Varus, who was governor of Syria, punished him, and, the people checked, Herod's children ruled a province divided into three between them. Under Tiberius it was quiet. Then after Gaius Caligula ordered that his statue be set up in the Temple they chose instead to take up arms – a rebellion that his death cut short. Claudius, after the kings were all dead or reduced to modest means, handed Judaea over to equestrians and freedmen; of these Antonius Felix exercised nearly regal power through every sort of cruelty and lust, a product of his servile temperament; having wed Drusilla, the granddaughter of Cleopatra and Antony, he was consequently Antony's grandson-in-law, while Claudius was Antony's grandson. Nevertheless, the patience of the Judaeans persevered until Gessius Florus was procurator; under him war broke out.[5]

Thus ends the brief history of Judaea under the Romans, before his extended (albeit as noted error-ridden) ethnography of the Jewish people. In contrast, Tacitus' general outline of the Roman conquest of Judaea is, in the main, correct.[6] Pompey the Great in the 60s BC was the first Roman to enter the province with an army during his conquest of Mithridates in Asia, after which he imposed a general settlement on the East.[7] The intervening civil wars between Pompey and Caesar, and then between the forces of Octavian and Antony against Caesar's assassins, led to instability in the region, resulting in invasions and destabilization by the Parthians, Rome's rival empire to the East.

C. Sosius restored order to the area and Augustus added it to Rome's possessions as a client state governed by King Herod the Great between 34 and 4 BC. Nearly fifty years later, during the reign of Claudius in AD 44, the line of Herod had mostly died out and ceased to rule in Judaea.

Regrettably, under first Claudius (AD 41–54) and then Nero (AD 54–68), Judaea had the misfortune to be a poorly run province, with a series of corrupt governors leading up to the momentous Revolt of AD 66–70.

However, it is the period in Tacitus' succinct sentence in Latin, *Sub Tiberio quies*, 'Under Tiberius it was quiet', that is our primary concern. Despite Josephus' sometimes breathless narrative of events in Judaea during Tiberius' rule, Tacitus is very reticent: the only mention Tacitus makes of the province in the first six books of the *Annals* (encompassing AD 14–37) is a notice under the year AD 17, when a delegation from the provinces of Syria and Judaea makes an appearance before the Senate, and 'worn out by their burdens, begged for a lessening of tribute'.[8] Part of the reason for Tacitus' reticence about Judea may have been due to the relative comparison a Roman would make to other parts of the empire during Tiberius' reign: under Tiberius there were initially serious mutinies among the armies of the Rhine and in Pannonia, and the horrific loss of legions in Germany was still a fresh memory with punitive expeditions still under way beyond the Rhine. On top of that, Tiberius' reign saw in the mid-20s two serious rebellions: the first was a protracted guerrilla insurgency in North Africa led by a native named Tacfarinas that took considerable time to crush, while the second was in Gaul under two rebel leaders, Julius Sacrovir and Julius Florus.[9] Both were far more serious than anything occurring in Judaea, given the revenue and resources of the African and Gallic provinces, and the position of the eight Rhine legions whose vigilance extended both west against the peoples of Gaul and east as a bulwark against the dangerous tribes of Germany. Judaea and its immediate environs – including Galilee and Peraea – were relatively insignificant, quiet (and generally impoverished) backwaters under Tiberius and any disorder could be met by the client kings, or by the governor in charge of the province.

Now, client kings such as Herod were nothing new to Roman administration.[10] Over time, as Rome expanded, a number of minor kingdoms were brought under Roman protection, with the kings often providing Rome with material assistance in the interest of maintaining a relative degree of autonomy. However, Rome never called her allied monarchs *cliens* or client – the more common term was *rex socius et amicus* ('allied king and friend') and the term *amicitia* ('friendship') was often used to describe relations between Rome and her friendly but unequal allies. Indeed, in 273 BC, about a decade before the outbreak of the First Punic War, we first find the term *amicitia* used between Rome and a monarch, in this case the Greek Ptolemid dynasty in Egypt, and the alliance appears to have been something of an acknowledgement by one of the Mediterranean's more formidable powers of Rome's growing prestige in the wake of Rome's victory over King Pyrrhus of Epirus, himself one of the most formidable Macedonian military talents of the day. For a variety of reasons, the Ptolemids under Ptolemy II Philadelphus (ruled 283–246 BC) may have been trying to isolate Pyrrhus politically and militarily.

A further example of how the system worked emerges from the First Punic War (264–241 BC). It was then that a Greek king of Sicily (traditionally ruled by Greek kings or tyrants), Hiero of Syracuse, sided with Rome against Carthage, a traditional foe of the Greeks in Sicily. At the end of the war Sicily was reduced to a Roman province, but Rome allowed Hiero to rule over south-east Sicily and a strip of coast as far north as Taurominium. He remained loyal until he died in 215 BC, supplying Rome material support and maintaining a robust fleet for the patrol and protection of the island. There are numerous instances in the course of Rome's history when client kings were used to maintain Roman hegemony over a region or province, and a semi-formal ceremony was established in which a client king or state would submit a golden crown in which the crown was usually deposited in the Temple of Jupiter Capitolinus.

Herod the Great, His Family, and the Client Kingdom of Judaea

Jesus himself was born into one such client kingdom. Notoriously the holy family had to flee the wrath of King Herod, also known as Herod the Great, and at the end of his life Jesus would face interrogation by Herod's son. That son's name was Herod Antipas (hereafter Antipas or Herod Antipas to avoid confusion with his father and other assorted Herods in his family), about whom we know a great deal thanks in large part to Josephus' *Jewish War* and *Jewish Antiquities*. Antipas was probably born around 20 BC. His father, Herod the Great, had nine wives over his lifetime. Antipas was the child of a Samaritan woman named Malthace, who also bore Herod another son, named Archelaus, and a daughter, Olympias.[11] Both Antipas and Archelaus were brought up in Rome 'by a certain Jew' according to Josephus while Herod continued to rule Judaea.[12] Of Antipas we hear but little until late in the reign of his father.

Herod the Great himself was born in 73 BC, the son of Antipater, an Idumean who had been made commissioner of all Judaea by Julius Caesar in 48 or 47 BC, and of Cypros, a Nabataean women (in what is now Jordan). Antipater's appointment notwithstanding, after Caesar's assassination in 44 BC he assisted C. Cassius, one of Caesar's assassins now facing off in a war against Marc Antony and Octavian, by raising 700 talents, a not inconsequential sum. The same year as the famous battle at Philippi in 42 BC, where Brutus, Cassius, and the forces of the republic fell before Caesar's avengers, Antipater was assassinated by one of the agents sent to help him collect the 700 talents, a man named Malichus, who dispatched Antipater with poison. Part of the reason for his assassination may have been the ruthless nature in which he and Cassius exacted money, enslaving the population of no fewer than four towns in an effort to extract revenue. In revenge, his son Herod had Malichus hacked to death and showed himself loyal to the Romans. Between 40 and 37 BC a period of civil strife erupted in Judaea, and Herod was compelled to flee to Rome early in the course of the conflict. In 40 BC, the Roman Senate declared him the rightful king over Judaea. By 37 BC, he had returned to Judaea and in the increasingly looming conflict between Marc Antony and Octavian sided with Antony. After the conclusion of hostilities in 30 BC, with Antony and Cleopatra now cold in their graves, Octavian pardoned him and allowed Herod a fair degree of autonomy in terms of how he ruled his kingdom, as long as he maintained a good relationship with Rome's other client kings, provinces, and regional interests.

Herod faced a number of challenges during his tenure, not the least of which was that he himself was raised Jewish, but, since he was half Nabatean Arab and half Idumean, Judaeans considered him a foreigner. However, the efforts he made in trying to reconcile the Jews to his rule were vigorous, and included a magnificent restoration of the Temple in Jerusalem, though at the same time he also built a splendid (pagan) temple to Augustus at his newly established port of Caesarea whose ruins are still visible today (see fig. 4.3).[13] In addition, he constructed a theatre and hippodrome in Jerusalem, structures associated with pagan festivals and religious observances, instituted great games that included musical contests and prizes, and gave *venationes* or wild animal hunts in these new venues.[14] The theatre itself he adorned with trophies of the nations he had conquered in silver and gold. While these large and ambitious construction projects will have had the effect of giving employment to the people of his kingdom, the pagan activities associated with these structures, in particular the adorning of them with images and the violence associated with the arena, deeply offended Jewish religious and ethical sensibilities according to Josephus.[15]

They are also emblematic of his attempt to walk the difficult line between Rome and the Jewish population he governed, at which he was not always successful. In fact, at the end of his life, when ailing, he faced violent resistance to his decision to dedicate a large golden eagle – a distinctly Roman symbol – over the great gate of the Temple.[16] Josephus tells us that two prominent Jews (both were respected teachers and interpreters of Jewish law), Judas, son of Sariphaeus and Matthias, son of Margalothus reacted by inciting the youth of Judaea, asserting that Herod's illness was due to his violation of Jewish law; a group of young men proceeded to tear the eagle down and destroy it, cutting it up with axes. In response, Herod put a temporary halt to the sedition and had the leaders arrested and burnt alive. In addition, he defended the dedication on the grounds that it had been he who had restored and adorned the Temple in the first place.[17] The conflict was to lay the groundwork for discord and instability for his successor, his son Archelaus, Herod Antipas' brother.

Regrettably, familial discord and instability seems to have been the order of the day for Herod and the Herodian dynasty in general. Herod had one of his wives, Miriam I (the first because he later had another wife named Miriam), executed in 29 BC, in part because she was a member of the Hasmonean Dynasty, a ruling family in and around Judaea that governed the region semi-autonomously by the grace of the Seleucids, the Greek ruling dynasty that controlled what is today Syria, Lebanon, Israel, and Jordan until its collapse and conquest by Pompey the Great in 63 BC. Herod's fear of a Hasmonean resurgence led in part to Miriam I's execution, though Herod's sister Salome (who was to become the grandmother of Herod Agrippa) had also accused her of adultery. Herod's sons by Miriam I, Alexander and Aristobulus, who had been raised in Rome, resented their father's treatment of their mother, and the tensions between Herod and his two sons with Miriam resulted in a rivalry so fraught that by 12 BC the family was compelled to travel to Italy in an effort to have Augustus mediate their dispute, ultimately to no avail.

It certainly did not help that there was no shortage of family members and courtiers eager to intrigue against Alexander and Aristobulus for their own motives: Herod's sister Salome hated them and put up her daughter, Berenice, who was married to Aristobulus, to spy on her husband. Berenice was only too happy to oblige and reported back that Aristobulus and Alexander planned to seize the kingdom for themselves upon Herod's death and reduce the rest of his children to 'village clerks'.[18] Alexander in turn was egged on by Pheroras, Herod's youngest brother, who fomented discord by attempting to incite Alexander to hatred against his father.[19] Entering into the mix was Herod's son with a woman named Doris (whom he divorced sometime between 43 and 40 BC), named Antipater, who accused both Aristobulus and Alexander of plotting to kill Herod, and exacerbated tensions between Herod and his sons, Alexander in particular.[20] Consequently, Herod's animus against Alexander and Aristobulus ultimately reached a boiling point, and after a forged letter was brought to Herod incriminating Alexander in a plot to overthrow him, he had both arrested.[21] Augustus, apprised of the situation, left it to Herod and the Roman officials on site to handle the matter, and in the end the two men, charged with conspiracy, were taken to Sebaste and executed by strangulation in 7 BC.[22] Even as he lay dying, Herod could not escape familial chaos. Taking advantage of his father's illness, Antipater proved too anxious to seize the throne. Herod took umbrage, and had him executed.[23] As Augustus was reported to have quipped, it was better on the whole to be Herod's swine than Herod's son.[24]

The Struggle for Succession among Herod's Successors and Revolt in Judaea

His family depleted, Herod was compelled to look to his sons from Malthace, who died the same year as he did in 4 BC. Initially he had settled on Antipas, but at the last minute changed his mind, and willed his kingdom to Archelaus, making Antipas the tetrarch of Galilee and Peraea instead.[25] This naturally set the groundwork for conflict among Herod's successors. However, before the conflict between the two could be resolved, Archelaus soon after, in the wake of Herod's death, already found himself dealing with a destabilized province whose people, angered over the recent brutal execution of Matthias and his followers, rioted in and around the city during Passover.[26] Archelaus sent in a cohort of legionnaires, but he initially hesitated: potential client kings, even if they were the sons of previous client kings, had to have the approval of Rome, and now Augustus, before taking so drastic a measure. They also needed to have their status fully ratified, and that would not happen until Archelaus had proven himself worthy of the title – Archelaus was still not the king. Furthermore, he wanted to be perceived as a competent administrator of his province (and inheritance) in the eyes of Augustus in order to prove worthy of his father's kingdom, and so he attempted to negotiate with those who still clamoured for justice for his father's actions, but the negotiations failed. Fearing the spread of sedition and disturbances, he at last sent in a cohort of legionary troops; initially the angry mob surrounded and stoned to death most of the soldiers. After this, Archelaus sent in numerous reinforcements – Josephus says his whole army, so perhaps a contingent as large as a legion with cavalry – and massacred 3,000 of Judas' and Matthias' rebellious followers in the Temple, as grotesque and egregious an act of impiety as could be imagined, while the rest were scattered throughout the surrounding countryside and ordered to return home.[27] The disorder quelled, the province was temporarily handed over to Syria's governor Quintilius Varus while Archelaus went to petition for his claim in person before Augustus in Rome. Antipas was close on his heels, not about to give up on what he believed to be his rightful inheritance of Herod's kingdom.[28]

Salome now interjected herself into the midst of the dispute and, according to Josephus, played a double game with Archelaus and Antipas: she had given Archelaus assurances that she would support his claim even as she encouraged Antipas' ambitions, asserting that because he had been designated successor earlier in Herod's will that she believed Antipas had the greater claim.[29] She may have simply been hedging her bets as she awaited Augustus' ultimate decision on the matter. Some of Antipas' followers while still in Judaea encouraged him to give up his claim since Archelaus was the older of the two, but once safely away from Archelaus dropped their opposition out of their dislike for him, believing Antipas would better serve their interests.[30] Meanwhile, Archelaus sent letters to Augustus to argue his claim and also sent him accounts of Herod's property for review; Augustus also carefully reviewed reports on the amounts of property and annual revenue from the kingdom that Varus had sent, and others from his lieutenant and subordinate Sabinus (whose report also included an accusatory missive against Archelaus) before he held his formal hearing in which Archelaus and Antipas both pleaded their cases in person.[31] The first to present their arguments was Salome's son Antipater, who was decidedly hostile to Archelaus: Antipater assailed Archelaus' usurpation of power, arguing that Herod had changed his will to favour Archelaus late in life when Herod himself was not of sound mind. He attacked Archelaus in particular for the massacre in the Temple, insufficiently mourning the dead Herod, and worst of all, behaving as though he already were king before Augustus' confirmation, thereby disrespecting Caesar's authority.[32]

Countering in the defence was the formidable Nicolas of Damascus, a close friend of Herod the Great and a noted historian who wrote a universal history and a biography of Augustus, among other works.[33] Nicolas asserted that the massacre had been brought on by the victims themselves, who were violent and lawless, and further argued that they had shown contempt for Jewish law, and for Caesar himself. Antipater's attack, he asserted, was driven by hatred against Archelaus, whose virtue he loathed. As for changing the will, proof of Herod's sound mind at the time of its writing was the place of Caesar in it, to whom he left the final decisions as to the fate and status of his kingdom. Augustus reaffirmed but did not confirm his inclination to judge in favour of Archelaus.

It is very likely that Augustus was in the midst of hearing the case when news arrived that the province was in a state of revolt.[34] Before Archelaus had left for Rome the governor of Syria, Quintilius Varus, and his lieutenant, Sabinus, had made arrangements for the governance of Judaea during Archelaus' absence: Sabinus had hoped to secure Herod's property, but Josephus tells us that Sabinus decided for the moment not to secure Herod's treasuries and citadels out of deference to Varus.[35] However, as soon as Archelaus departed for Rome, Varus, having helped Archelaus clean up the remnants of the rebels from the Passover riots, returned to Antioch, Syria's capital; Sabinus, contrary to his promise to remain in Caesarea, moved into Jerusalem. There he took control of Herod's palace, and proceeded to seize fortified positions and any royal treasuries he could lay his hands on, in addition to deliberately harassing the Jewish population of the province.[36]

At the end of May, a great number of Jews from Galilee, Idumaea, Jericho and the Transjordan, as well as Judaea itself, assembled in Jerusalem for Pentecost and also to take action against Sabinus' provocations.[37] Organizing themselves into three groups, one occupied the hippodrome, the other two the eastern and western ends of the Temple, thereby hemming in and surrounding Sabinus' troops. Sabinus now seized and occupied the highest tower of the fortress of Herod's palace called Phaesel, then sent word to Varus about the situation, and from the safety of the tower proceeded to order his men to the attack. The bulk of the fighting took place in and around the porticoes of the Temple, where the rebels held the high ground and used archers to ward off the Roman infantry whose javelins were unable to meet their targets because of their elevated and well-defended positions. Finally, the Romans out of desperation resorted to fire, setting the portico of the Temple ablaze; the combustible materials from which the roof of the portico was constructed, including sealants of pitch and wax, collapsed on the defenders, many of them choosing suicide, while the Roman soldiery did its savage best to kill any who survived. The Romans cut a path of destruction through the fire and slaughter to the Temple's treasury, most of which the soldiers looted for themselves, with Sabinus keeping 400 talents for himself, a phenomenal sum of money. Retreating to the palace, Sabinus and his men now found themselves besieged by yet another group of rebels, but decided to try to stick it out until Varus arrived with reinforcements. Meanwhile, disturbances began to spread throughout Judaea.

Brigands took advantage of the rebellion to plunder the countryside, such as those under the leadership of a certain Judas, son of Ezekias.[38] Simon, a former slave of Herod's, even usurped the crown. After he set Herod's diadem on his head, his followers proclaimed him king, after which he proceeded to burn Herod's royal palace in Jericho, plunder its valuables, and set fire to a number of royal residences throughout the country.[39] Eventually, Simon was intercepted by Gratus, a member of Herod's royal troops, but also a Roman loyalist, and was decapitated.[40] Another pretender, a certain Athronges of humble origin, also took advantage of the province's chaos to proclaim himself king with the help of a formidable band of armed followers, and like Simon, dared to put on the royal diadem, and proceeded to harass both Roman legionnaires and Herod's royal troops; however, Athronges and his followers made themselves hated and feared by Roman and provincial alike due to their sheer savagery.[41]

It was amidst this state of affairs that Varus arrived with two legions to Sabinus' rescue, gathering auxiliary troops from the people of Berytus (modern Beirut), and from Aretas, king of Petra as well (who hated Herod but was eager to cultivate his friendship with the Romans). Varus employed Aretas and his son to pacify the region of Galilee, while Varus proceeded south to Samaria and then back into Judaea; along the way he had the town of Emmaus burnt as reprisal for the cooperation of its people with brigands, who had attacked and killed a Roman supply party. Advancing to the outskirts of Jerusalem, those active rebels besieging Sabinus' men now fled. Varus marched into the city and dressed down the populace for the rebellion; the people defended themselves, asserting that the disturbances were the result of outsiders who involved them in a war of which they wanted no part. Then the Romans and royal troops who had remained loyal emerged from the fortified position where they had been besieged to meet Varus – excepting Sabinus, who had surreptitiously left the city and headed for the coast. Now came the mopping-up operations: Varus' army scoured the country for the remainder of the rebel forces; some were pardoned and released, but the more egregious offenders were crucified to the number of 2,000.[42] Varus then left a garrison in Jerusalem and returned to Antioch.

Soon after the end of the revolt, Archelaus, who had been given reasons to be hopeful from Augustus' generally positive reassurances, once again found himself in some jeopardy. Varus had allowed a delegation of Jews to travel to Rome to request autonomy, and they now appeared on the scene.[43] Augustus received the delegation in the Temple of Apollo on the Palatine. On the opposing side stood Archelaus and his circle of friends, including Philip, later known as Philip the tetrarch, who, as the son of Herod the Great and Cleopatra of Jerusalem (Herod's fifth wife), was Archelaus' half-brother.[44] The Jewish delegation, which desired the dissolution of the kingdom, began by rehearsing the offences of King Herod's regime.[45] They assailed Herod's extravagant expenditure, his reduction of his kingdom to poverty as a result, and his cruelty. His officials, in their effort to extract revenue, resorted to extorting bribes and were not above rape, something his victims had to endure in silence as long as the king lived. While they initially welcomed the succession of Archelaus thinking anything would be better than Herod, his actions in carrying out the massacre in the Temple proved their hopes delusional. They begged Augustus to attach Judaea to the province of Syria that they might be subject to its Roman governor.[46]

Once again, Nicolas of Damascus arose to defend both Archelaus and Herod's legacy. He assailed the delegation for not bringing up charges against Herod while he was still alive, choosing instead to attack him now that he was safely dead and buried. And he again attacked the rebels as responsible for the fate they had brought on themselves. After the two sides made their case, Augustus deliberated for some days before coming to his decision: Archelaus would not be appointed king, but he would be ethnarch of half of Herod's territory encompassing Samaria, Judaea and Idumaea, which included much of the central and northern portions of modern Israel and all of the West Bank; in addition, he made certain cities directly subject to him, including Jerusalem, while others, such as Gaza and Gadara, were made part of the province of Syria.[47] The total annual revenue from Archelaus' territory was a healthy 600 talents. If Archelaus proved capable as ethnarch, then Augustus promised that he would later be appointed king. Augustus took the further step of remitting a quarter of the tribute for Samaria as reward for not having joined the recent revolt. Antipas for his part was to govern Galilee and Peraea with its annual tribute of 200 talents, while Philip was to control Batanaea, Trachonitis, Auranitis, and an area called the kingdom of Zenodorus as tetrarch, all of which covered (roughly) a small portion of modern northern Jordan and southern Syria, and yielded an annual income of 100 talents.

There are numerous reasons why Antipas ultimately lost his case and Hoehner discusses them in his study in close detail.[48] Among the reasons for Antipas' loss are that Salome was a close friend to Livia, Augustus' empress, and though Salome did not want to see Archelaus on the throne the consolation prizes bestowed on her, possibly through Livia's influence, included monetary additions to the terms of Herod the Great's will, a royal palace, and the enormous personal stipend of 60 talents annually. Another reason for Augustus' decision may have been the youthful age of Antipas, who was still only barely 20. On top of that, he had less influential support and less clout with Augustus than those who made the case for Archelaus. Yet it was not all bad for Antipas as Hoehner notes.[49] Archelaus did not inherit all, but merely half, of Herod the Great's realm (Judaea and Samaria) and was not designated king but ethnarch, which may indicate that he represented all Jews before Rome and before the Sanhedrin, possibly granting him some oversight of the remaining half of Herod the Great's kingdom that Antipas and Philip shared, although after Archelaus' deposition they gained full charge of their territories. It may not have been what Antipas wanted, but it was by no means entirely bleak.

Once Archelaus was ensconced as ethnarch, one of his first acts was to marry a Cappadocian princess named Glaphyra, who had once been married to Alexander, (son of Herod and Miriam I) with whom she had had children, and she had later married King Juba II of Mauretania. After Juba apparently divorced her she returned to Cappadocia to live with her father and the marriage to Archelaus took place not long afterwards.[50] The marriage was offensive to the Jews because it was contrary to Jewish law for a man to marry his deceased brother's wife (unless childless).[51] His actions proved no less offensive over time and by AD 6 the Jews and Samaritans had had enough. They accused him of oppressive tyranny and cruelty before Augustus, and the charges must have been severe because Josephus tells us that they elicited Augustus' wrath.[52] Augustus immediately summoned Archelaus from Judaea to answer the charges in person and Augustus, after giving a fair hearing to his accusers and then to Archelaus himself, banished him to Vienna (modern Vienne) in Gaul and appropriated his property into the imperial treasury. An important result of this event was that Antipas now received the name Herod, since up until AD 6 he had always been referred to as simply Antipas in our sources, but now becomes Herod Antipas.[53]

Herod Antipas Becomes Tetrarch

Archelaus' corruption was to have enormous consequences. For the next nearly 600 years, until the Sassanid Persian and then subsequent Muslim conquest, Jerusalem and Judaea were to be under direct Roman control. Judaea, Samaria, and Idumaea were all rolled into the province of Syria, now governed by Publius Sulpicius Quirinius, a man of consular standing, whose first duties were to carry out a census in his province and to sell off Archelaus' estates.[54] He then sent Coponius – a man Josephus tells us was of equestrian status but about whom otherwise little is known – to be the first Roman prefect of Judaea under its changed status, granting him full authority to govern the Jews as he saw fit.[55] Quirinius, however, was himself present with Coponius initially to help oversee not just the liquidation of Archelaus' estates and property but also to make an assessment of Jewish property in order to exact tax and tribute for Roman coffers, a move that deeply offended Jewish sentiment. In opposition to Roman rule and taxation there arose a man named Judas from Galilee, who enlisted the help of a Pharisee named Saddok.[56] He attempted to rouse the Jews to rebellion against the Romans, asserting submission to the assessment was tantamount to servitude.[57] The result of Judas' attempted rebellion included his execution and the dispersal of his followers, according to *Acts*. However, Josephus also tells us, likely anachronistically and in hindsight, that this set in motion an almost pathological desire on the part of the inhabitants of Judaea, and Jews even beyond it, to violently divest themselves of Roman rule, and further set in motion a trend that was to culminate in the horrific rebellion of AD 66–70 about which Josephus wrote.[58] In addition, Josephus goes so far as to include Judas' and Saddok's rebellious doctrine, in which they viewed taxation as a form of servitude, as a fourth among the three other major sects – the Pharisees, Sadducees, and Essenes – of Jewish religious thought.[59]

At the same time as Quirinius was touring Judaea, Herod Antipas started to rule as tetrarch: he began by fortifying and beautifying Sepphoris which he intended to be the capital of Galilee, renaming it Autocratoris ('Imperial City'), and fortified Betharamphtha (biblical Beth-haram) with a wall and renamed it Livias, in honour of the wife and empress of Augustus.[60] After Augustus' death in AD 14, Herod Antipas quickly earned an elevated position among the friends of the emperor Tiberius, and in his honour built and named a city after him on Lake Gennesaritis appropriately called Tiberias.[61] He settled it with people from Galilee, some of them forcibly, including local magistrates, though some were poorer inhabitants of his kingdom who received houses and land at his own expense. The reason for the generous offer was that the city was apparently on the site of a large necropolis that had been destroyed to make way for the settlement, and the Jews (as was the case too for ancient Greek and Roman peoples) considered having the dead within one's city as taboo, even bringing pollution. Finally, early in his reign Antipas had married a local princess, the daughter of Aretas IV, the King of Nabataea (an independent border state on Rome's south-eastern frontier that included parts of modern Jordan, Sinai, and Saudi Arabia), a marriage that was to later end on a bitter note for Antipas.

Yet by the mid-20s AD things seemed to be going well for Herod Antipas. He ruled a stable region that regardless of the reputation of Galilee for having a fanatical and restive populace was doing relatively well, and he himself had made a good marriage.[62] Despite the appearance of prosperity, however, there are some caveats: we are uncertain about his reaction to some of the provocative moves Pilate made upon assuming the governorship of Judaea in 26, and we are equally uncertain about his involvement, if any, in the various efforts to oppose some of Pilate's actions. He was almost certainly among the four princes who approached Pilate concerning his dedication of a series of golden shields in Herod's palace in Jerusalem, which likely happened after AD 31 since the embassy threatens to go to Tiberius, his prefect Sejanus apparently now out of the picture.[63]

Prior to that incident, however, sometime well before Pilate's arrival, we cannot be sure when, Herod Antipas made a journey to Rome.[64] Before he even set sail he fell in love with a woman named Herodias, wife to his half-brother Herod II (sometimes called Herod Philip, but not to be confused with Philip the tetrarch), who was son of Herod the Great and Miriam II (daughter of Simon Boethus, the high priest).[65] So smitten was Antipas that he immediately brought up the subject of marriage with her during his visit, and she welcomed the idea, suggesting that they marry upon his return from Rome provided he divorce Aretas' daughter. Our sources remain silent on what Herod II felt about all of this but there is no indication of his resisting the idea. At about the same time there arose a strange movement led by a peculiar religious figure, who was none other than John the Baptist.

An Eater of Locusts and Wild Honey Dons a Goat Skin and Sees God

However, to call John the Baptist a peculiar figure is not entirely fair. In the ancient world he would have been readily recognizable as a character type – one in a line of men with strange habits, who would take on the role of a counter-cultural gadfly and whose message and actions the authorities could come to view as politically deviant if not downright dangerous and rebellious. John's eccentricities included standing knee deep in the Jordan preaching the impending arrival of the kingdom of heaven and of God, wearing the skin of a wild camel about his loins with a leather strap to hold it up, and eating locusts and wild honey for nourishment. Figures such as the famous Socrates (known to us from Plato and Xenephon) and the less famous Apollonius of Tyana (for whom our main source is Philostratus) were equally alienated from their peers: thus we hear in Plato's *Symposium* from the thoroughly inebriated Athenian statesman Alcibiades that Socrates for one was incredibly ugly, resembling a snub nose satyr, who could fall into trances barefoot in the snow for hours on end, whose capacity for wine was such that he never got drunk, was impervious to the advances of beautiful young men (an oddity in Athens with its virtually institutionalized pederasty), while later, in Plato's *Apology*, Plato has Socrates claim to have heard a divine voice that stopped him whenever he was about to do anything considered unethical or unjust, and who portrays Socrates as someone who annoyed his fellow citizens by exposing their ignorance on a variety of subjects.

According to Philostratus, Apollonius of Tyana, who may or may not have been fictional, had the gift of distant sight, hence was witness to the assassination of the emperor Domitian in AD 96 in Rome even though he was nearly a thousand miles away in the market place at Ephesus, in Asia, at the time. He could reportedly identify the souls of great men which had transmigrated into animals after their deaths, as when he identified the soul of Pythagoras in a lion. He could magically slip out of any irons with which any guards might try to restrain him. Finally, he lived to a great old age. Both Apollonius and Socrates were considered threatening enough to face punishment at the hands of the authorities. For Socrates that resulted in death, although Apollonius, by virtue of his ability to escape chains and even to transmigrate himself from one place to another, was more fortunate. The ancient world abounded with examples of the strange and the exotic, including witches, magicians, and zealous devotees of mystery cults who bore witness and attested to the powers of, say, Isis or the Magna Mater, and it is in this context, in part, in which John the Baptist – and Jesus – must be appreciated. It was a universe where the strange and miraculous was expected, and though not always accepted, was given much greater credence than we in the modern world might expect.

Josephus tells us that John had exhorted the Jews to live righteously, to practise justice and piety and that this was a preliminary to baptism – the soul and body should both be cleansed by proper behaviour.[66] In the New Testament, John's wrath in his fiery sermons was directed in particular against the Sadducees and Pharisees.[67] But John's preaching as depicted in the gospels also included another target, Herod Antipas and his recently wedded wife Herodias, since their marriage went against Judaic law, which prohibited a man from marrying his brother's wife if his brother were still living.[68] When he started to draw crowds – as he was reported to have done, of everyone from Pharisees to centurions, from soldiers to tax collectors – Herod Antipas became alarmed about the possibility for sedition, even revolution (*epi stasei* in Greek) as Josephus tells us.[69] Yet he feared both John as a righteous man and the crowds that he was attracting.[70]

Eventually, possibly both for personal reasons and reasons of public order, Antipas had him arrested, cast into chains, and imprisoned in a fortress at Machaerus, just east of the Dead Sea in what is modern Jordan, where some scant remains of the fortress still survive.[71] While John was in prison he was reported to have sent two of his disciples to Jesus (whose baptism based on *Luke* 3:1 will have taken place in the fifteenth year of Tiberius' reign, hence approximately AD 29) to inquire whether he was the Messiah (*Matthew* 11.1–3; *Luke* 7:18–20), implying that his imprisonment was not all that secure.[72] Jesus' response was one that was hardly conciliatory towards Antipas, hence *Matthew* 11:12 has Jesus state at one point, 'And from the days of John the Baptist until now the kingdom of heaven suffereth violence, and the violent take it by force.' But according to *Matthew*, Herod Antipas' hands were tied; even though he had the Baptist in custody, he feared the mob and its response should he put John to death.

Then an (in)famously unfortunate event took place: Herod Antipas had promised on oath to Herodias' daughter by Philip (hence Antipas' niece and also Herod the Great's granddaughter), Salome, that he would give her anything she asked if she danced in his honour for his birthday; Herodias instructed her to ask for the Baptist's head.[73] Herod complied

Fig. 5.1: Salome holds a silver platter as the executioner places the head of John the Baptist on it. By Caravaggio, National Gallery, London. (Public domain via *Wikimedia Commons*)

and had John's head brought to her on a platter, a subject of occasional if somewhat grim treatment by Renaissance artists (see fig. 5.1). A question arises concerning who really wanted to see John executed. *Matthew* (14:5) tells us it was Antipas, while *Mark* (6:19) indicates it was Herodias.[74] *Luke* (9:9) indicates that it was ultimately Antipas who was responsible for John's death, although *Matthew* (14:3) and *Mark* (6:17) say that Antipas ultimately executed John 'on account of Herodias'. But Herodias was exceedingly anxious to get rid of John whom she hated, and as Hoehner has pointed out, she does not appear to miss a heartbeat when Salome asks her for what she ought to ask.[75]

The head itself was to have a much storied afterlife: Josephus claimed it was simply buried at the fortress of Machaerus, yet by the sixth century it was reportedly discovered and sent to Damascus as a sacred relic to honour the Christian church that had replaced a Greek temple to Zeus, after which the church was dedicated to the Baptist. After the Muslim conquest in AD 634, it was converted to the Ummayad Mosque,

Fig. 5.2: One of several purported tombs of John the Baptist, this one in the Umayyad Mosque, Damascus, Syria. (James Gordon via *Wikimedia Commons*)

a masterpiece of Islamic art and architecture, where Muslim pilgrims and worshippers still venerate the shrine containing the Baptist's tomb (see fig. 5.2). Other traditions have the head transferred from Jerusalem to Alexandria where it was buried at a basilica dedicated to John on top of the former Serapeum (the famous shrine to the god Serapis) which was destroyed in AD 391, while still other accounts have the head fall into the hands of the Knights Templar, and others have it spirited off from Constantinople to France after the Fourth Crusade and the sack of Constantinople in 1204 by Wallon de Sarton and now resting in the cathedral of Amiens. Modern popes have become involved, with Pope John Paul II giving authority to the authenticity of the site in Damascus, but Pope Benedict XVI subsequently declared the skull in the church of San Silvestro in Capite in Rome, where it reportedly came to rest in the twelfth century, as authentic.

Herod Antipas' Disappointment with Jesus

Of course the other central event of Herod Antipas' storied life for those of the Christian faith, apart from the beheading of the Baptist, was the hearing that he gave to Jesus. According to The New Testament (*Matthew* 14:1–12; *Mark* 6:14–29), when reports concerning Jesus reached him he feared another 'John the Baptist' moment, stating that 'This is John the Baptist: he is risen from the dead.'[76] He was not, according to tradition, the only one to think this. In Matthew's gospel (16:13–14) some of his disciples identified Jesus with John, and there is indication that this opinion was not limited to his disciples alone, the scripture passage stating rather vaguely 'some say'. Antipas may have been intent on arresting him, and some scholars argue this influenced where Jesus preached and taught, although this is a matter of some controversy.[77]

It is unclear, however, to what extent (if any) Antipas might have been involved in the hearing and execution of Jesus, though there are indications that he was concerned about his ministry, the crowds and support he attracted, and the general consternation he was causing among Jewish authorities, since *Mark* 12:13 says that both the Pharisees and followers of Antipas were intent on catching Jesus up with his own words, and there is indication of Antipas' anxiety if not actual animus elsewhere, as in *Luke* 13:31, where Jesus is warned in a village near Jerusalem that Herod Antipas was intent on killing him, which was probably little more than a threat given the trouble he had incurred with John the Baptist's execution.[78] Jesus' response was dismissive, perhaps rightly so: 'Go ye, and tell that fox, Behold I cast out devils, and I do cures to day and to morrow, and the third day I shall be perfected.'[79] It was only after Jesus' arrest during his hearing that Antipas had a chance to meet Jesus face to face. One of the controversies concerning Herod Antipas surrounds the 'trial' of Jesus, and that is to what extent Antipas had jurisdiction as opposed to Pilate over the accusations against Jesus.

The question hinges on *Luke* 23:6–15, the only gospel that interjects Herod Antipas into the Passion narrative, which states that Pilate, upon discovering that Jesus was from Galilee, sent him to Herod Antipas as under his jurisdiction.[80] Antipas happened to be in Jerusalem at the time, likely due to the Passover holiday, and some scholars have argued that Pilate will have sent Jesus to Antipas as a courtesy, and it may have been a favour well-received if we can trust *Luke*, which states that previously there had been enmity between Pilate and Antipas but after that day they became friends.[81] However, there is the other possibility that Pilate was trying to divest himself of a very troublesome problem and intended to pass the buck to Antipas.[82] Herod Antipas was excited to meet Jesus and anxious to see him perform one of his many miracles bruited about by the people at large, but in the end he was frustrated and disappointed by his unwillingness not only to perform any miracle but even to speak to him, handed him over to his soldiers who reportedly mocked him, arrayed him in an elaborate robe, and then sent him back to Pilate. That Jesus suffered a mere beating and a mocking of his pretensions as king with a robe is possible further proof of his innocence and could potentially have been understood as such by Pilate.[83] The writer of *Acts* (4:27) was not so forgiving though, since Antipas and Pilate are arguably blamed, along with the Jews and the Gentiles, for Jesus' death.[84]

Another possible reason for Pilate to send him to Antipas may have been that Pilate saw Jesus' case as one that was a matter of Jewish law since one of the charges was blasphemy – although there was, of course, the famous accusation that Jesus was seeking to make himself king. Herod Antipas himself may have had very good motives for not wanting to take the case in hand himself: he had been hesitant to execute John out of prudence and concern for the response of John's followers and the people at large, and with his execution fresh in mind, he might have been all too happy to have Pilate carry it out. His execution of John certainly indicates that he possessed the authority and the standing – if not the political capital – to carry out the execution of someone in his jurisdiction, though they were in Jerusalem at the time (hence the possibility that Pilate's 'courtesy' was in his sending someone to Antipas who was from Galilee, though currently in the jurisdiction of Jerusalem). Whatever the reason for Antipas' hesitation, he appears to have escaped another situation such as the one he had faced with John the Baptist.

Herod Antipas' Final Years in Power and Deposition

Unfortunately for Antipas, according to one popular tradition, John the Baptist was the gift that kept on giving. If Jesus is a person of anonymity in Josephus, John, his contemporary, certainly was not. John had been a vocal critic of Antipas' marriage to Herodias, but some also saw in Aretas IV, the king of neighbouring Nabataea and the truly offended party, the hand of God working vengeance for John's execution. Aretas had held his peace for some years after Antipas had divorced his daughter.

That changed in AD 34, when a conflict arose between Aretas and Antipas over a disputed boundary between Antipas' and Aretas' kingdoms. Josephus further adds that Antipas' former wife (Aretas IV's daughter), had been incensed by her former husband's casting her aside for Herodias and added fuel to the fire through her complaints to her father.[85] The two prepared for war and when, in that same year of AD 34 the two armies clashed, Aretas resoundingly defeated Antipas.[86]

This prompted Antipas to send a letter complaining bitterly to Tiberius about Aretas' hostilities, and Tiberius obligingly ordered a three-time consul, Lucius Vitellius to either send Aretas to him alive in chains if captured, or his head if slain. Tiberius had given Vitellius a general mandate over affairs in the East in AD 35 with a view to dealing with the perennial dispute between Rome and Parthia over Armenia; Vitellius negotiated a peace treaty with the Parthians. Details are few, but Antipas was clearly involved in the negotiations and provoked Vitellius' wrath (which Vitellius apparently kept well hidden) when Antipas sent a detailed letter to Tiberius, with whom he appears to have had a strong and enduring friendship, about the success of the mission.[87] Vitellius believed, as governor in charge of Syria and of the burdensome management of eastern affairs, that it was his and not Antipas' place to send reports to the emperor. In the end, Vitellius' anger notwithstanding, his campaign against Aretas was broken off before he could capture him due to Tiberius' death, and Vitellius was subsequently recalled by Gaius.[88] Vitellius went on to be one of the most sycophantic members of Caligula's and Claudius' court, and father of one of Rome's more loathsome emperors.[89] According to Josephus, some viewed Antipas' defeat as divine vengeance for John's execution, since John was viewed as a righteous man who exhorted his Jewish compatriots to pursue lives of justice, righteousness, and piety towards God.[90]

After Tiberius' death things took an ominous turn for Antipas: Herod Agrippa, (the grandson of Herod the Great and son of Aristobulus IV and Berenice), present at the court of Tiberius in the emperor's last year (AD 36–37), started to poison Tiberius' opinion of Antipas. He had an excellent foot in the door at court, since he had been brought up in the house of Tiberius and was a close friend of Tiberius' son Drusus; he also had a close friendship with Antonia, wife of Tiberius' brother Drusus, as well as a friendship with Antonia's son, the future emperor Claudius.[91]

After the death of Herod Agrippa's mother, Berenice, according to Josephus, Herod Agrippa gave way to extravagant living, went deeply into debt, and was compelled to leave Rome when he was reduced to poverty.[92] In addition, he was forbidden to enter the presence of Tiberius as he was formerly accustomed to, reportedly due to Tiberius being too grief stricken at the death of his son Drusus in AD 23 to endure the sight of his friends. Agrippa reportedly retired to a fortress in Idumaea in despair. Herodias, Antipas' wife, rescued him and assigned him a place in Tiberias, fixing him an allowance and giving him the office of *agoranomos* (in Greek), or *aedile* (in Latin), an official who oversaw the workings of the market place.[93] Antipas, however, subjected his benighted nephew to insults, taunting him at a feast while in his cups with his poverty and dependence.[94] Agrippa had enough and went to live with an old friend, L. Pomponius Flaccus, now the governor of Syria (between AD 32–33), but they soon had a falling out.[95] Eventually, Agrippa managed to secure funds to make his way back to Italy, and, notifying Tiberius of his presence, he was now forgiven and warmly welcomed back into the emperor's company on Capri – after he had paid off some debts incurred in the East with the help of Antonia, who had a soft spot for Agrippa as a family friend.[96]

While in Italy, Herod Agrippa began to cultivate the friendship of the future emperor Caligula, popular due to the celebrity status of his father, the late Germanicus Caesar, and now the presumptive heir apparent. Unfortunately for Agrippa, he was indiscreet of tongue and openly expressed the hope that Tiberius would abdicate and Caligula soon take power and execute Gemellus, Tiberius' grandson and Caligula's potential rival claimant to the throne.[97] Overheard by a servant, Agrippa was denounced to Tiberius who promptly had him cast into chains and thrown into prison.[98] During his six-month imprisonment, he was well taken care of due once again to the intervention of Antonia.[99] It was with presumed relief that Agrippa, after not too long a time (in March of AD 37), heard the words, 'The lion is dead' from his freedman Marsyas, meaning Tiberius was dead and Caligula emperor.[100]

Within days of Tiberius' funeral, Caligula sent for Agrippa and crowned him as king of Philip's tetrarchy, adding the territory of Lysinias into the bargain, taking away his iron chains, presenting him with ones of equal weight in gold, and placing the diadem on his head.[101]

In the next year (AD 38) Agrippa left to take control of his kingdom.[102] Regrettably, Caligula's elevation of Agrippa substantially above the position and power of Antipas' provoked the resentment of Herodias, Antipas' wife, and she urged him to go to Rome in person to press his claim.[103] The laidback Antipas – now nearly 60 and enjoying the ease and luxury of a stable kingdom – reportedly resisted the ambitious Herodias' envious promptings, but her badgering finally broke his will, and they embarked for Rome to plead their case.[104] In response Agrippa sent one of his freedman, Fortunatus, to Rome to counter their claim. Herod Agrippa armed Fortunatus with gifts for the emperor and with accusatory letters.[105]

Those letters were to prove Antipas' downfall, and Josephus vividly relates his end: both Fortunatus and Antipas along with Herodias arrived at the posh Roman resort of Baiae on the northern end of the Bay of Naples at the same time. Even as Antipas pleaded his case, Caligula was perusing the accusatory letters. The charges included that Antipas had conspired with Sejanus and was now giving aid to Artabanus, the King of Parthia, against Rome, which included the creation of an armoury with sufficient means to equip 70,000 heavy infantry.[106] Josephus does not tell us if Antipas confessed to deliberate aid of the Parthians, but he was forced to confess that there was indeed an armoury with the equipment set forth in the letter. That was enough for Caligula. Antipas was relieved of his tetrarchy, which was added to Herod Agrippa's kingdom, his property was confiscated and handed over to Agrippa, and Antipas was exiled permanently either to Lugdunum in Gaul (modern Lyons in France) or to Spain, and steps off history's stage never to be heard from again.[107] Ironically, Herodias as the sister of Herod Agrippa was protected, and she was allowed to keep her personal property, but upon receiving an ungracious and proud reaction from Herodias, Caligula rescinded his more lenient response, sent her into exile with her husband, and handed over her property to the newly installed Herod Agrippa as well.[108] Taken on balance, Antipas was a relatively good dependent of the Roman realm: his failings were minor, and are offset by the quiet he was able to bring to his province, miniscule though it was, for nearly four decades.[109] Ruling from AD 40–44, Herod Agrippa was not as fortunate, and was destined to be Judaea's last king – one might say the last, but by no means most famous, King of the Jews.

Chapter 6

The Resistance

> Then Simon Peter having a sword drew it and smote the high priest's servant, and cut off his right ear. The servant's name was Malchus. Then said Jesus unto Peter, 'Put up thy sword into the sheath; the cup which my Father hath given me, shall I not drink it?'
>
> *John* 18: 10–11

In one of the magnificent fresco panels of the Scrovegni Chapel in Padua, painted in vivid colours by the great artist Giotto in the fourteenth century (fig. 6.1), you can see him. He is one of two figures with a halo. The central haloed figure is Christ, whom Judas, himself attended by soldiers, priests, and assorted servants and officials, kisses. The other, on the left side of the panel, is Saint Peter, doing something that one would scarcely consider saintly, as he cuts off the ear of one of the men come to arrest Jesus. In all of the gospel accounts, it is a servant of the high priest whose ear is struck off, and only in *John*, cited above, is his name reported. Peter's is the sort of resistance one is used to in Rome's sprawling empire – violent, armed, and bloody. However, this singular instance of violence committed by a disciple of Jesus stands out by virtue of its being at odds with Jesus' teachings in general and the broadly pacific mission of his disciples. It is the sole act of physical violence against a person in the course of his ministry as it has come down to us and stands out accordingly.

Not that there were not tense moments, threats of violence, and flaring tempers in New Testament scripture: Jesus knows full well his apostles will at times be rejected by the communities they visit, perhaps violently so, and tells them to shake the dust of those places off their feet; he himself famously overturned the money-changers' tables in a fit of pique, and the apostles and Paul have plenty of hostile encounters, such as when Paul is shouted down in Ephesus by the men who earn a livelihood by making bronze and terracotta votive offerings at the Temple of Artemis

Fig. 6.1: Judas kisses Christ as Peter cuts off the ear of an attendant in Giotto's *Arrest of Christ*. The Scrovegni Chapel, Padua, Italy. (Public domain via *Wikimedia Commons*)

of the Ephesians, one of the seven wonders of the ancient world, and who were fearful of losing their livelihoods if Paul's subversive message gained traction. As one minister once told me, Jesus can get irritable and grumpy in a 'you-kids-get-off-of-my-lawn' sort of way. His occasional irascibility aside, however, one of the best ways in which to understand and appreciate the profoundly radical nature of Jesus' ministry and message – which, as I will later explain in this chapter, I take as a given, stood in opposition to Rome – is to ground it in its larger historical and cultural context. Only when one considers and compares it to other resistance movements in the empire can we appreciate and bring into focus the deeply atypical nature of Jesus' movement and message.

'Traditional' Forms of Violent Resistance to Rome

Resistance to Rome took a number of forms that were usually violent and driven by political and economic considerations, or motivated by local ethnic conflicts. Additionally, sometimes these rebellions were influenced and partly driven by nativist religious elements that could be enmeshed with the various motives for revolution and rebellion. Part of the reason for this is simply the nature of ancient societies, where the political and military authorities were also not infrequently the religious leaders as well. During Rome's republic, before the advent of Caesar and Augustus, there had been a history of rebellion in recently conquered provinces or in regions in the process of being subdued, and there is little that can be detected as any sort of specifically 'spiritual' opposition; although those elements were very likely present, they are often simply lost to us. One of the earliest of these rebellions took place in Spain in the 150s under the charismatic Variathus, a native of Lusitania, now modern Portugal, in the wake of the treacherous and deliberate massacre of Lusitanians, who were betrayed after agreeing to surrender to the proconsul Ser. Sulpicius Galba.[1] At about the same time, in Greece in 149 BC, a rebellion erupted led by the Macedonian pretender Andriscus.[2]

Over half a century later, Rome's Italian allies, impatient of their obligation to support Rome without the advantages of full Roman citizenship, broke into a fierce rebellion that resulted in a bloody and hard-fought war from 91–88 BC. It was during this time that an eastern potentate, Mithridates, king of Pontus (located in northern Turkey), exploited discord in Italy to make a grab for Rome's richest province, Asia, which had come into Rome's possession in 133 BC.[3] His invasion opened a powder keg of animus in Rome between the factions of two warlords, C. Marius, a popular commander and hero of the German Wars in which he fought between 105 and 100 BC, and L. Cornelius Sulla, a ruthless conservative blue-blood, champion of the nobility and senatorial privilege who had offended Marius while his lieutenant during the war against the Numidian king Jugurtha, fought between 112 and 106 BC.[4]

The war with Mithridates and the re-conquest of Asia was brutal and ferocious, and had the long-term result of bringing Judaea for the first time into the Roman sphere. As a preview of the war's ferocity, early in the war a Roman commander, Manius Aquillius, had the misfortune of being captured, only to have Mithridates humiliate him by forcing him to ride a mule before pouring molten gold down his throat.[5] Once in control of Asia, Mithridates coordinated a massacre of as many Romans and Italians now living and doing business in the province as he could get his hands on. Sources put the body count of what became known as the 'Asian Vespers' at 88,000, surely exaggerated, but nonetheless surely a testament, regardless of the number, to the profound hatred felt by the province's inhabitants against these Italian neophytes. The stories are singularly gruesome: at Ephesus those who took refuge in the Temple of Artemis were removed from the sanctuary by force and butchered; at Pergamum those seeking the sacred protection of Aesculapius, a prominent healing deity, were shot with arrows even as they grasped statues of the god invoking his protection; the inhabitants of Adramyttea pursued and massacred those Romans and Italians who sought to escape by swimming into the sea, and had their children drowned; similar outrages were repeated throughout the province of Asia.[6]

It took numerous commanders and nearly twenty-five years to finally bring Mithridates to heel before he ended his days by suicide when capture was imminent. It was one of the few times in which there may have been at least an incipient attempt to thwart Rome from one end of the empire to the next. The Roman historian Sallust, writing in the time of Julius Caesar and during the rise of Augustus, tells us of a letter Mithridates sent to a Roman turned rebel in Spain, Q. Sertorius, in which Mithridates suggested the two act in conjunction with one another. But the coordinated effort came to nothing. Indeed, there was never any attempt at an empire-wide rebellion in the course of Rome's history by provincials, even though during some rebellions rumours were spread to that effect.[7] That is perhaps unsurprising, given the problematic nature of communications in antiquity, not to mention a diversity of cultural, social, political, and economic conditions and interests.

Still, this did not discourage provincials from rebellion. Caesar, even in the midst of the conquest of Gaul, faced a major rebellion in 52 BC, which may have had a religious element to it (see p. 146). As already discussed, the Dalmatians and the Pannonians between AD 6 and 9 had taken arms up against Rome and posed a serious threat that took Tiberius some time to control. No sooner was the region pacified than the German chieftain and rebel Arminius took up arms against Rome, luring three legions into an ambush that Rome never forgot.[8] It could be argued that this was one of the few successful instances of rebellion and resistance to Rome, since Arminius managed to thwart Augustus' ambitions of extending the Roman frontier to the Elbe, and forced the Romans to withdraw permanently to the Rhine, which became, along with the Danube, Rome's northern boundary. Tiberius himself faced a number of rebellions that had to be put down in the AD 20s after he was well entrenched in power. The first of these was in Gaul led by Julius Florus and Julius Sacrovir in AD 21, which was quickly and handily crushed.[9] The other started several years before, in 17, in North Africa, whose leader Tacfarinas, a Numidian, had once served as an auxiliary fighter in the Roman army.[10] Tacfarinas used guerrilla tactics, and it was only after years of fighting with varying degrees of success that the governor of Africa, P. Cornelius Dolabella, with the help of the client king of Mauretania, Ptolemy, managed to defeat him in AD 24. Taking Tacfarinas and his forces by surprise, his men were scattered, his bodyguard cut down to a man, his son captured, and Tacfarinas himself, in his final despair, rushed into the thick of Roman spears and perished. It is worth noting that the revolts in Pannonia between AD 6 and 9, by the Germans between the Rhine and Elba in AD 9, of Julius Florus and Julius Sacrovir in Gaul in AD 21, of Tacfarinas in Africa in the 20s, all took place within the lifetime of Jesus.

Despite the merciless repression of rebellious provincials, Romans were at times remarkably capable of self-criticism, and understood full well the hostile sentiments of some provincial natives towards their empire. While they may not have empathized with those who rebelled, there are certainly instances when our sources are quite blunt about the cost of Roman power to other peoples. One of the most famous instances of this is found in Tacitus in a work titled the *Agricola*, a biography of his father-in-law, Cn. Julius Agricola, who while governor of Britain between AD 78 and 85 attempted to complete the long, slow conquest of Britain started under Claudius in AD 43.[11] Building on earlier Roman successes, Agricola took Roman arms for the first time into what is now modern Scotland, known then as Caledonia. He there met with stiff native resistance, and in an encounter in Agricola's last year as governor between the Caledonians and the Romans at what became known as the Battle of Mons Graupius, Tacitus attributes a speech to the leader of the Caledonian resistance, a man named Calgacus, that constitutes a starkly candid and honest reckoning of what Roman conquest meant to native peoples.[12] It bears noting that the speech is a complete fiction by Tacitus: there is absolutely no way that any Roman will have heard the speech, and at most it will have been a second-hand report by a native captive. Even if that were the case, we may still rightly ask how much interest the captive will have had in a true representation of events, and equally important, how good were the Roman translator's Celtic language skills. The matter need not concern us too much, since set speeches of dubious accuracy intended merely to present a particular perspective or elucidate and bring to life a historical personality were all too common in ancient historians.

The speech can be summarized as follows: Calgacus begins by telling his warriors that the battle will be the beginning of liberty for all of Britain; none who have gathered for the fight against the invading Romans have any experience of servitude – at the ends of the earth, they are the final bastion of freedom, though now they are besieged by Rome's might, and threatened by land and sea. Our eyes, he says, have not been violated by the contagion of servitude, and our very remoteness has defended us – until now. All that remained beyond them, Calgacus reminded them, were the waves and the barren rocks – and the hostile Romans, whose arrogance one flees in vain through obedience and humility. Calgacus then turned to their greed, calling the Romans the world's brigands who, when the land fails to satiate them, look to the sea. If an enemy is rich the Roman turns avaricious, but if he is poor then he will conquer for mere glory – neither the East nor the West has filled Rome's appetite. He then concludes the opening of his speech with one of the most magnificent and quotable sentences in all of Roman literature: *auferre trucidare rapere falsis nominibus imperium atque ubi solitudinem faciunt pacem appellant*, 'To steal, to butcher, to plunder they call by false names "empire", and where they make a desert they call it peace!' It is a stunning and exhilarating conclusion to Calgacus' preface, and in the speech's remaining two paragraphs never reaches such a crescendo again.

Instead, Calgacus diverges into the consequences of defeat, which were dire indeed. He reminds his men:

> your women and children will become mere sexual chattel for the Romans, even if they are fortunate enough to escape rape by the soldiery; your property will become tribute; your land will go

> to feed Rome; your hands and bodies will be worn down as you fortify their frontiers, even as you endure blows and insults; Britain as the last conquered province will be treated like a lowly and newly acquired household slave, and as such subjected to the worst possible treatment; we will be forced, asserts Calgacus, to toil in our own fields and mines and harbours; our ferocity and courage will render us suspect, as will our long distance on the edges of empire.

Calgacus continues:[13]

> A woman once led the revolt of the Brigantes: she burnt down a colony, attacked Roman camps, and would have stripped off the Roman yoke had not her good fortune turned to carelessness.[14] We on the other hand will remain unconquered and fresh in our strength, not wage war to our regret. Let us now show them what sort of men Caledonia has set in store for them! The Romans depend on their opposition, especially when a combination of different peoples, to be at variance with one another, and they depend on that opposition to vanish once matters turn against their opponent's favour. Fear and terror are weak bonds of affection: once they are removed, who has feared begins to hate. But we now have all inducements to victory before us: the Romans have no wives to incite them, no parents who will reproach flight, most no other fatherland. Few in number, ignorant of the country, looking around themselves at the very climate, sea, and forests, the gods have virtually handed them over to us ensnared like beasts and already subdued. Fear not the empty sheen of their gold and silver armour that neither protects nor wounds; in the very line of battle we will find our instruments – their British, Gallic, and German auxiliaries will remember their freedom, and their own cause, and will desert.[15] There is nothing further to fear: their forts are empty, their colonies full of old men, their cities feeble and full of discord, and caught between those unwilling to obey and those ruling unjustly. On our side we have a leader, we have an army: they offer only tribute, and the mines, and other punishments for the enslaved, which either you shall forever endure or avenge at once on this field. Advancing from here into the line of battle, think on your ancestors, and your posterity!

With this, Calgacus' exhortation ends. Tacitus is disparaging of the Briton's response to Calgacus' oration: 'They welcomed his speech enthusiastically, as is the custom with barbarians, with a loud roar of approval and discordant shouting.'[16] Calgacus and his band were defeated, and the devastation was reportedly widespread. Ten thousand of the enemy lay dead to the Romans' 360. By morning, the surrounding hills were deserted, the fires of burnt-out homesteads still smouldered, and an eerie silence hung over what was now a desolate landscape.[17] Tacitus says that a vast silence (*vastum … silentium*) hung over the countryside, both fulfilling and echoing Calgacus' warning that Roman peace brought only a desert.[18] In despair, some burnt their homes and fled, while others slew their wives and children, and then, presumably, themselves.

This native response of utter despair, including turning against one's own, was not an isolated event in the Roman world. Famously, the holdouts at Masada during the Jewish rebellion of AD 66–70 did the same, as did other communities in the course of Rome's conquest from Spain to Greece.[19] In 206 BC, the city of Astapa in Spain, chose mass suicide over enslavement at the hands of Scipio Africanus, one of Rome's greatest generals who went on to defeat Hannibal four years later at the Battle of Zama in North Africa.[20] Many Numantines in north-eastern Spain chose death rather than captivity, after a great war that lasted twenty years, in 133 BC.[21] Another Spanish tribe, the Cantabrians, after their failed rebellion collapsed in 22 BC, chose suicide over enslavement.[22] During the civil wars following Caesar's death between 44 and 42 BC, Marcus Brutus besieged Xanthus, a city in Asia Minor whose citizens chose suicide over defeat at Roman hands.[23] In almost ritualistic patterns, such a response to impending Roman conquest generally entailed the inhabitants of a town gathering and piling up all their wealth and movable valuables into the centre of town, and lighting the heap ablaze, after which the men would slaughter the women and children before killing themselves. After Trajan's defeat of the Dacians in AD 106, many chose mass suicide over enslavement, and some of the final panels on Trajan's Column in Rome depict mass suicide by some Dacian nobility who share poison from a cauldron (fig. 6.2). It was a better alternative than being worked to death in the mines or abused and raped repeatedly by one's Roman owner. When in 146 BC Scipio Aemilianus finally captured and sacked Carthage, Rome's greatest and deadliest foe, the city's defender, Hasdrubal, cravenly

Fig. 6.2: A mass suicide of the Dacian leadership, from Trajan's Column (AD 113) in the Forum of Trajan, Rome. (Public domain via *Wikimedia Commons*)

begged the Romans for mercy while his wife verbally assailed him for his cowardice before, like Dido, the city's mythic founder, she threw her two sons and then herself into the fires that blazed around the city; deserters from the Romans also chose suicide, casting themselves into the flames that engulfed the Temple of Eshmun – possibly set by Hasdrubal's wife.[24]

Roman rage against rebels is well documented in the archaeological record. In 125 BC, for reasons that are not entirely known, the city of Fragellae, a Latin colony that did not have full Roman citizenship rights, rebelled, standing alone against Rome. Today, excavations of the city, which is roughly halfway between Rome and Naples, speak volumes about the violence a community could face: there is nothing there. Roof tiles, the occasional earring found in a drain, three-inch high foundation walls, the periodic fragment of pottery or of a terracotta oil lamp, remnants of a floor here and there, and evidence of fire – and that is all. The paucity of material is perhaps a testament to Roman efficiency when it came to annihilating her opponents. When Carthage was finally captured in 146 BC, they took their time burning and razing the entire city to the ground over the course of seventeen days.[25] Long sieges in particular – Carthage in 146 BC, Numantia in 133 BC, Jerusalem in AD 70 – provoked a wrath among the Roman soldiery that transcended the bestial and veered into the demonic, in which entire communities were flattened and cast into outer darkness, a *damnatio memoriae* that sought to erase not just communities, but the most basic presence of their existence from history.

Violent Resistance and Divine Assistance

There was at times another aspect to this resistance: a religious one, although here some distinctions and difficulties concerning a religious element to ancient warfare need some addressing. Unlike the Christian era, the pagan world of the Greeks, Romans, and other pagan communities with which they came into contact, did not go to war for theological reasons: no one quarrelled over the nature of God (as in Alexandria in the fourth century in which Christian schism over the divine nature of Jesus resulted in the deaths of scores in violent conflict). Ancient peoples of Europe and the Mediterranean in general did not dispute, as in the Middle Ages, with centralized religious institutions over control of territory, religious as opposed to secular jurisdiction, or control of religious sites, with one or two significant exceptions.[26] In addition, the status of religious offices were rarely a fraught bone of contention, again with some rare but notable exceptions.[27] Nor were there religious wars over schisms in theological doctrine. The nature of religious conflict in antiquity, when it did arise, was quite different. There were, to be sure, conflicts over religion, even religious authority internally within Greek and Roman society.[28] Yet despite the lack of 'wars of religion' the divine and religious both cast a shadow over ancient conflicts in general.

Part of this is due to the inherent lack of separation between religious and secular institutions. Rome, for example, had a group of priests known as the *fetiales*. These were in charge of the sacred ceremonies by which war was formally declared and by which peace was ratified, and included sacred ceremonies at both the commencement of hostilities and their conclusion. Crudely put, imagine US senators who were also priests and running the Pentagon or State Department ratifying treaties by sacrificing farm animals, or casting spears and uttering sacred formulaic curses, and one will get the general idea. Religious ceremonies were imperative at every step of the way in warfare. In Rome, a commander before departing for war was obligated to take the auspices on the Capitoline before departing from the city on campaign; this could entail observing weather phenomena in the heavens or the behaviour of birds. He was obligated at virtually every step of the way, before, sometimes during, and after battle to perform religious ceremonies whose neglect could have dire consequences. Cicero, in fact, devoted half of an entire philosophical treatise, the *De Divinatione* (*On Divination*) to this phenomenon, and cited numerous examples of men who neglected their religious duties only to come to grief. Appius Claudius Pulcher was among the more renowned examples he cites: he not only failed to take the auspices when admiral of the Roman fleet fighting Carthage in 255 BC, he grew impatient at the sacred chickens when they refused to eat and tossed them into the Mediterranean. He was defeated that very day. One after the other Roman defeats are explained away by religious irregularities. After battle a pig, ram, and bull would be sacrificed in a purification ceremony known as a *suovetaurilia*, of which there is a particularly outstanding example in sculpted relief now in the Louvre (see fig. 6.3). At the end of a victorious campaign, the Romans offered thanks to Jupiter, and the victorious general, at least in Rome's early history, embodied the god himself for a day in the ceremony of the triumph, after which he sacrificed to Jupiter on the Capitoline.[29]

Here a brief word should be had concerning precisely how sacrifice could take place. In its crudest form it could be the simple slaughter of a small animal – say a suckling pig – at a small altar. For a large formal sacrifice it was something quite more elaborate. Sometimes the horns of bulls would be gilded and the animals adorned with garlands. There would be a number of officiants who would process with the animals

Fig. 6.3: A *suovetaurilia* (a purification sacrifice of a bull, ram, and pig) from part of a sculpture relief dating to the first century AD, now in the Louvre. (Daderot via *Wikimedia Commons*)

that would hopefully head to the altar willingly. On occasion a group of attendants would sing hymns, chant, or ululate, and a *tibicens* or flute player might attend to help drown out any words of ill omen. An attendant would carry a basket of grain which the animal would presumably follow, and from it would produce a flint knife with which some hairs would be cut from the animal's head and then tossed into the fire. An attendant called a *camillus* who carried a box of incense might also toss precious fragrances such as frankincense (which came from Yemen) on to the fire (worship always took place outside at an altar). Then a large beefy man called a *popa* would stun the animal on the head with a mallet and an equally beefy man called a *cultifer* would slit the stunned animal's throat. Throughout this process there would be singing and the playing of music. Blood might be caught in a basin and saved for sausages and puddings. Then the animal's organs would be inspected for omens by an *augur*, or a *haruspex*, who was a type of religious officiant of Etruscan origin who specialized in divining the will of the gods through the inspection of particularly the liver. The animal would be carved up, the thigh bones wrapped in fat and burnt as an offering to the gods while the priests and other attendants – and sometimes the whole community in the case of large festivals – would feast on the animal(s). Other offerings, such as milk, blood, wine, and oil, might also be poured on the altar. As noted, this was a frequent occurrence in political and other aspects of life – and in warfare.

A victor in war or battle simply assumed, in general, that their gods were more powerful and had rendered them assistance, and war was at times interpreted as having taken part on a divine scale and the outcome driven by divine intervention. This was true both for the Greeks and the Romans. Perhaps the best example of this is the Greek historian Herodotus' account of the wars between Greece and Persia: the Athenians had assisted Ionians, Greeks living on the coast of Asia Minor, in an attempt to liberate themselves from Persian domination between 499 and 494 BC.[30] During their revolt, they burnt down an important temple to Athena (or, rather, her Lydian equivalent) in Sardis. Although the Athenians withdrew from the revolt soon afterwards (early on in 498), King Darius of Persia swore revenge, a revenge not entirely fulfilled until his son, Xerxes, invaded Greece in 480 – but Xerxes himself made war against the gods, lashing the sacred waters of the Hellespont after a storm destroyed his pontoon bridge, and then burning Athens to the ground, including its temples. His reward was defeat at the hands of the Greeks at Salamis, Plataea, and Mycale, and a disastrous retreat back to Asia. Herodotus and doubtless other contemporaries saw the hands of the gods in this, and the place of religion in the wars between Greeks and Persians between 498 and 479 BC is worthy of its own discrete study.

On the Roman side of things, Livy, in the preface to his epic history of Rome, attributes the city's success to Roman piety and the favour of the gods, putting his history, too, on a semi-divine plain. Apart from the various standard priestly sacrifices and rituals, there were other religious aspects of warfare in ancient Rome. Before, during, and after battle, temples and offerings were vowed to numerous deities, and in Rome these vows were often directed towards Jupiter or Mars; indeed, in one of the suggested years of Jesus' birth, 4 BC, the emperor Augustus dedicated the Temple of Mars Ultor, Mars the Avenger. He had vowed the temple the night before the Battle of Philippi in 42 BC as a thanks-offering to the god for his assistance in defeating Brutus and Cassius, and completing the punishment of his father Julius Caesar's assassins. Similarly, Augustus vowed and dedicated the Temple of Apollo Actium to celebrate his defeat of Antony and Cleopatra at the Battle of Actium in 31 BC, a temple directly connected to Augustus' residence on the Palatine. The battle itself was one that was viewed in Augustan poets such as Horace and Propertius as one that took place on a divine scale, with Roman deities soundly thrashing the half-bestial gods and goddesses of the barbaric and effete Egyptians. How popular the view was that the gods took an active interest and role in human affairs, and how widespread such views were, is of course open to argument, though even Tacitus, a relatively sophisticated mind, holds out that the wrath of the gods was at work against Rome in the civil war of AD 68–69. Yet the gods, on the whole, remain ancillary powers in war – they are never the actual cause of it. Once a people was defeated, the Romans would complete their subjugation by on occasion (at least twice but possibly more) performing a ceremony known as *evocatio*, in which the defeated enemy's god(s) were invited to leave their vanquished city and serve Rome: this happened we know at Veii in 396 BC, and at Carthage in 146 BC.[31]

Neither Greek nor Roman society was immune during the enormous stress of warfare from bouts of religious fervour and hysteria. Hence, as the Persian invasions loomed over Greece, oracles were consulted and their interpretations became points of contention, while during the Persian occupation the presence of the Greek hero Ajax was thought to have helped the Greeks to victory.[32] The day after the Persians cut down an ancient olive tree on Athena's sacred acropolis the tree had already sprung up – a miracle, since the olive is a very slow growing tree.[33] During the Peloponnesian War between Athens and Sparta, Thucydides tells us in the wake of the plague in 430–29 BC that oracles and disputes over them arose in both Athens and Sparta.[34] In Rome, the exhausting and destructive Hannibalic War (220–202 BC) that ruined Italy impelled the Romans, towards its end, to the consultation of the sacred and oracular Sibylline Books, which resulted in the importation of the Magna Mater, the Great Mother goddess, to Rome from Asia Minor.[35] She was to act as a talisman that would supposedly prevent an enemy from ever making war on Italian soil again.

We can say in general that religion, given the structure of ancient society, was integral to warfare, and that the gods were often ancillary to the conflict at large or a means towards making sense of the conflict. We should be cautious and hesitate to say, however, that they were at any point a causal basis for ancient conflict: there are no Crusades, and as noted, no battles over theological issues, no great schisms. At best there are territorial conflicts over the control of sacred sites or the invocation of the gods for understanding the reasons behind the outcomes of conflicts and certain events during their course. At the same time, however, we need to exercise some prudence: the nature of our ancient sources are problematic. They are often sparse, and fall far short when it comes to teasing out the deep complexities of the causes of warfare in the ancient world. Even Thucydides, one of our most sophisticated of ancient historians, is problematic in his presentation concerning the outbreak of the Peloponnesian War, a relatively well-documented conflict. We often lack the information that would allow us to assess in more accurate and precise terms the complexity of reasons for warfare during classical antiquity, and the current state of our evidence urges caution, agnosticism, and sober conjecture.

Mona, Boudicca, and the Rebellion of the Britons

What are at times readily detectable in the historic record are distinctively nativist religious elements in warfare, and as it happens these are perhaps most notable in a number of rebellions in the first century AD: these include the revolts in Britain in AD 60–61, Gaul and Germania in AD 69–70, and that of Judaea in AD 66–70. The difficulty with the first of these, Britain, is perhaps the most problematic, though only slightly so.[36] It was then that the Iceni and Trinobantes, two tribes that lived directly to the north-east of London, rebelled under the leadership of Queen Boudicca (see fig. 6.4).[37] Part of the reason for the rebellion was an aggressive calling in of loans by Roman money lenders from Britons, something that is attributed to the machinations of Nero's courtier Seneca the Younger, but which also was potentially connected with financial difficulties during Nero's regime.[38]

Fig. 6.4: A late nineteenth-century rendering in bronze of Queen Boudicca in her chariot with her two daughters next to her. Westminster, London. (Paul Walter via *Wikimedia Commons*)

The background to the rebellion as related in our ancient sources is as follows: Prasutagus, king of the Iceni, had made the emperor Nero co-heir in hopes of preserving his kingdom and household, to no avail. Once Prasutagus was dead there was no protection against the avarice of Roman officials, and his widow, Queen Boudicca – who later became the leader of the rebellion – was flogged and her daughters raped. Iceni chieftains were deprived of their estates and the king's relatives treated in a manner befitting slaves. The Iceni and the Trinobantes, enraged at such mistreatment, joined forces and attacked Camulodunum (modern Colchester), the capital of the Roman province and probably Britain's first genuine city.

Just prior to the attack, as news of the rebellion spread, a wave of religious hysteria struck the city after a statue of Victory – presumably in the Temple of Claudius and at that time the largest temple in Britain – inexplicably fell with its back turned as though in flight. This was perhaps significant in more ways than one, since the actual name of the city itself was *Colonia Victricensis*, or Colony of Victory.[39] While likely named after the victory of Claudius that gave the Romans a firm footing on the island in AD 43, the name had equal significance for the Britons, since it was the ancient seat of the goddess Adraste (also called Andraste), a Celtic warrior goddess, to whom the place was sacred. Religious fervour hit the Roman women of the town hardest, and they reportedly went into deliriums, chanting of imminent destruction, attesting that they had heard loud cries from the local senate house, and had seen visions of a phantom city that lay in ruins at the mouth of the Thames. Most ominously of all, the sea had turned a blood red and shapes resembling human corpses were seen at the ebb tide. While the Roman inhabitants of Camulodunum were in despair at these reports and the dire portents, they encouraged the natives who were sympathetic to Boudicca and her cause. Roman concerns at the time were well placed. The imperial agent from whom the Roman residents of the town had asked assistance, Catus Decianus, was an incompetent, and sent just 200 men to help fortify the un-walled city. The rebels easily stormed it and massacred the inhabitants, including the garrison that had sought to make a last stand in the temple. When a commander of some talent, Q. Petilius Cerealis, attempted to relieve the town, his entire infantry force was slaughtered and he was forced to withdraw with his cavalry to his camp and reinforce it as best he could, while Catus Decianus, now humiliated, high-tailed it over the English Channel to Gaul.[40]

Boudicca then mustered her forces and prepared for the attack. In Dio's version of events, Boudicca gives a lengthy speech to her 120,000 strong army (surely a much exaggerated number), and exhorted it to take up arms against the Romans prior to the attack on Camulodunum. Dio also gives a vivid description of a queen who was a most striking force of nature: tall and terrifying in appearance, she had ferocious eyes and a harsh voice, and her blonde hair fell down to her waist. She wore a golden necklace, a thick multicoloured tunic with a heavy mantle fastened with a brooch, and sported a spear, cutting a figure no doubt resembling a Celtic Athena or Bellona. In her speech she rebuked her people for accepting the domination of the Romans and forgetting their ancient ancestral liberty.[41] She reminded them that poverty and freedom were preferable to slavery and wealth, and deprecated the suffering of the Britons since the Romans' arrival: the taxation, the mortgaging of their persons into debt servitude, the agricultural labour demanded, the general and complete despoiling of their wealth even beyond the grave. The Romans, she continued, knew nothing of the world the Britons inhabited, only how to extract a profit; while there was still time, she urged the Britons to hand over to their children the patrimony of their freedom before they too, born and raised in bondage, forgot their ancient liberty. She concluded by urging her people, oppressed by fear and hate, to turn their rage against the Romans who, although heavily armed, would be no match for their courage; their enemy was not as hardy or capable of as much endurance, since they had been ennervated by wealth and luxury – mere hares and foxes trying to govern over dogs and wolves! After the speech she performed a type of divination as she set loose a hare from the fold of her dress and it ran in a direction deemed auspicious. Boudicca now raised her hands to heaven, gave thanks to Andraste for the good omen, and appealed to her to be their leader in the coming fight, attacking the Romans once more for their effeminacy and casting insults at the emperor Nero, calling the Romans 'slaves to a lyre player, and a bad one at that', and impugning his masculinity.[42]

Among ancient peoples there was nothing unusual about Boudicca functioning in her capacity as a military commander as an important religious leader as well, and in some respects it was the order of the day.

Trajan and Claudius, when they took the field, were after all Pontifex Maximus as well as emperor. But here Boudicca's role and actions may take on an added significance.[43] It is suspicious that the Roman governor, C. Suetonius Paulinus, was away at Mona (the modern Isle of Anglesey) when Boudicca broke into rebellion. We are unclear why Suetonius attacked it: Tacitus states that he was ambitious for glory and concerned to hold his own with another commander of outstanding repute, Cn. Domitius Corbulo, who had won renown while campaigning in Armenia. The island of Mona, sacred to Britain's inhabitants, was strong by virtue of its population that was augmented when it became a refuge for those displaced by Rome's conquest. As the Romans approached the island, the British defenders drew up a dense battle line of assorted warriors with women running about in their midst in the manner of Furies, wearing funerary clothes, their hair dishevelled, and brandishing torches. Druids stood around them too, uttering frightening prayers, their hands raised to heaven. Suetonius' soldiers were paralyzed with terror until he urged them on; they advanced, laid the enemy low, and in the confusion some of the Britons were enveloped in the flames of their own torches. The Romans then proceeded to cut down the sacred groves on the island where, Tacitus says, they practised the cruel superstitions of their sacred rites (*saevis superstitionibus sacri*): 'For they deemed it right to honour their altars with the blood of captives and to consult their gods through human organs.'[44]

It is not too much to think that the attack on this sacred site was one of the possible motives for rebellion, even though neither Tacitus nor Dio make the connection, although we must note that this is conjecture. Tacitus, in particular, is rarely sensitive to the religious traditions of other people as noted elsewhere (p. 36), so we would not necessarily expect him to be any more sensitive to the potential for religious sentiment among northern barbarians. The reason to be suspicious of a connection is the chronology of the episode in Tacitus, who indicates that Suetonius had planned and launched his attack against Mona before Boudicca launched her rebellion, even taking his time to construct a fleet for his campaign against the island. He was barely in the course of mopping-up operations when he was brought news of the rebellion in the south-east, and Tacitus indicates that the news was unexpected.[45] Dyson may be right to suspect that rather than being connected, the revolt may have received further impetus by the attack on Mona which was, he argues, simply a part of the operations ongoing in Wales as the Romans slowly subdued the island.[46]

Yet there is also the possibility here of a carefully coordinated operation between Boudicca and the religious leadership on Mona, since in his earlier work, the *Agricola*, Tacitus appears to connect the two events, although his presentation is maddeningly vague: he states in reviewing the history of Roman governorship in Britain that Suetonius Paulinus deliberately attacked Mona, *Monam insulam ut vires rebellibus ministrantem adgressus terga occasioni patefecit* ('He left his rear guard exposed to the enemy while attacking the island Mona, on the grounds it was supporting rebels.')[47] He then digresses briefly on the reasons for the revolt before introducing Boudicca and briefly covering the rebellion in the course of a single paragraph. However, the premeditated attack on Mona and its timing, taken in conjunction with the omen of the Roman goddess of Victory at Camulodunum and Boudicca's own invocation to Andraste, give Boudicca and her rebellion the distinct feel that there was spiritual leadership in this rebellion of a sort that is simply not highlighted in the resistance led by other committed rebels discussed earlier, such as Andriscus, Mithridates, or Calgacus, though we can by no means have absolute certainty about this. Suetonius' assault on Mona and its destruction, however, very possibly implies that this was a sacred centre and that Suetonius may have believed, given the risk involved, that its destruction could effectively decapitate the rebellion and was worth taking the chance of exposing his rear guard. Perhaps most importantly, Mona was a religious centre of Druidic worship, and in Britain at this time it appears that this class within Celtic society still maintained a prestigious leadership role, as it had in Gaul in the time of Caesar a century earlier. Caesar had faced rebellion in Gaul in 52 BC and as Cunliffe has pointed out, felt compelled to attack the tribe of the Carnutes first and their capital Cenabum (modern Orléans); it was somewhere in this region in a consecrated spot (Caesar is imprecise as to where) that the Druids held an annual pan-Gallic assembly and considered this place as the centre of all of Gaul.[48] Suetonius may have known full well that the province was restive and to pacify it required violent action against the leadership centred on Mona, just as Caesar had assaulted Cenabum as a Druidic religious centre a century before.

As for the remainder of the revolt: Suetonius Paulinus soon came to the province's rescue after a forced march from the island of Mona. Tacitus says that Suetonius evacuated Londinium as best he could (the earliest mention we have of what was to become London), but the old, the infirm, and those attached to the place stayed. The rebels soon destroyed it, as well as nearby Verulamium (modern St Albans). Tacitus reports that the rebels went for places where there was wealth rather than attacking forts or garrisons, looking for the weakest places that were easy pickings. Along the way they variously burnt, crucified, or cut the throats of Romans and provincials alike, and Tacitus puts the number of dead at 70,000. Cassius Dio gives a more ghoulish account: the Britons hung the noblest of their women captives naked, cut off their breasts, and sewed them to their mouths to give the appearance as though they were eating them. Others were impaled on sharp stakes running through their entire body. This too, may have had a religious significance to it, since Dio tells us that they did this while sacrificing, indulging in banquets and (more vaguely) 'outrageous behaviour' (*hubrizontes*) in all their sacred places, but in particular in the Grove of Andate (possibly a mistake by Dio for Andraste).[49] In addition, in Suetonius' speech to his men as reported by Dio (62.11), he urges his soldiers that if the fortunes of battle are against them, to avoid capture: 'It is better that you fall bravely while fighting than being captured to be impaled, see your guts cut out to be spitted on red hot skewers, and to perish melted in boiling water.'[50] Taken together with Tacitus' reference to human sacrifice, it is not too much to think that their captives will have had a religious significance as offering to the gods; indeed, Celtic and Germanic people both employed human sacrifice of captives as a religious offering.[51]

Suetonius' concerns were groundless, since once Roman forces engaged with Boudicca's it was no contest. The Romans annihilated the enemy, including the women (and presumably children) whom the Britons had brought to watch the battle and left at the baggage train, which in fact also proved an impediment to the Britons when they tried to retreat. Even the pack animals were slaughtered. Again the disproportionate casualties – as was the case at Mons Graupius years later – were staggering: 80,000 enemy dead to the Romans' 400. This might sound dubious to those not familiar with ancient warfare, however, the nature of ancient warfare in the Greek and Roman periods at least appears such that, once an enemy's ranks were broken or their flanks and rears surrounded, a thoroughly unequal bloodbath was not uncommonly the order of the day. Even if the numbers are exaggerated, the lop-sided nature of the victory remains highly plausible. The Romans themselves had been on the receiving end of similar massacres in the course of their history, most famously at the hands of Hannibal during the Second Punic War between 220 and 202 BC. Names of places such as Trasimene (where the Romans lost 20,000 men) and Cannae (with possibly as many as 60,000 Roman dead) haunted the Roman imagination, as did Aurasio (modern L'Orange in the South of France) just over a century later, where the Romans suffered a massive defeat at the hands of the Germanic Cimbri and Teutones in 105 BC in southern Gaul, with a reported loss of 80,000 Romans and Italian allies. At Marathon, the Athenians defeated the Persian host, who lost more than 6,000 men to Athens' 192; the Athenians buried the men on the spot and rightly celebrated it as one of their most magnificent victories. There was no substitute in battle in antiquity for discipline, training, and experience, and much of the course of ancient history can be traced to the breaking of ranks, unexpected appearance of cavalry, careless armies deceived by weak centres and oblivious of strong flanks, or the experience of veterans set against green, raw, and young recruits. The Britons were resoundingly defeated, and Boudicca committed suicide by ingesting poison.

Civilis, Veleda, and the Revolt of the Batavians

Eight years later, in AD 69, came another rebellion in which religion again appears to have played a part. The revolt was led by a man named Julius Civilis, a Batavian of royal stock, the Batavians being a Germanic tribe living in the Rhine delta, in what are now the Netherlands. Under the emperor Nero he had been charged with fomenting rebellion, likely in the ultimately abortive revolt of Julius Vindex against Nero in Gaul in AD 67 or 68, and sent to the emperor in chains, only to be released by Galba who had succeeded Nero after Nero's suicide. Galba sent Civilis back to the Batavians, who were now under the jurisdiction of Vitellius, governor of Lower Germany and briefly emperor from April until December of AD 69; Vitellius dared not punish Civilis for fear of alienating a people who supplied significant cavalry auxiliaries to the Roman army.[52] But under Vitellius' command the soldiery demanded his punishment. To avoid this, Civilis proceeded to foment revolution by virtue of a short, nasty civil war fought in the wake of Nero's suicide between June AD 68, after Nero was declared a public enemy and the armies of Spain had rebelled and chosen Galba as their emperor, and late December AD 69. Civilis proceeded to invite Batavian chieftains and the most determined of the commoners to a sacred grove, and after they became heated by a night's entertainment, Civilis addressed them, playing on their resentments, rehearsing all the injustices Roman officials had visited on them, and reminding them of their glorious past and current servitude.[53] He bound them into alliance using 'barbarous ritual and ancestral curses', hence creating a bond through religious ceremony; that was, one suspects, not unusual. He also took a vow: he would let his hair grow wild until he could claim victory.[54]

The revolt gained allies, both among the tribes of Germania east of the Rhine and in Gaul; the rebels even gained possession of twenty-four ships from Rome's fleet on the Rhine. Their success was aided by the feckless, incompetent, and inert governor of Upper Germany, Hordeonius Flaccus, who failed to coordinate with Herennius Gallus, commander of the first legion stationed at Bonn.[55] Duillius Vocula, commander of the twenty-second legion was more effective, but failed to exploit opportunities or to follow up on his successes.[56] Worst of all, Rome's armies on the Rhine were torn with civil dissensions, some supporting as candidate for Emperor Vitellius, and others supporting Vespasian, the no-nonsense soldierly commander of the legions in Judaea and recently (as of 1 July AD 69) declared emperor in Alexandria, Egypt. Roman failure against Civilis, civil war over the imperial succession, legions consequently torn apart by divided loyalties, and mutinous troops anxious for their donatives from imperial pretenders had made for a toxic stew. The mood of the Rhine legions grew ugly, and Flaccus the governor was murdered. However, Flaccus may have had no one but himself to blame, since he made the impolitic move of giving them a promised donative in Vespasian's name, even though it had been sent by Vitellius – a move Tacitus says, more than any other, that led the troops to murder Flaccus.[57]

Here a brief word is necessary concerning Vitellius. According to our sources, Vespasian appears a stalwart, earthy and affable man, one supremely competent as a general. His rival Vitellius could not have been more different. From a corrupt and ancient aristocratic family, his father, Lucius Vitellius, was the most servile of courtiers under Caligula and

Claudius: he reportedly instituted the practice of worshipping Caligula as a god, and received the privilege under his successor, Claudius, of removing the empress', Messalina's, shoes, which he reportedly fondled and kissed.[58] His son and the future emperor, Aulus Vitellius, was no better if not worse: he came to Caligula's attention for his skill as a charioteer, to Claudius' for his proficiency at dice, and was one of the basest of flatterers at Nero's theatrical performances.[59] When Galba succeeded Nero in 68 he made Vitellius governor of the important and powerful province of Lower Germany, not considering him a menace. Galba was assassinated in January of 68 and succeeded by M. Salvius Otho, governor of Lusitania under Nero as well as Nero's formerly close friend.[60] Soon a confrontation between Otho and Vitellius became imminent. Their forces clashed at Bedriacum, modern Cremona; yet before the outcome was certain Otho bravely and nobly committed suicide, not wanting to sacrifice more lives on the altar of his ambition.[61]

Vitellius took a gruesome delight in touring the battlefield when he arrived some weeks later, the corpses now filling the air with a stench so awful that he swigged undiluted wine to help himself withstand it, despite commenting that the only thing that smelled sweeter than a dead enemy was a dead fellow citizen.[62] In fact, Suetonius states that his two ruling vices were cruelty and gluttonous extravagance, which included alcoholism, something Suetonius says gave his face a constantly flushed appearance.[63] Upon entrance into Rome his brother, Lucius Vitellius (named after their father), gave an outrageous feast to celebrate his victory that sported 2,000 exotic fish and 7,000 game birds, but the show-stopper was 'Minerva's Shield', a concoction served on a ridiculously large platter, and consisting of pike livers, pheasant and peacock brains, flamingo tongues, and lamprey milt.[64] It was little wonder his reign only lasted eight months, and ended as sordidly as Vitellius himself had lived (see p. 151).

Vespasian's forces defeated the Vitellians on 24 October at a second battle at Cremona. Forcing their way into Rome, there was violent street fighting, hair-raisingly described by Tacitus – brothels, baths, and eating houses functioned as usual in the midst of the melee, with the Roman people urging on now one side, now the other, as though the bloody urban conflict were sport.[65] One of the casualties of the fighting was the Temple of Jupiter Capitolinus, the most revered temple in the city that loomed atop the Capitoline over the Roman Forum, but which had become a battleground in December of 69.[66] Vespasian's brother, the city prefect Flavius Sabinus, was captured and executed, but in the end Vespasian's forces prevailed.[67] Vitellius, whose previous attempt to abdicate had been rejected (no emperor abdicated again until Diocletian in AD 305), was soon deserted by all. The events as Suetonius and Tacitus depict them are unforgettably lurid – Vitellius' isolation in the imperial quarters on the Palatine, his terror at the deafening silence, his dressing in befouled clothes to escape detection, his hiding in the imperial kennels (or a latrine) before finally Julius Placidus, a tribune of the praetorians, dragged him out of the palace. A noose was put around his neck, a sword under his chin. He was paraded in his filthy garments that had been made bloody since he had been attacked by the dogs where he hid; pelted with refuse and excrement by the mob, he was summarily butchered next to the Gemonian Steps in the Forum.[68] His only saving grace, according to Tacitus, is that he found the courage in his last words to say to his executioner, 'Yet I was your emperor.'

Soon after, in the early weeks of January AD 70, news of Vitellius' lynching reached the armies – and the rebels. The news gave new life to Civilis' rebellion, possibly infusing it with a religious element up until now somewhat muted, and the Gauls now, along with the Germans, felt encouraged.[69] Rumours spread that the Dacians and Sarmatians, tribes that lived north of the Danube in what is now modern Hungary and Romania, were also in arms against the Roman provinces of Moesia and Pannonia in the Balkans; stories circulated that Britain was wavering in its loyalty; above all, that the Capitoline had burnt, the site where every Roman triumph culminated with a sacrifice to Jupiter in thanksgiving for victory over Rome's vanquished foes, was welcome as a sign of the inevitable demise of Rome's empire. The Druids in Gaul inflamed the sense of religious fervour when they recalled that even when their Gallic forebears had captured Rome nearly 500 years earlier, in 390 BC, the Capitoline had stood firm as Rome's citadel, protected by powerful gods.[70] The fire was a sign of divine rage; the Roman world was soon to pass, replaced by a Gallic one – not far ultimately from the truth, but hundreds of years too soon. The burning of Rome's Holy of Holies was a sign from the gods, an indication of divine favour towards Rome's subjected peoples.

Now a number of Gallic chieftains joined the revolt, including Julius Classicus, a commander of Roman auxiliary cavalry of the Treverii (from the Moselle Valley), and Julius Tutor, a fellow Treveri.[71] These proceeded to send agents throughout Gaul to incite the province to rebellion, and in the process hired a Roman deserter, Aemilius Longinus, who assassinated the Roman commander Vocula.[72] Civilis, Classicus, and Tutor now stood at the head of a formidable rebellion: Tutor besieged Colonia Agrippinensis (modern Cologne) and, once taken, forced the Roman soldiers there and its inhabitants to swear allegiance to the new Gallic empire. At Moguntiacum (modern Mainz), he killed the Roman tribunes and expelled the camp prefects when they refused to swear the loyalty oath, and then besieged the camp.[73] After he received the surrender of the starving men he forced them to swear allegiance as with those at Cologne, but subsequently he treacherously attacked them, killing most. With much of the Rhineland, i.e., Rome's German provinces, under the control of Germans and their Gallic lieutenants, Civilis now cut his hair which he had dyed red. To help celebrate his massacre of Rome's legions he handed over some Roman prisoners to his son to use as targets as he practised his skill with the bow, an action that may have had some religious significance as a form of sacrifice.[74]

It is at this juncture in Tacitus' narrative that a religious element most obviously intrudes: as a thanksgiving offering Civilis sent one of the legionary commanders, Munius Lupercus, to a woman named Veleda.[75] The woman, whose virgin status Tacitus remarks upon and which was possibly an aspect of her status as a spiritual leader (something she held in common with Rome's Vestal Virgins), was famed as a prophetess. Of German origin, she was a member of the Bructeri, a tribe that inhabited what is now eastern Holland. Tacitus tells us that it was a German custom to consider women of Veleda's ilk not simply a prophetess, but even a goddess, and that at this particular juncture her fame and repute were at their height, since she had foretold the rise of Germanic power and the overthrow of the Roman army. It did not hurt that some of the legions, decimated by the revolt and by divisions brought on by the rivalry between Vespasian and Vitellius, had now submitted to and in essence joined Civilis' rebellion. The rebels now turned once again on Cologne, one of the most powerful Roman colonies in the region; the besieged inhabitants, many whom were German, were at a loss concerning what to do and entered into negotiations, requesting that Civilis and Veleda act as chief negotiators.[76] Offering gifts to Civilis and Veleda, the people of Cologne obtained a reprieve. However, they were not allowed even to see Veleda, who lived atop a tower in isolation to instil a greater sense of awe and mystery around her person and to bolster her religious authority.[77] Tacitus tells us that mediators went between Veleda and any who wished to speak with her, as though emissaries between the gods and men. Indeed, Veleda's authority was such that at one point during the rebellion the Germans offered the captured Roman flagship of Rome's Rhine fleet as an offering to her.[78]

It was at about this time, however, that the political situation in Rome stabilized, and the Roman government was able to rise to the threat. Petilius Cerealis, a veteran of Suetonius' campaign against Boudicca, was sent to deal with the crisis.[79] He inflicted a serious defeat on Civilis at Augusta Treverorum (modern Trier in western Germany), and then again at the site of the old camp at Vetera (modern Xanten).[80] After a few more minor encounters, Cerealis entered into negotiations with Civilis, secretly promising him a pardon and putting pressure on Veleda and those close to her to use their influence to help end a catastrophic war and do a good service to Rome.[81] Tacitus' manuscript breaks off not long (about two paragraphs) after this episode, but it appears reprisals were less severe than normal. The fate of Civilis, however, remains unknown.

Both Veleda and the Druids of Mona share in common that they acted as religious advisors to military and tribal leadership, and in the case of Mona may have actually constituted a part of that leadership. We find this, too, in the historical record among other northern peoples, such as with the Dacians we encounter in Strabo, writing in the first century AD. In the 80s BC under the leadership of King Burebista, a number of disparate regional tribes, including the Daci, the Getae, and the Buri, consolidated into a single state encompassing the general region of modern Romania.[82] Assisting Burebista in this was a man named Decenaeus, a religious advisor to Burebista. About Decenaeus and his role among these tribes, Strabo tells us the following: the institution of the religious sage *qua* advisor to the king had been inherited from the Getae and its origins, by Strabo's time, stretched back hundreds of years to a man named Zamolxis (also spelt Zalmoxis), who had been a slave but also a student of Pythagoras and was even said to have studied in

Egypt. His studies lead him to an understanding of celestial phenomena and how to interpret it to divine the future. How he came to be with the Getae is anyone's guess, but once among them Strabo says his talent gained him great influence with their king who took him as a partner in government since he understood the will of their gods, and he was soon made priest of the god most honoured among the Getae. As was the case with Veleda, he took up habitation in an isolated spot, a mountain the people soon believed itself sacred called Cogaeonum. Also like Veleda, he was eventually honoured as a god himself, and was accessible only to the king and his attendants, no doubt creating an aura of religious awe and mystery. The king's prestige grew by degrees because the community now believed his decrees were in accordance with the counsels of the gods through this new intermediary.

After Zamolxis' death, the institution persisted hundreds of years, though how is uncertain, since Strabo indicates only in the most vague terms that it abided down to his own time 'with some such person of this sort in respect to their character always being found'.[83] Under the joint leadership of Burebista and Decenaeus this newly founded confederacy began to cause the Romans serious problems in the lower Danube and Balkan frontiers, as they raided into Macedonia, Thrace, and Illyria, and starting around 60 BC began to expand westward.[84] Indeed, the situation was so serious that, by the eve of his assassination in 44 BC, Julius Caesar was not only planning an expedition against the Parthians, but against this newly formed Dacian state on the lower Danube as well.[85] Strabo calls Decenaeus a wizard (a *göēs* in Greek) who like Zamolxis had studied in Egypt, learned to prognosticate the will of the gods, and himself was honoured as one. However, Burebista was deposed around the time of Caesar's assassination, his kingdom broken up, and nothing more is heard of Decenaeus.

The Jewish Rebellion of AD 66

A similarly religious element intrudes in the rebellion of Judaea in AD 66–70, in which religious tensions contributed to the outbreak of the Jewish rebellion against Rome, as had been the case with earlier rebellions and unrest in the province (see pp. 80–7 and 110–16). Before embarking on this discussion, we should note that two magisterial studies have recently been published on this conflict, the first by Vasily Rudich in 2015, the second by Steve Mason in 2016, and regrettably neither appears aware of either work as they progressed. Both take somewhat different approaches, with Rudich looking at the Jewish Revolt's religious motivations, and viewing it, as the title of his work implies, as an example of religious dissidence, while Mason's approach is somewhat more reserved. As Mason has noted, our main source for the rebellion, Josephus, weds 'cosmic drama' to a real-life event, but we need to clarify that despite the aspect of the divine in Josephus' explanation, religious tension was by no means the sole cause of the conflict, although it was certainly a stressor and even a flashpoint that contributed to it.[86]

At the same time, Mason rightly admonishes against seeing Judaea as a province that was constantly seething with resentment in which conflict was inevitable, and as noted elsewhere in this study, from a number of perspectives the native ruling authorities in Judaea were anxious to maintain good relations with Rome and generally managed to walk a tightrope between regional religious and ethnic chauvinism, and Roman domination.[87] He is right, too, I believe, to see some of this war's root causes not in resistance or animus to Rome, but in internecine ethnic strife that traditionally plagued the region and that served in the end to impel Rome's intervention and the clash between Romans and Jews, with Jerusalem as the focal point.[88] Rudich, however, makes a very compelling argument for seeing the conflict of AD 66–70 in very stark religious terms. He dives deeply into the background of previous tensions and conflicts between the Jews and Romans: the rage at Herod the Great for desecrating the Temple with an imperial golden eagle, the demonstrations before Pilate for his violation of the sacrosanct space of the Temple and its treasury, and the bitter expressions of resentment at Caligula's ultimately unrealized demand for imperial cult worship in the Temple itself, all are evidence of simmering religious tensions and potential flashpoints between Romans and Jews prior to the outbreak of the rebellion in AD 66.[89] It is far from my intention here, unlike those more focused studies, to give a detailed history of the war itself and its origins. However, before proceeding further in investigating the religious elements of the rebellion, a summary of Josephus' narrative, our main source for the war, is in order, a source, it should be noted, that is not always easy to follow.

According to Josephus, the conflict erupted when some of the Jewish community living in Caesarea took offence at a Greek who lived next to a synagogue: he had built a workshop next to the synagogue rendering access difficult, and possibly as a wilful act of provocation.[90] Tensions rose, and Jewish attempts to resolve the situation by involving Gessius Florus, a corrupt governor of Judaea notorious for his avarice, and even bribing him, did not help. He reportedly refused to check brigandage, a serious problem in the province, and was himself brutally extractive in his taxation of the provincials. Indeed, Josephus says Florus was sufficiently concerned about accusations of provincial maladministration by the Jewish population that he intentionally exacerbated the volatile situation in order to try to drive the province to revolt and provide a screen for his corruption.[91] Cestius Gallus, the governor of Syria at the time, may have been under pressure simultaneously to extract greater revenues from the neighbouring province, a pressure that will have devolved also to Florus, and the same excessive taxation that helped provoke open rebellion in Britain under Nero may also have been at work in Judaea.[92]

Visiting Jerusalem, the people crowded Cestius (probably during Passover in AD 65) and denounced Florus.[93] Cestius did his best to reassure the people that they would enjoy a more moderate governance in the future before he returned to Antioch, the provincial capital of Syria, while Florus went back to the Judaean capital at Caesarea, where tensions simmered between the Jewish and Greek population, not just over the incident concerning the synagogue but also over who had the right to govern the city – Jews or the Syrian Greek population – and both sides started to incite the other to violence.[94] Eventually, someone wilfully provoked the Jewish population of Caesarea by sacrificing two birds on an overturned chamber pot in a deliberate act of desecration.[95] A riot broke out and the Jews seized their sacred books and fled 7 miles away from Caesarea to Narbata, while twelve of the top Jewish leaders of Caesarea went to Sebaste where Florus was staying to complain and beg his assistance, only to be thrown into irons for their trouble – and charged with unlawfully removing copies of the Jewish law from Caesarea.[96]

News of the riots and disorders in Caesarea and of Florus' response reached Jerusalem and tensions mounted, with fuel added to the fire when Florus appropriated 17 talents from the Temple's treasury.[97] In this instance, however, as opposed to Veleda and Boudicca, who functioned as religious authorities inciting rebellion, the high priests of the Temple attempted to calm matters, and urged a submissive demeanour towards Florus, who was not inclined to sympathize with the Jewish populace. Josephus even tells us that:

> every priest and every minister of God brought out the sacred vessels and put on the robes they always wore when officiating, the harpers and singers appeared with their instruments, and they all fell down and implored the people to preserve their sacred ornaments and not provoke the Romans to plunder the treasures of God.[98]

But when Florus entered the city a riot erupted; he soon withdrew in the face of opposition but left a large garrison and extracted a promise from the chief priests and Sanhedrin to maintain order in the city.[99] As Mason points out, Florus' actions in Jerusalem may have been the tinder box that caused a regional explosion.[100] In the meantime, Florus sent a missive to Cestius Gallus in Antioch, accusing the Jews of rebellion, while letters also came to him from local magistrates that accused Florus of malice, and Cestius sent an official, a tribune named Neopolitanus, to investigate.[101]

The agent satisfied himself that the Jews were sincere in their desire to stay loyal to Rome, did his best to mollify the people of Jerusalem, and returned to Cestius to make his report.[102] In addition, Herod Agrippa II, who was in control of Peraea and Galilee and a staunch Roman loyalist, also tried to assuage the population in Jerusalem who demanded that an embassy be sent to Nero to accuse Florus and excuse the damage done by rioting and violence in the city.[103] For the moment Agrippa mollified the people, whom he advised to restore the damage done by civic unrest and to pay their usual tribute to Rome.[104] But violent insurrection metastasized throughout the region with astonishing speed, first south into Idumaea where insurgents seized the impregnable fortress of Masada and massacred its Roman garrison, then north into Syria, where unspeakable violence erupted between the Syrian and Jewish populations, spreading even into Agrippa II's petty kingdom and to Alexandria in Egypt.[105]

Meanwhile, back in Jerusalem, Eleazar, son of the high priest Ananias and temple captain, prohibited foreigners from sacrifice or bestowal of gifts on the Temple, including sacrifices offered on behalf of Caesar.[106]

This forced a meeting of the foremost citizens of the city, including the Pharisees and chief priests who saw Eleazar's move as contrary to custom and unprecedented.[107] The city now fell into factions, with the lower city and Temple in the hands of Eleazar and the insurgents. Meanwhile, Herod Agrippa II had arrived with an auxiliary of 2,000 horse, and supported the faction now forming around the leading men and chief priests who had advocated peace. Full civil strife had now broken out.[108] The insurgents quickly gained the upper hand, and broke out into full vandalism and arson during which Ananias was murdered and his house burnt to the ground.[109] As these events were unfolding in Jerusalem, the Syrian Greek population of Caesarea undertook a brutal massacre of the Jews there, and news of the slaughter spread throughout the region, catapulting the region's cities into a frenzy of violence in which Jews and Syrians massacred each other in breathtaking numbers, according to Josephus.[110] It was at about this time, motivated by a petition of Agrippa II and by unrest spreading among the Jewish population in Syria, Egypt, and throughout the region, that the Romans, under the leadership of Cestius Gallus, governor of Syria, decided to take action, marching first against Caesarea and Joppa, among other hot spots, before heading to Jerusalem.[111]

As the Romans encamped near the city, the new high priest, Ananus, son of Jonathan (possibly high priest in the 50s), tried to open negotiations with Cestius and as a result was attacked by an angry mob, while Cestius led an unsuccessful assault on the city and was forced into retreat.[112] A free Judaean government was now set up, with the region divided between a number of prominent men, many of them from families that had held priesthoods, including the high priesthood in Jerusalem: at the time Ananus, the high priest, took full charge of matters in Jerusalem, along with a certain Joseph son of Gorion. Regional priests and commanders, such as Jeshua son of Sapphas, a chief priest in Idumaea, were put in charge of particular districts.[113] Josephus, however, is quite clear that Ananus did not favour war entirely, and was attempting to drag his feet when he saw dejection among the people in Jerusalem and when omens were reported that further depressed popular sentiment from embracing rebellion, although those factions eager for war, including the Zealots, were not to be dissuaded.[114] The war continued apace, and soon Vespasian (who was welcomed by Agrippa II) and his son Titus arrived on the scene to crush the rebellion. While Vespasian and Titus reduced Galilee, there was trouble in Jerusalem. Factionalism had broken out among the rebels there, exacerbated by the lawless brigands who had infiltrated the city.

The lawless elements now attempted to usurp the authority of the high priest, appointing individuals of obscure origin to high religious office, and went so far as to make the Temple their stronghold.[115] Josephus claims that they attempted to consolidate their authority by appointing priesthoods by lot rather than succession, which had been the traditional means. The Temple's priests were shocked at this sacrilege and now Ananus and Jeshua, son of Gamaliel, whom Josephus calls the most respected of the high priests, attempted to incite the people against the Zealots and their followers.[116] Fighting erupted and the Zealots and their supporters were forced to take refuge in the inner court of the Temple after being forced out of the first outer court, however, Ananus could not bring himself to commit the sacrilege of forcing the gate of the inner court.[117] It was a lost opportunity: the leader of the Zealots, John, enlisted Eleazar son of Simon and Zachariah son of Amphicaleus, both from priestly families, and also called in the Idumaeans from the south to help reinforce them.[118] In a horrific assault, the faction led by Ananus found himself attacked now by the Zealots and Idumaeans; in the bloodbath that followed (Josephus says there were 8,500 corpses in the Temple courtyard), Ananus and Jeshua were butchered and their bodies, contrary to Jewish religious custom, were cast out without burial.[119] Subsequently, the city broke into factions and the rebellion was only crushed after a brutal and lengthy siege in AD 70, culminating in the destruction of the Temple.

We need not bother with the military details during the course of the rebellion. More importantly for our purposes, we need to step back and ask, can we call this a war that was religiously inspired or under religious leadership? It is clear that religious tensions contributed to the outbreak of war, as we see in the situation at Caesarea, and, in a sense, in the very real religious tensions that appear to have perennially been at issue in the Jewish community, not just in Judaea but in the larger region as a whole, dating back to Greek domination under the Seleucid dynasty of Syria. Such tensions were most violently expressed in the rebellion against the Seleucids under the leadership of the Maccabees between 167 and 160 BC, which erupted in part over Jewish resentment of the chauvinistic

Hellenistic paganism asserted under Seleucid rule. In the conflict of 66–70 there is an undercurrent of complicity with Roman policy on the part of some of the elite Jewish elements in the province. The religious authorities in Jerusalem clearly were less than enthusiastic about rebellion – fearing the wrath not only of the Romans, but of their Jewish God as well – and had by tradition cooperated with Roman authorities. In the war's aftermath, many, including Josephus, believed that the rebellion itself was God's instrument for the destruction of Jerusalem and the Temple. In other words, the war was part of a cosmic and eschatological conflict. From this perspective Josephus' analysis is not entirely different from other ancient historians such as Herodotus, who explained the causes of the Greco-Persian wars nearly 600 years before both in human and divine terms.

It is clear, though, that if the war were to have larger support, the leaders needed to combine their political, military, and spiritual roles, otherwise it would make little sense for the Zealots to be so eager to usurp the divine authority of the priests and themselves lay claim to that title. Resistance demanded divine authority stand behind it and particularly telling in this regard is the Temple as a focal point of the conflict. Indeed, in the final analysis the Romans themselves may have viewed this as a religious war, given the complete annihilation of Jerusalem and of the Temple as a central cult site.[120] From this perspective it shares in common with the rebellion in Britain the very deliberate destruction of an enemy's central sacred site, although the destruction of the Temple is far more shocking and profound if we set it in its larger context: the Romans and the Jewish elites who were the Temple's priests had fostered – or tried to foster – good governance and accommodation and the Romans themselves certainly recognized the Temple's central importance and sacred nature over a period of nearly a century and a half, starting with Pompey's eastern settlement in the late 60s BC. This was, after all, not some northern barbaric grove strewn with human body parts. Given that, it makes the Roman destruction of the Temple all the more shocking, and very unlikely not to have been deliberate although that is a matter of some controversy. However, the Temple was never rebuilt, and the new emperor of AD 70, Vespasian, established what became known as the *fiscus Judaicus*, or Jewish Treasury, in which Jews were now ordered to pay their annual tithe instead to what became an imperial treasury for the emperor's appropriation.[121] The appearance in the course of the war of a group known as the *sicarii*, translated by Rudich as 'terrorists', whose religious fanaticism was without parallel, further attests to the deep religious underpinnings of this conflict.[122] Yet one must note that while religion, as Rudich compellingly argues, was likely the central contributor to this conflict, other factors were also in play whose origins, as Steve Mason's study has brilliantly teased out, were numerous, complex, and profoundly interwoven with regional history, ethnicity, and particularism.

Before we take our leave of Josephus and this conflict, one point bears repeating: one of the more remarkable aspects of Josephus' text is that, as noted, we obtain the perspective of an outsider. Josephus was a Jew who was involved with the opposition, only to betray his people and end up a client of his former foe, Vespasian. He was, in short, a member of the elite, and his acquiescence to and cooperation with the Roman authorities is not too surprising given the history of elite Jewish cooperation with the Romans. If we consider the list of names of provincials elsewhere we find local royalty, priestly castes, and members of the elite are sometimes the ones who resist Roman power (though by no means always, as in the case of slave rebellions), and it is vital to recall that that resistance is always violent in nature, as it was in Judaea.

The New Testament as Resistance Literature

The historic background discussed above is important to recall by way of comparison when considering the New Testament, whose gospels emerged at a time of sometimes quite violent unrest in Judaea: the Jewish War of 66–70 AD is ever present as a ghost that stalks the gospels. Jesus, the gospels' protagonist, straddles a role between lowly carpenter's son who kept equally low company and an individual of princely status, a descendant of David and a figure of portended greatness, the King of the Jews. Hence, we have the story of the divine appearance of the Star of Bethlehem upon his birth and the visitation of the three *magi*. The star serves as an omen, as was the case with the comet that appeared shortly after Julius Caesar's death, which some Romans took as an indication of Caesar's divinity and godhead; the portentous interpretation of heavenly phenomenon continued into the Christian era, when Halley's Comet appeared in the momentous year of 1066. So, too, at Jesus' execution, astrological portents appeared in the form of an eclipse, and moved a Roman soldier to interpret Jesus' status as divine. This is perhaps not surprising, given that the common soldiery in antiquity had a general fear of unusual astronomical phenomenon, as did even military commanders. In addition, as was the case in other stories throughout history or mythology of a royal who threatens the established order of things, such as we hear in the tales of Oedipus, Romulus and Remus, or Cyrus the Great, King Herod took measures to exterminate his divinely sanctioned rival, forcing Jesus' family into refugee status as they escaped to Egypt. Jesus' birth, hence his very presence, threatened the established order.

But the far more outstanding and overwhelming aspect of the gospel as a resistance text is the ministry of Jesus itself, and – as the philosopher Hannah Arendt noted many years ago – his central and radical message of forgiveness. Jesus was a part of an imperial system whose founder, Augustus, actively celebrated violence and revenge, or what we might call in current parlance toxic masculinity on steroids. Indeed, his largest building project by far in Rome was his forum where the Temple of Mars Ultor, Mars the Avenger, celebrating the violent deaths of Julius Caesar's assassins, had pride of place. A system of such ethics, with its literal enshrining of violence, would have no room for the forgiveness of Paul by Jesus' disciples for his past persecution of the emergent Christian community in Jerusalem. The gospels are arguably a singular challenge to a culture and a system where violence along with strict class hierarchy and almost no regard for any sort of social safety net were front and centre. Centuries later, Julian the Apostate (emperor from AD 361–363) admitted that the pagan ethos, with its disregard for the social squalor and inequities that pervaded the empire, could not compete with Christian concern for the poor, the widow, the outcast. Pagan temples, unlike Christian churches, were hardly charitable institutions.

More remarkable still are the characters that make up the gospels. The apostles and the other men and women who appear in the gospel accounts are not the stuff of epic poetry, not of grand and sweeping history, not even of a picaresque Greek or Roman novel, with its handsome youths and perilous adventures. Instead, it is peopled with those whom members of the so-called respectable classes would avoid, or at whom they would look askance: men who eke out a dangerous living by fishing; prostitutes; serving women; tax collectors; the plain-spoken and gruff centurion; the disconsolate, the sick, the mentally ill, the weak, the leper. No ancient historian, or biographer for that matter, would concern himself with the anguished decision of the tax collector Matthew to follow Jesus, or with men who fished and mended nets, or with women disgruntled that some must serve dinner while others listened to the teachings of a charismatic. These are variously comforted, cured, or treated with profound, even radical compassion, empathy, and solicitude.

The low who populate ancient classical literature in Plautus' comedies for example, or Petronius' risqué picaresque novel *The Satyricon*, or Apuleius' equally bawdy *The Golden Ass* (or *Metamorphoses*) and who are on the margins include clever slaves who by virtue of their superior intellect are deemed comic, thieves and murderers who ultimately receive their come-uppance, small-town intellectuals ridiculed as half-learned, witches, eunuch priests, and pimps in comedy whose destiny is the gibbet; only a few prostitutes who populate Roman comedy are occasionally treated with some sympathy. Nowhere else in the surviving ancient literary record do we see a parade of such characters in such numbers, and certainly not with a call to feel compassion for them – and most certainly not from an individual such as Jesus whose life story is punctuated with divine portents. That is the exclusive province of princes, kings, and emperors. That in and of itself constitutes a radical departure from any other literature that we have in the Roman Empire. This is no doubt the case in part because Jesus and the authors of the gospels emerged from a deep tradition within Judaism that expressed profound concerns over human ethics, justice, and equality. We might further add that Judaism also had a long tradition of resistance to outside powers, such as the Greek kings of Syria who tried to impose Hellenistic culture on Jewish communities, albeit, as was the case with the famous Maccabee rebellion, such resistance was not always pacific.

Furthermore, we should not be shy about reading the gospels as a form of resistance literature – indeed the Romans themselves were inclined to critique power throughout their own literature, itself an arguably 'soft' form of resistance. Classicists have long since recognized that the subtleties of Vergil's depiction of Aeneas, of Horace's poems that occasionally address current events, and Tacitus' hostile depiction of emperors, among others, constitute potential critiques of Roman power with varying degrees of candour. In addition, the pages of Tacitus are packed with instances of executions, book burnings, and censorship for those whose perceived criticism went too far. Yet their resistance – and given the fraught relationship of literature and power in ancient Rome it is not entirely unfair to call it such – was scarcely more than a critique of the current regime with little desire to tinker with most of its basic mechanisms, let alone to undermine it completely. By contrast, the four gospels for obvious historic reasons are far more radical. That they portray Jesus' ethical teachings in a generally consistent manner and as a man of peace and radical empathy is in many respects shocking by any standard, including contemporary ones, but particularly in the context of the date of their historical composition, after the Jewish War of AD 66–70; and the one caveat to this radicalism's singularity has nothing to do with Roman but Jewish culture, which as noted above, had a deep and abiding concern with human ethics – Jesus surely stands in the context of that ethos. The gospels emerge from this ethical tradition, and thus preach forgiveness and love of one's enemies, something driven in part as well by the early Christian community's concern for spiritual purity as the coming of God's kingdom loomed.

Yet for all that, some of the violent animus against Rome lurks in the gospels like hot embers embedded in ash – how could it not, after the Jews and the writers of the gospels endured the shocking horrors of the siege of Jerusalem and its destruction in that *annus horribilis* of AD 70? What, after all, are we to make of the somewhat muddled story about the swine of the Gadarene? Jesus, coming to Gadarene, confronted a man possessed by demons who lurked among the tombstones. When Jesus asked his name he replied, 'I am legion.' The demon 'legion' was driven out of him and into a herd of pigs that promptly ran over a cliff and drowned in the sea below. The collective trauma of the war, and the destruction of Jerusalem and its Temple, made the writers of the gospels hedge and compromise at times with Jesus' more pacific principles. Hence, Jesus' claim not to bring peace but a sword, and that he will set son against father. In *Luke* (22:38) at the end of the Last Supper as they leave to head to Gethsemane the disciples say to Jesus, 'Lord, behold, here are two swords. And he said unto them, "It is enough."' And that is the extent of the gospel's relatively superficial violence on Jesus' end of things: Jesus' confession that he is an instigator – almost certainly attributed to him in light of the Jewish Rebellion as was his statement about the Temple's destruction, some money-changers' tables overturned, two swords for twelve men, a servant's ear cut off and immediately cured with the disciples admonished to put away their swords into the bargain, and a metaphoric fantasy about the destruction of a Roman legion – Quintilius Varus in pig-skin.

Far more subversive of the Roman system, ultimately, was the message of forgiveness, of love, of seeing the image of God in the least in human society, of rejection of material over spiritual comfort, of the embrace of divine over temporal power. A man like Pilate, or his emperor, or the ruling elite of which they were a part saw little of value outside of worldly status expressed by the size of a great man's retinue, the colour and width of the stripe on his toga, the gold or iron rings indicative of senatorial or equestrian status, the elegance of a great house with its fountains, gardens, porticoes, and images of ancestors who had served the *imperium Romanum*. The world of Rome was fundamentally at odds with the traditions of Judaism as understood and interpreted by the heretical rabbi who lived under Rome's power.

Chapter 7

The Collaborators: Informants, Tax Collectors, and Centurions

1st Soldier – I was surprised how he acted.

3rd Soldier – The part I don't like is the nailing them on. You know, that must get you pretty bad.

2nd Soldier – It isn't that that's so bad, as when they first lift 'em up. [He makes a lifting gesture with his two palms together.] When the weight starts to pull on 'em. That's when it gets 'em.

Today is Friday, by Ernest Hemingway

The short play *Today is Friday*, first published in 1926 then reappearing in 1927 in a collection of short stories titled *Men Without Women*, is not the first work that comes to mind when we think of its iconic author, Ernest Hemingway. It is, nonetheless, an interesting and puzzling work of historical fiction. The brief play, which would probably take the whole of three to five minutes in performance, has a deceptively simple plot: three Roman soldiers stationed in Jerusalem are sitting in a drinking establishment late one night. They ask the establishment's proprietor, George, for a round of red wine, while the characters named 'first soldier' and 'second soldier' attempt to accommodate their compatriot, the 'third soldier', who has a sour stomach. They then begin to discuss the day's events, a crucifixion: they banter about how their victim, obviously Christ, endured his execution reasonably well, about his followers and how they refused to stay to the end, and about the women, presumably his mother Mary and Mary Magdalene, who did stay until he died. At one point the first soldier boasts about spearing him in the side to end his misery, but then George interrupts them that it is getting time for closing, and the three men end the play with a brief dialogue in the street before returning to their barracks.

It is, of course, a work that is inevitably anachronistic and problematic, as when at one point one of the soldiers uses the expression 'Jesus Christ!' after he takes a swig of some disagreeable wine.[1] Yet for all of its difficulties and its purely fictional nature, as with many works of fiction it contains some compelling truths: the soldiers are bluff professional types who give the impression of having had experience, and plenty of it, with death and torture, and we might even say that they have some modicum of admiration if not sympathy, for their victims, despite their prejudice against provincials; their expressions are laconic, and their grammar sometimes leaves something to be desired; they express simple concerns – over bad water, illness, pay, the wine being too weak; one soldier, drawing on the later tradition that Mary Magdalene was a prostitute, implies that he used to make use of her services as such. The great historical theorist John Lukasc once noted that historical fiction can at times better capture the sense of a historic period than actual history itself, and Hemingway here is perhaps an excellent example of this phenomenon. The Roman soldiery, who often built the infrastructure – the roads, sewers, and bridges – and even at times baked the bricks with which Roman buildings were constructed, was but one pillar of the power structure on which Rome was built. We could, of course, cite more, since Rome had its share of functionaries who participated in the workings of empire – its policing, its tax collection, its bureaucratic and judicial administration, to name but a few of the functions necessary in the day to day workings of government. Some of these functionaries, such as the freed slaves known as freedmen (*liberti* in Latin), oversaw the bureaucracy of the imperial palace; some, such as public slaves, cleaned sewers or baths, or worked the furnaces to heat them up; some, such as Roman soldiers, tied and nailed flesh to wooden crosses to mete out Roman justice to non-citizens.

This chapter will explore three categories of imperial functionaries that we encounter in the New Testament during the time of Jesus' ministry: first, we will look at the place of the informant, a role filled by Judas Iscariot, perhaps the most notorious figure in the four canonical gospels, and place him in his Roman context. Informants and activities closely associated with such persons, including witnesses and prosecutors, played a significant role in the workings of the Roman state and the maintenance of law enforcement and order within the empire. We will then consider one of Jesus' disciples, Matthew, who is famously tied to a group known in Latin as *publicani*, (*telonēs* in the Greek of the New Testament), i.e., tax farmers who collected revenue for Rome's imperial purse as well as for the workings of the provinces and even local towns. *Publicani* were a significant and powerful group in the Roman republic, and continued to have a vital role under the empire in filling Roman and provincial coffers, providing the fiscal sinews for the creation of infrastructure and the support of the military, and it was to this group that Matthew belonged. Finally, we will turn to the simple centurion. These were men of hardened and tested experience who had often risen through the ranks to a position of high responsibility, best represented in the New Testament by the gruff centurion who entreats Jesus to heal his sick servant and who receives the simplest but highest of praise for his faith from Jesus himself.

The Delator: Judas Isacariot and Roman Informants.

> And when they had bound him, they led him away, and delivered him to Pontius Pilate the governor. Then Judas, which had betrayed him, when he saw that he was condemned, repented himself, and brought again the thirty pieces of silver to the chief priests and elders. Saying, I have sinned in that I have betrayed the innocent blood. And they said, What is that to us? see thou to that. And he cast down the pieces of silver in the temple, and departed, and went and hanged himself.
>
> *Matthew* 27.2–5

Of all the characters in the gospels, Judas Iscariot is one of the least in need of introduction. The betrayer of Christ infamously accepted 30 pieces of silver, recognized his sin for what it was, and committed himself to the noose. In Dante's *Inferno* he is in the ninth circle of the fourth ring of Hell, slowly masticated for eternity in one of Lucifer's three jaws, the other two occupied by Brutus and Cassius, Julius Caesar's principal assassins. Yet Judas – who was used as an informant by the local Jewish authorities to denounce what was perceived as a dangerous cabal – was only part of a much larger phenomenon: the imperial administration at numerous levels throughout the vast empire it governed relied on an array of informants and prosecutors to help in law enforcement, the maintenance of order, and the administration of justice, such as it was. In the imperial capital and in the Senate, these men were known as *delatores*, a rhetorical term used to define anyone who informs or prosecutes usually, though not always, a fellow senator, and a word with decidedly negative connotations, similar to our word 'shyster' in reference to an ethically challenged or money-grubbing lawyer.[2] For the great Roman historian Tacitus they constitute a central element to the tyranny of the early emperors. Indeed, at the opening of his first major historical work, *The Histories*, Tacitus counts the activity of *delatores* as among the worst catastrophes of the age, competing with the civil wars of AD 69, the eruption of Mount Vesuvius, and the attendant destruction of parts of Campania as among the foremost evils. However, it is important to note that the term *delator* encompassed a number of diverse individuals: it included *accusatores* – accusers – who acted as prosecutors in the Senate; it signified the backroom courtier or freedman who denounced an individual privately to the emperor; it referred to the witness (*testis*) willing to embellish testimony, or the informant (*index*) who named names to the authorities, occasionally with particular relish.

In the case of Judas we are decidedly dealing with the genus *index*, a term that almost always refers strictly to an informant – although the term *delator* was also at times applied to an *index*. Similar unnamed characters also appear in the context of the 'trial' of Jesus bearing false witness against him according to the New Testament. The *index* has direct information, could himself actually be involved in the crime, and denounces but does not prosecute it – unlike the prosecutor who could, but did not necessarily initiate a case by a preliminary denunciation before the appropriate magistrate, and who had no involvement in the legal transgression he prosecuted. The *delator* is often a categorized type, and Tacitus presents a portrait of a paradigmatic sort in the opening of his *Annals*, with his portrait of an ambitious prosecutor named Caepio Crispinus. Early in Tiberius' reign Caepio, Tacitus tells us, created a pattern of life that was to be followed by others:[3]

> [Not much later] Caepio Crispinus accused Granius Marcellus of treason; Granius was the former praetor of Bithynia under whom Caepio had served as quaestor, and Romanus Hispo acted as supporting prosecutor: Caepio entered upon a form of life which the miseries of the times and the daring of men afterwards made

> famous.[4] For without means, unknown, restless, he wormed his way into the emperor's cruelty by means of secret letters, and he soon endangered anyone of high rank. Having obtained power with the emperor, he won hatred among all. He gave an example that made those who followed it rich men from poor, men to be feared instead of despised; they destroyed others and afterwards themselves. But he was accusing Marcellus of having held sinister conversations about Tiberius, an inescapable charge, since the accuser chose the vilest aspects of Tiberius' character to cast against the defendant.

There, in Tacitus' description of Caepio, is the archetypal *delator*. He is one who is a fierce opportunist, a ruthless careerist who will climb to the top and create peril for all who cross his path, who disregards danger to himself, who gains access to the imperial ear. He is lowborn, advances from poverty to wealth, and is a threat to those of high rank. Implicit in Tacitus' description is the sense of proximity and betrayal in Caepio's prosecution – the close relationship between the two men renders the prosecution a betrayal of sorts in which bonds of any kind of solidarity are snapped. In short, *delatores* constitute a negative social category, often constructed based on the social and political prejudices, as well as the status-conscious nature of Roman society; it was a way Romans communicated with one another concerning perceived abuses of the legal system and of political privilege as well.

The activities of the *delator* or *index* are almost always cast in a sinister or malicious light, however, in this regard our sources are problematic, since writers such as Tacitus often saw the interests and privileges of the Senate as ranged against the emperor. That means that even when a prosecutor is undertaking a legitimate and important court case, such as one that sought to hold accountable malicious governors genuinely guilty of wrongdoing, Tacitus will often prove more sympathetic to the accused than to the provincials who may have suffered under the heel of brutal or corrupt administrators. This is despite the fact that Tacitus himself prosecuted at least one similar case in the Senate, and possibly more, during his career.[5] Yet in fairness to Tacitus, *delatores*, who are perhaps best attested in his work the *Annals*, were often trying to press Rome's legal and judicial limits as they tried to criminalize and distort all manner of actions: they tried to criminalize, imply sinister intent to and even render treasonous things said in conversation or writing about the emperor or his family, to criminalize the replacing of heads on imperial statue portraits, and the consultation of astrologers, among other malicious attempts to ensnare their fellow Romans for the sake of power and often rich remuneration. Indeed, our sources are replete with such characters who – as today with certain political operatives – became too important and experienced in the imperial administration not to be tapped by more than one emperor. Hence, characters such as Eprius Marcellus, Vibius Crispus, and Fabricius Veiento, notorious prosecutors under Nero in the 50s, are still found active under Vespasian into the mid-70s or even into the reign of his son, Domitian, in the 90s.[6]

The *delator* and its various cognates and associated phenomenon, rightly or wrongly, therefore constitutes a negative construction; it is a term of abuse for those involved in some capacity in the Roman legal system. Even outside the Senate, *delatores* of lower status are no less prone to depiction as creatures that break the strict social bonds governing Roman society. The attempt to delegitimize the *delator* takes on a much more dramatic form in our sources, since their behaviour is often equated with law-breaking; prosecutions are frequently referred to as crimes (*scelera*), and *delatores* are depicted as destroying, rather than enforcing, the very legal bonds they in theory ought to protect. Finally, it is worth noting that many of the terms Tacitus uses for *delatores* and *accusatores* have contemptuous associations that border on the criminal, such as *condemnator* (a procurer of condemnations), *criminator* (slanderer), or *calumniator* (false accuser). In addition, moral reservations are expressed concerning launching accusations throughout our sources, including the great statesman Cicero, and Quintilian, a noted and famous grammarian and rhetorician of the first century AD. Yet any concerns Quintilian had over accusation were qualified by his own admission that it was a necessary and important activity for the welfare of the state.[7]

Of course, a prosecution at Rome before the courts or the imperial Senate or even the emperor himself was a far different affair from a summary hearing before local officials or a governor in the provinces, and it is that phenomenon that Judas' case represents. So, how did this work on a provincial level? In the provinces themselves, *delatores* were a constant presence from the republic through the empire, and even the likes of Pliny the Younger, a relatively genteel and mild-mannered personality as noted previously, relied on them from time to time (see pp. 69–70). Yet, in addition to Pliny's correspondence, there exists an interesting and eclectic array of sources, including Cicero's speech against Verres, Dio of Prusa's (Chrysostomus') rhetorical works, and the New Testament itself, that offers a relative wealth of material illustrative of how informing and prosecuting worked in the provinces during the late republic and into the imperial period, giving us an occasionally lurid picture of how those such as Judas and other similar operatives functioned.

Well before the advent of the emperors we have a window into how informants might work in the context of Roman provincial administration thanks in part to Cicero's orations against Verres, already discussed in Chapter 4 (pp. 74–8). According to Cicero, Verres, it appears, kept a number of informants (which in Cicero go by the name *quadruplatores*) and accusers (*accusatores*) on his staff in the interest of making a killing by profiting from his governorship, and it is reasonable to imagine that any governor would have his share of agents in order to keep himself informed about significant issues that might arise and need addressing throughout his province. However, such agents in the hands of a corrupt governor could potentially be employed for nefarious means, and such was the case with Verres, who as noted put his agents to work to keep an eye out for those provincials with particularly fine household furnishings or works of art, or to spy out who had recently come into a particularly lucrative inheritance, and bring it to Verres' attention. One of Verres' freedmen, Timarchides, was the apparent overseer of Verres' 'staff' of these creatures and used them to fulfil both his own and Verres' desires.[8] Timarchides was not an isolated case for Verres. Before he was governor of Sicily, Verres had spent time in Asia, where he employed a certain Rubrius, who fulfilled the same office.[9] While Cicero informs us only of the most negative aspects of this activity – and we could cite further cases – such characters will have also served a vital if unpopular function in helping to enforce justice in the province or in the collection of revenues (see p. 180).

Perhaps the finest example of the provincial informant in action under Verres is a certain Naevius Turpio: a Sicilian provincial, Dio of Halasaea, had received a large legacy, and Verres put up Naevius to lay a false charge against Dio for not erecting statues in the local forum upon receipt of the legacy as his public duty apparently demanded, and to argue that, having failed to do so, his inheritance was forfeit to Venus of Eryx (a local cult dedicated to Venus that sat atop a dizzyingly precipitous height in north-western Sicily – today the site still preserves the goddess' name, Castello di Venere, Venus' Castle). The outcome of the case was that Dio, in order that he not forfeit his entire legacy, paid a very large sum to Verres instead, and had his estate looted of its thoroughbred mares, silver, and tapestries.[10] The employment of prosecutors and informants for the laying of false charges was not an isolated incident; they were occasionally suborned to accuse others in order to divert suspicion of various offences from Verres himself, although such procedures were little more than pro-forma kangaroo courts. Hence, Verres suborned one anonymous agent in the case of a 'theft' (really Verres' own appropriation) of a statue of Ceres at Catina; in this instance an accuser was suborned to testify against a slave, and false witnesses were put up to corroborate the story.[11]

Such abuses continued into the imperial period. According to Philo, Avillius Flaccus, prefect of Egypt late in Tiberius' reign, made use of two agents, Isidorus and Lampo in Alexandria for the purposes of informing and prosecuting, and Flaccus was less than diligent in his oversight of the cases they brought before him.[12] Unfortunately, Philo is quite vague over their precise activities, but they appear to have been working on Flaccus' antipathies against Alexandria's Jewish population. Years later, under Vespasian (emperor AD 69–79), Josephus relates the case of Catullus, governor of Libyan Pentapolis in what is today modern Libya.[13] There was a Jewish community there, but it was torn by factional strife. A particularly obnoxious ringleader of one of the factions, Jonathan, who led a group known as the *sicarii* (assassins), was arrested; to save himself, he denounced (probably falsely) the wealthiest members of the Jewish community in Cyrene, whom Catullus proceeded to have murdered (Josephus puts the number of his victims at 3,000), and then confiscated their possessions for the imperial treasury. The accusations spread to encompass Jews in Rome and Alexandria as well, until Vespasian, after a personal interview with Catullus, Jonathan, and his followers, detected their wrongdoing. Jonathan was executed, but Catullus got off with only a reprimand, (although he died soon after).

The New Testament, with its denunciation, arrest, and hearing of Jesus, gives us yet another window into how local informants and prosecutors could prove useful to a governor in his province, though some circumspection is warranted given that the work is not intended to be a historical text. However, given the comparisons that we have available in the cases already mentioned in Cicero and other sources, the New Testament appears to present a reasonably credible pattern in which a local dispute is brought to the attention of the Roman authorities during which some conflict arose over jurisdiction and punishment. The hearing started first on a local level: Judas was notoriously bribed by the authorities to disclose the location of Jesus and his followers to the chief priests and elders of the people in order to effect Jesus' arrest (*Matthew* 26:47; *Mark* 14:43). In *Mark* and *Matthew* Jesus' accusers charge him before the Sanhedrin with blasphemy. According to *Matthew* (26:59–61) the elders held a series of interviews in an effort to find an individual who would act as a false witness (*ezetoun pseudomartyrian*) and state false evidence that he had heard Jesus boast that he would destroy the Temple and rebuild it in three days; Jesus' response to the charge was ambiguous, and this infuriated the high priest, who accused him of blasphemy. *Mark*'s version (14:56–64) agrees in essence with *Matthew*'s although he adds the detail that the false witnesses were not able to produce a coherent version of Jesus' crimes. After the preliminary hearing before the Sanhedrin, Jesus was taken to Pilate whose encounter with Christ we discussed in Chapter 4.

Reading between the lines, we actually see in Jesus' ordeal an example of how informants and false accusers (*Mark* 15:3 and *Luke* 23:1 use the Greek verb *katagorein*, meaning 'to accuse') could act in what they believed was imperial interest, and at the same time serve the interest of their own community. Yet the gospel accounts also indicate that the accusers were skilful manipulators, putting a sinister spin on his actions: The telling phrase – 'If you let this man go you are not Caesar's friend' – recalls the frequent manipulation of the treason law for political ends in Roman public life, and uses a notable political turn – *Caesaris amicus* – to enforce its point.[14] In Jesus' encounter with Pilate, the writers of the gospels depict the Jewish leadership as skilfully manipulating Pilate's very worldly concerns for his own position. Furthermore, as noted, the Jewish leadership in Jerusalem reportedly conducted their own inquiry and set their preliminary charges before Pilate. As we saw in Chapter 4, any formal trial has been called into question, and Jesus' punishment was probably relatively summary, perhaps in the nature of an informal investigation (what was known as a *cognitio extra ordinem*) followed by the same sort of punishment that Pliny meted out two generations later to the Christians in Bithynia (see pp. 68–9) – though in the rougher neighbourhood of Judaea, where there had been recent unrest within living memory of Judas of Galilee, John the Baptist, and others, less legal formalities may have been in order, and Pilate will probably have had – as did Pliny – a rather free hand. The arrest and hearing plausibly represents an example of how *delatores* on a provincial level helped to meet opposition and resistance to Roman rule, and of their utility in disarming potentially dangerous subversives – or in being allowed to commit serious acts of injustice, another difficulty to which Pliny alludes in his letters.

We should note that a very different process, as is well known, took place in the case of Paul, who as a Roman citizen, which Jesus was not, was entitled to special consideration by Felix, governor of Judaea between 52 and 60. Felix, according to *Acts*, gave Paul special consideration after his arrest, and waited to put Paul on trial until his accusers arrived; they were headed by Ananias, the high priest, the elders of the community, and Tertullus, an orator who formally presented the charge that Paul had profaned the Temple and was to be counted among the remnants of Jesus' followers (*Acts* 24:1; 24:5–6): 'We have found this man a pestilent fellow, and a mover of sedition among the Jews throughout the world, and a ringleader of the sect of the Nazarenes' (*Acts* 24:5). It has been plausibly asserted that, inasmuch as governors were generally unwilling to convict on purely religious grounds, the accuser in this instance was attempting to change a religious into a political case by adding the charge of sedition. The investigation did not go well for the plaintiffs. Felix was willing to listen to Paul's defence and reasoning, according to the author of *Acts*, because his wife, Drusilla, was Jewish, and Felix let the case hang fire for two years until his successor, Festus, took command of the province in AD 60 (*Acts* 24:10–27). By the time the case finally came before Festus, Paul had made his appeal to Caesar; Festus could have acquitted Paul, but instead sent him to Rome. This was not the first time Paul had been the victim of *accusatores*. Several years before, in Corinth, the governor Annius Gallio (who was the brother of Seneca the Younger, a noted philosopher and playwright and tutor of the emperor Nero) refused to entertain the denunciations by the Jewish community there against Paul (*Acts* 18:12–16). *Acts* is unclear on the precise nature of the charges, but they appear to have been strictly religious in nature. As Sherwin-White points out, one of the reasons for Gallio's dismissal of the charges may have been that there were no formalized rights to which the Jews could lay claim by which they could force compliance with Jewish religious custom on fellow Jews.[15] Whatever the nature of the case, Paul as a citizen was more privileged and consequently received better treatment than the friend Judas Iscariot betrayed.

Matthew and the Publicani

> And as Jesus passed forth from thence, he saw a man, named Matthew, sitting at the receipt of custom: and he saith unto him, Follow me. And he arose, and followed him. And it came to pass, as Jesus sat at meat in the house, behold, many publicans and sinners came and sat down with him and his disciples. And when the Pharisees saw it, they said unto his disciples, Why eateth your Master with publicans and sinners?
>
> *Matthew* 9:9–11

You see the soon-to-be-apostle's face in Caravaggio's *Calling of Saint Matthew* in half-shade and half-light, a masterful use of chiaroscuro colours that was to become the hallmark of late Renaissance painters (see fig. 7.1). The mostly invisible face, that of Saint Matthew, stares down at the table as he counts coins, and the viewer is uncertain whether he is still unaware of the presence of a lean Christ whose hand is outstretched and beckoning him: is Matthew engrossed in counting coin, about to look up in a moment of spiritual revelation, and relinquish a life of ease – an ease betrayed by his clean, white hands, his finery of an immaculate shirt of striped and luxuriant silk and velvet, his well-tailored tan vest and hose, and the sumptuous vestments of those who surround him, with their velvet, fur, and plumed hats? Or has he already had that moment, and is he brooding over the coins as he weighs what will be the most momentous decision of his life, leaving his wealth and position in favour of a very different path? Caravaggio is cagey in his depiction of this moment and it is difficult to decipher: the spectators give us no help. Have they just seen Jesus and is Matthew too intent on counting his coins yet to have noticed? Or are they awaiting his decision, some, like the young boy, with

Fig. 7.1: *The Calling of Saint Matthew*, by Caravaggio. From the Contarelli Chapel, Church of San Luigi dei Francesi, Rome. (Public domain via *Wikimedia Commons*)

a bemused ironic expression as he leans his elbow on the elderly gentleman seated next to him? *The Calling of Saint Matthew* is one of the typically powerful moments of New Testament narrative that Caravaggio was so adept at depicting, with an exquisite eye for psychological complexity, an earthy sense of worldliness, and emotional heft, where the viewer can fill in a myriad of stories about each individual's background. Yet we do know something about Matthew, simply by virtue of his profession.

Matthew was a tax farmer (*publicanus*), a name that was so detested that it was paired directly with sinners and prostitutes (*pornai*) in the New Testament, and in one ancient encyclopedia is grouped with pimps, among others of morally dubious professions.[16] The word *publicanus* itself was a term taken from the fact that these men dealt with public property – that which was *publica*, as one well-known Roman historian has pointed out.[17] It is important to note that because of the primitive nature of Roman society and ancient society in general, Rome's administrative capacities were somewhat limited, and the sort of taxation to which one might be subject, at least during the republican period, included contributions to a *stipendium* or levy paid out by a city in either a lump sum, or as *decumae* (tithes on crops), *scriptura* (pasture dues), or as indirect taxes such as sales tax, excise, or customs fees – tax farmers tended to be in charge of the collection of these less direct taxes.[18] The state, embodied by the Senate in the republican period, was the primary principal (i.e., the actor who chooses the agent or company – *collegium* in Latin), just as the emperor often was during the empire.

During the republic, the collection of revenue was normally sold as a public contract to those who had the wherewithal to compete for bids. The purchaser then tried to make back his bid, paid to the state, and to garner a profit in the process. The same men also bid on contracts for public works, and this money would often be recovered by the investor(s) through the levying of taxes. During the early and middle republic, as Rome emerged victorious over Hannibal, most of the *publicani* likely made their money from contracts for goods and services provided to the state, especially army supplies.[19] When Rome started to extract revenues from its provinces (Rome's first province was established in Sicily after the First Punic War, 264–241 BC), she justified her extraction by right of conquest and on the premise that a conquered province had resisted Roman might.[20] Under the empire the justification shifted, and Rome argued her right to taxation by virtue of the benefits of the renowned *Pax Romana* or Roman Peace.[21]

Publicani gained a great deal of power under the reformer C. Gracchus in the early 120s BC. It was then that he opened up the recently acquired province of Asia for the first time to very lucrative four-year contracts for these men; second, the recently established (149 BC) court for trying provincial maladministration (*repetundae*) was opened up to the *publicani*, putting a check on senatorial corruption and giving them enhanced power. This, in turn, gave rise to a class of extremely wealthy financiers and businessmen by the time of Cicero and Caesar in the 70s BC. Indeed, by Cicero's day, large companies of *publicani* had emerged to arrange for special contracts with specific privileges enshrined in law. *Socii*, which translates literally as 'allies', but which we can extend no doubt to include friends, acquaintances, and various other interested parties, would furnish much of the upfront expenditure for the contract and were beholden to a *magister* (a managing director) who would often (but not necessarily always) act as what was known as a *manceps* for the contract, that is, the representative of the company who acted as agent and bid on the contract. Many of these were from the equestrian class, a rank technically below that of senator, although there were plenty of equestrians who far outstripped their senatorial contemporaries in wealth. In the provinces, the *publicani* were under a coordinator called a *pro magistro* whose staff would consist of numerous equestrians, but also of *liberti* and *servi* (freedmen and slaves); they acted as bankers for governors and collectively as institutions for large-scale financial transactions, and anyone in Rome with the wherewithal could purchase shares in their companies, with Asia considered particularly lucrative, at least in the late republic.

Of course, *publicani* were state contractors, and they were not above dishonest practices. Livy reports that during the Second Punic War against Carthage (220–202 BC) some unscrupulous *publicani* had been committing fraud, loading poor vessels with cheap goods, arranging for their wreckage, and then exaggerating the amount of the loss to turn a profit.[22] Individually and collectively they could turn greedy: in the 60s BC *publicani* had over-speculated on public contracts by so much that they were demanding debt relief. Because many of these *publicani* were of the equestrian class, it was creating a serious breach between their order and the Senate, which refused to grant the *publicani* their request.[23] In 60 BC, the ruthless M. Licinius Crassus was motivated to join an alliance with Rome's then greatest living general, Pompey the Great, and an ambitious rising star, Julius Caesar, creating the First Triumvirate – Crassus, in return for his support of the two men and their ambitions (he was reportedly the richest man in Rome and could use his resources to purchase political backing for both), demanded relief for the equestrians in the Senate. Indeed, by Caesar's time the *publicani* constituted a virtual order in Rome in service to the state, and were also involved in a variety of private financial activities.[24] Elite members of that order will have had inheritances and incomes that allowed them to live not just off the interest they charged through lending to others but from assorted investments they made in land, livestock, and other enterprises.

Publicani by Matthew's day – during the early empire of the late 20s and early 30s AD – had therefore already enjoyed a long and storied past, and under the empire were somewhat less formidable than their counterparts during the republic – but are also somewhat less well attested in the literary record.[25] Part of what put the curb on their power was that senators now came to depend on imperial favour and so had less incentive to court *publicani* as a group for political support; in turn, *publicani*, too, came to rely more on the goodwill of those within the imperial court or Roman officials in their province who were well connected in order to secure business deals and contracts.[26] The quaestors and procurators now collected tribute in their province as one of their central functions, and *publicani* were employed on a more local level, becoming a part of the highly bureaucratic system of the collection of revenues of all sorts.[27] One scholar, P.A. Brunt, sums up the situation succinctly: 'The emperors gradually created a kind of civil service consisting of their own freedmen and slaves, who were able, under the direction of generally equestrian procurators, to control the publicans more closely than had been possible under the republic.'[28] A bureaucracy was set in place that consisted of many layers of accounting and extensive staff for assessment and record keeping.[29] A governor would thus potentially have his hands full managing the oversight of this bureaucracy.[30] *Publicani* would enforce payment of assorted taxes and fees, and navigate any judicial disputes concerning collection due to them; they likely would have taken a percentage of the proceeds of the taxes they farmed, and regulating and managing the percentage of their cut introduced yet another level of bureaucracy, since they would need to be scrutinized to ensure they received only their contractual due, while *delatores* (see earlier) were in turn employed at times to expose *publicani* guilty of taking more than their stipulated percentage.[31] If *publicani* crossed too far over the line, they risked imperial intervention, as in AD 58, when the emperor Nero felt compelled to demand transparency by open publication of their agreements with local companies when they grew too extortionate in their exactions.[32] Procurators also could potentially lease contracts for various services to *publicani* and received the payment due in instalments, necessitating employment of a large staff in order to audit their books;

these will have included accountants, cashiers, scribes, copyists, and archivists, among others.[33] Slaves and freedmen were increasingly employed in the occupation, and this accelerated under Claudius (AD 41–54).[34] The Romans also depended on the collaboration of local elites to help manage this activity, and we can imagine that, as loathed as they were, many of them will have been respectable and respected bourgeois businessmen of varying sorts, perhaps our Matthew included.[35]

Under the empire, the system offered the fortunate astute and ambitious opportunities to advance quite far: the emperor Vespasian's father started off his career as a *publicanus*, collecting port duties in Asia and going on to become a moneylender which allowed him to marry up when he was wed to Vespasia Polla, whose brother was no less than a Roman senator.[36] Such ambition and social climbing came with a cost, since some well-placed Romans developed a healthy social prejudice against the various *publicani* who became parvenus as they accrued wealth and influence. Juvenal, the renowned satirist who lived from the mid-first to the early second century AD, had the character Umbricius, an equestrian, lament that low characters such as *publicani* achieved wealth and status as great as his own.[37] Indeed, Davenport notes that *publicani* could rise from men of lesser substance and standing to become self-made men and rise to prominence in their community, even to a level of respectability, as honorary inscriptions show.[38] Yet, in status-conscious Rome, freedmen becoming prominent and successful did not always sit well. Consequently, between the seemingly innate human antipathy against taxation and the status dissonance that *publicani* could cast into relief, for all the curbs on their potential abuses, they remained unpopular from the period of the late republic throughout the early imperial period. Occasionally, however, the hatred against *publicani* was well-deserved, in particular when the less scrupulous ones would employ street toughs and thugs among their staff and violently enter houses to appropriate property by force, as references in Rabbinic texts attest.[39]

It is consequently not hard to see why the *publicani* would have been so persistently and stubbornly hated. From the perspective of provincials, the New Testament provides a window into the sort of abusive denunciations the *publicani* conducted with a passage in *Luke* proving especially instructive of the trouble they could and did make for others: when passing through Jericho, in Judaea, Jesus was reproached for going to dinner at the house of Zacchaeus, an apparently detested and rich *publicanus* (*architelonēs*).[40] The gospel reports that during Jesus' stay, Zacchaeus repented of his past activities as a tax farmer – and as one who had viciously gone after his quarry in the courts as well: 'Behold, Lord, the half of my goods I give to the poor; and if I have taken any thing from any man by false accusation (*esykophantesa*), I restore him fourfold.'[41] Zacchaeus' remarks may be illustrative of how some *publicani* will have made extra money on the side, if not actually a fair percentage of their profits, through corrupt practices. Nor is this an isolated example. Bringing false charges in the interests of gaining the property of opponents was an occasional problem in the provinces, according to Dio Chrysostomus (see e.g., Or. 43.6), and it is not past thinking that this could have motivated some of the *publicani* in his own province to denounce others in the interest of collecting revenue. Again, Dio Chrysostomus could use as a defence when being attacked by the mob for the high price of grain in Prusa that he had never placed anyone in jeopardy of losing their estate by accusing them under the pretence that it belonged to Caesar, or 'as an advocate had played false to anyone'.[42] What Chrysostomus here refers to is the activity of malicious accusers who denounced others (falsely) of encroaching on imperial estates; their property – or a part of it – would likely have been confiscated and turned over to the state, with the accuser getting a cut. One finds it easy to imagine the unscrupulous *publicanus* turning to the courts for the purposes of profit, though as noted above, this will have also occurred in the case of trying to collect taxes from tax evaders. Thus, when the *publicani* came to hear John the Baptist preaching at the Jordan, and asked him as he urges repentance what they ought to do, he replied: 'Exact no more than that which is appointed you', (*Luke* 3.12–13). We may wonder if Matthew was among those present.

The taxes *publicani* collected – through legitimate and legal means, violently, dishonestly, or otherwise – went towards all manner of infrastructure, civic improvements, and the military, and only very minimally to anything we would understand as 'social welfare' – although sewers, baths, roads, and other infrastructure certainly helped towards the public's well-being. There were, as well, subsidies towards grain, public games and festivals, donatives to troops, and the upkeep of the military (by far the largest expense in the Roman budget) – and this list is far from complete. There was also a hefty dose of private patronage, too, for the construction of baths and other infrastructure, as well as religious festivals and spectacles in the circuses and amphitheatres. Cities, unless they were fortunate enough to receive imperial patronage, often had to make do with the largess of local grandees, as we see in communities from as small as Pompeii to cosmopolitan centres such as Athens, where construction projects large and small were proof of the benefaction and power of local elites. To fill Roman coffers, both on an empire-wide and local basis, the *publicani*'s exactions would have included those for income tax, poll tax, city tax, water tax, taxes on meat and salt, taxes on roads, houses, and on markets, and would have further included tolls on roads and bridges – and this is by no means an exhaustive list.[43] They also collected indirect taxes that included custom tolls known as *portoria* gathered on ports and at regional borders, a 5 per cent tax on manumitted slaves who became freedmen (called a *vicesima libertatis*), and a 5 per cent tax on inheritances (called a *vicesima hereditatis*).[44] All of this required a large staff of experienced and educated people adept at keeping good records.[45] It should be noted that, given the diversity of the provinces, the amount of revenue and their sources could vary – not every province had the mineral wealth of Spain or the grain-producing capacity of Africa or Egypt, and local conditions will have influenced both revenue sources and management, and Judaea was no exception.[46]

Now Judaea was exempt from much of this as long as Herod the Great was in power, during which time he made Judaea a relatively stable and secure place that enjoyed a fair level of wealth and prosperity. During Herod's tenure, the taxes and tribute he extracted from his subjects went to beautify the country he ruled, building cities such as the great port Caesarea, beautifying Jerusalem and restoring the Temple, and invigorating the spice trade with Arabia.[47] All of this was done, as noted elsewhere (see pp. 108–109), with a view to delicately balancing Roman and Jewish sentiment. After Herod's death and Archelaus' deposition, the first Roman census of the province will have taken place in AD 6 under Quirinius, the governor of Syria, and Coponius, his prefect who was in charge of Judaea, since the province then came under direct Roman rule for the first time – an event famously confused in the gospel of *Luke*, presented as occurring contemporaneously with the birth of Jesus in the same year as Herod's death in 4 BC. As noted in Chapter 4, the census was understood as a preliminary step towards taxation by the Romans, and not only was it unwelcome, but gave rise to an incipient though ultimately (for the moment) aborted rebellion. While from AD 6 some of the money went for infrastructure in Judaea and the region, most of it likely went to the imperial treasury, although as P. A. Brunt points out, we cannot be entirely certain of this. Some may have gone for local taxes to support cities which themselves may have been in charge of collecting tribute. He notes, for example, that *publicani* in Galilee were likely farming taxes for the tetrarch or local authorities rather than for Rome, further noting that Rabbinic texts could ambiguously be referring to liturgical officials or tax farmers, and concluding that 'it is not always clear whether they were acting for Rome or for a city.'[48] The case is more clear cut for Judaea itself, since it had been rolled into the jurisdiction of the province of Syria by AD 6. Yet already by AD 17 Syria and Judaea (by then governed by the prefect Valerius Gratus) both felt compelled to send delegations to Rome to ask for relief from tax burdens.[49] We are by no means certain of the response since there is no further mention of this delegation, but it may not have been as severe as we might anticipate. Tiberius did move at some point in his reign to put the brakes on rapacious governors and exaction of revenue, since when they at one point requested that they be allowed to exact amounts he deemed burdensome his simple reply was, 'A shepherd must shear his flock not flay it.'[50] Later on, the method of taxation in Judaea may have changed: as was the case with Asia under Caesar in 47 BC, the cities of Judaea appear to have been given charge of collecting tribute, since as of AD 66 we know that the priestly class in Jerusalem was mandated with the management of its collection.[51] Yet it clearly made little difference to the people of Judaea, who in AD 66 rebelled against Rome and set in motion a rolling catastrophe for the Jewish people under Roman rule that would in many respects never again abate.

The Centurion

> And when Jesus was entered into Capernaum, there came unto him a centurion, beseeching him, and saying, Lord, my servant lieth at home sick of the palsy, grievously tormented. And Jesus saith unto him, I will come and heal him. The centurion answered and said, Lord, I am not worthy that thou shouldest come under my roof: but speak the word only, and my servant shall be healed. For I am a man

under authority, having soldiers under me: and I say to this man, Go, and he goeth; and to another, Come, and he cometh; and to my servant, Do this, and he doeth it. When Jesus heard it, he marvelled, and said to them that followed, Verily I say unto you, I have not found so great faith, no, not in Israel.

Matthew 8:5–10

By AD 14, the patience of the legions of the Rhine and in Pannonia had reached a breaking point. Augustus' ashes were barely deposited in his mausoleum and Tiberius seemingly at the head of the government when the legions, disgruntled over pay, their lengthy terms of service, and (in their view) scant remuneration as veterans, exploded into mutiny. The Pannonian legions proceeded to vent their rage and frustration on the commanders of their individual units, the centurions, whom they accused of venality and cruelty, since a number of them had extorted bribes from soldiers in exchange for leave or for more lenient terms of service.[52] One of them, the camp commander Aufidienus Rufus, was particularly targeted because of his insistence on harsh, old-school discipline. After looting the camp and beating up some other centurions, the soldiers turned to looting nearby towns and marched Rufus at their head, loading him with heavy packs, asking him mockingly if he enjoyed his heavy burden and the long march.[53] The soldiery then murdered another centurion, Lucilius, who had earned the grim moniker *Cedo alterum*, or 'Give me another', since he was infamous for breaking his signature staff of office, a vine rod, over the backs of soldiers marked for punishment.[54] In the course of the mutiny, the soldiers nearly came to blows with one another over the fate of yet another centurion named Sirpicus, demanded by the eighth legion for execution, while protected from punishment by the fifteenth. Meanwhile, another centurion, Julius Clemens, was elected to act as a negotiator with imperial agents (which included Tiberius' son, Drusus) concerning the mutinous soldiers' demands.[55] The mutiny in Pannonia was finally quelled, and centurions were ordered to effect punishments for the ringleaders, a task they doubtless conducted with relish.[56] On the Rhine, one legion vented its fury against its centurions by having them all thrown to the ground and giving each one sixty lashes, one for each of the legion's centurions.[57] In order to finally quell the mutiny, one of the terms to which the imperial authorities agreed was a review of the conduct of centurions throughout the legions, during which each centurion was to give his commander-in-chief, his name, company, country, number of campaigns, distinctions in battle, and his military decorations, if any.[58]

Fast forward some fifteen years after the mutiny, sometime between AD 29 and 31, and it is not impossible that the centurion Jesus encountered was a participant or himself witness to this brief, violent episode. In turn, we might also wonder – given the mutinous soldiers' complaints about corrupt venality and brutality – whether he was among the soldiers who asked of John the Baptist as he preached and baptized in the Jordan, 'And what shall we do? And he said unto them, Do violence to no man, neither accuse any falsely; and be content with your wages' (*Luke* 3:14).

The Roman legion to which such soldiers and centurions belonged at the time of Augustus, as well as the time of John and Jesus, normally consisted of 5,000 infantry and 120 cavalry. All men were citizens and served for sixteen years with four in reserve until Augustus changed the terms of service to twenty years with five in reserve in AD 5; given life expectancy, the army was a lifetime career, or sentence depending on one's perspective. A legion itself was divided into ten cohorts that in turn were divided into six 'centuries' of eighty men; it was over these individual century units of eighty that centurions commanded. At the time of Augustus, there were roughly 1,800 men belonging to the 'club' of centurion rank scattered throughout the legions of Rome's empire.

A centurion's career trajectory was very much dependent on his status and the class from which he came, although the precise means by which a man achieved this rank is not entirely certain. During the republic the consul chose the centurions, while centurions in turn chose their own second in command and standard bearers, though it also appears that the *hastati*, *principes*, and *triarii*, the three most significant ranks of Roman soldiery, also elected centurions. In the empire, this changed and legionary centurions could be nominated by the province's governor, but were ultimately approved by the emperor himself, though occasionally they could receive direct appointment, as was the case for Arrius Varus, who won the rank of chief centurion of the legion, known as the *primipilus*, for denouncing his own commander, Domitius Corbulo, to Nero, when he accused Corbulo of conspiracy.[59] It also appears during the empire that men of equestrian status generally entered the army by holding the office of centurion through direct commission, as was the case with a certain

Tiberius Claudius Vitalis, who did so in the second century AD.[60] In addition, former members of the praetorian guard also had the privilege of entering the army with this title, as was the case with M. Vettius Valens, one of the dramatic personae of the tumultuous events of AD 69, a year in which Rome elevated and toppled no less than four emperors.[61]

Some centurions, however, will have attained their office through promotion by rising directly from the ranks of the legionary soldiers, and could even occasionally achieve the status of camp prefect, though our current state of the evidence indicates that this was the least common means of promotion and required advancement via junior officer and clerical posts. The career of Petronius Fortunatus gives us an example of one such centurion who had climbed the legionary ladder from soldier to centurion: he had served as *librarius* (a junior officer post who kept the unit's administrative and financial records and dealt with the unit's clerical work), *tesserarius* (a clerk who was keeper of the watchword), *optio* (an orderly who was second in command to a centurion), and *signifer* (the standard bearer for the century), and then finally obtained his post by a vote of the legion (*ex suffragio leg*[*ionum*]).[62] Afterwards Petronius served in over a dozen legions from Britain, to the Danube, to Lower Germany, to the eastern provinces, and received the *corona muralis* (a crown awarded to the first man over the wall of an enemy city), and, in addition, won various visible honours, such as the award of torques and *phalerae* (necklaces and medals worn on the soldier's breast). Fortunatus died at the age of 80, presumably in North Africa where his tombstone was discovered, and outlived a son who died at age 35 who was also himself a centurion (possibly commissioned due to Fortunatus' own status). Julius Caesar in his *Gallic War Commentaries* further affirms that centurions from the lower orders of other legions could fill vacant centurion posts by virtue of their valour.[63] Perhaps one of the more remarkable examples of an award for bravery is a centurion named Scaeva, who, during the civil war between Caesar and Pompey, fought at Dyrrachium on the Adriatic coast. After the various engagements around the camp and city, Scaeva brought Caesar his shield, which had 120 holes in it.[64] According to Suetonius, Scaeva lost an eye and was injured in both the shoulder and thigh.[65] For his service to the state and himself, Caesar awarded him a whopping 100,000 sesterces and promoted him from centurion of the eighth cohort to chief centurion of the legion.

Men in the auxiliary units certainly reached the rank of centurion, as one notable inscription shows: a soldier had started as a legionary grunt in *legio III Augusta*, gone on to be promoted as a soldier at double pay (*duplicarius*) in the Pannonian division (*ala Pannoniorum*), thence to status of *decurio* (a cavalry commander), and then back to the *legio III Augusta* as centurion.[66] Auxiliary centurions will have come from the wealthier clans of local elites of conquered provincials, such as the native Gauls mentioned in Tacitus' *Histories*.[67] Goldsworthy plausibly argues that most auxiliary enlisted men would have been illiterate, hence not suitable for promotion, noting that the Vindolanda letters, a corpus of remarkable correspondence that have come down to us written by the men who manned this distant Roman military outpost in Britain, were not composed by any below the rank of a *principalis*; local elites will have been the only auxiliaries to have had a modicum of literacy, hence the qualifications for a centurion's numerous duties.[68] Centurions could then be enrolled in the senate or council of their native cities upon retirement.[69]

After army reforms were put in place under Augustus, regardless of their status, centurions were answerable to a tribune (the *tribunus angusticlavii*), of which there were five to a legion of equestrian rank, and these answered in turn to the camp prefect (*praefectus castrorum*), usually, as noted, a former centurion, and he, in turn, answered to the second in command, the *tribunus laticlavus*, who was usually a young senator with no prior military experience in his twenties, while the commander of the legion was the *legatus legionis*, usually a senatorial officer in his early thirties.[70] As a soldier, the centurion was supplied, like every soldier, with the standard equipment of helmet, body armour, skirt, tunic, knee breeches, underclothes, belt, sword, dagger, shield and shield cover, javelins, shoes, probably socks, and a cloak, but in addition would be supplied with greaves.[71] Centurions were given the privilege of wearing whiter, brighter clothing than most, which had been specially treated, and centurions in the late republic and early empire were distinguished by wearing a transverse crest on a Gallic-style metal helmet with cheek and neck guards (see fig. 7.2). In addition to their distinct helmet and medals, centurions carried a vine rod as a staff of office, such as the very distinct one that Marcus Caelius holds, displayed on his tombstone and symbolizing his office and authority (fig. 7.3). The centurions, like the military tribunes, will have had a status that clearly demarcated them

Fig. 7.2: The tomb of Titus Calidius Severus; note the greaves and the Gallic style helmet, indicative of his status as a centurion. A translation of the inscription reads: 'Titus Calidius Severus, son of Publius of the Camilian tribe, first an equestrian, then an *optio* and decurion of the First Cohort of the Alpini, then a centurion of the Fifteenth Legion Apollonaris age 58 with thirty-four years of service is buried here. Quintus Calidius his brother put this tomb up.' (User: MatthiasKabel via *Wikimedia Commons*)

as prominent by their insignia, even to their own demise, as was the case in the aftermath of the Teutoberg disaster in AD 9, when tribunes and centurions were sacrificed at the altars of the German gods in the wake of the defeat of three legions.[72]

In addition to their notable insignia, centurions in the republic received a double rate of pay over the other soldiers, something that may have continued into the empire.[73] Other forms of remuneration will have come in the form of loot from captured cities and vanquished enemies. Although we cannot be certain, Tacitus indicates that if a city were plundered, the lion's share of the spoils went to the common soldiery, while negotiated surrender meant rich rewards for the tribunes and centurions. Hence, Tacitus reports that at the siege of Cremona in AD 69 the enlisted men rattled and clashed their arms in order that the pleas of the tribunes and centurions for negotiation might be drowned out.[74] Within a legion itself, the centurions were ranked with specific titles based on seniority, experience, and ability. The *primus pilus* was a legion's senior centurion and would normally be first centurion of the first cohort (out of ten in a legion); this cohort in turn had five double-strength centuries of 160 men and the five centuries were ranked: *primus pilus*, *princeps*, *princeps hastatus*, *hastatus*, and *hastatus posterior*. The remaining nine cohorts each had six centuries with eighty men with a total of 480 per cohort, and each cohort had centurions ranked by seniority: the *pilus prior*, *pilus posterior*, *princeps prior*, *princeps posterior*, *hastatus prior*, *hastatus posterior*. However, it remains somewhat uncertain if this constitutes a strict grading of posts,

Fig. 7.3: The tomb of the centurion Marcus Caelius with two of his freedmen. Killed at the battle of the Teutoberg Forest in AD 9, the inscription translates: 'To Marcus Caelius, of the Lemonian tribe, born in Bologna, a centurion of the first order of the Eighteenth Legion, 53 and a half years of age. He fell in the Varine War. It is permitted that his freedmen's bones rest here. Publius Caelius, son of Titus of the Lemonian tribe, his brother, set up this monument.' (Agnete via *Wikimedia Commons*)

starting with the centurions of the tenth cohort as most junior and moving up, or not. On the march, centurions were positioned at the rear of their century. Each century required eight tents for the men in the ranks and a larger tent for the centurion. The children of a high-ranking centurion could rise to great prominence, as was the case with Helvidius Priscus, a vocal and courageous critic first of Nero, then later of Vespasian, whose father had worked his way to *primus pilus* status, a position that could also elevate the centurion to rank of equestrian upon completion of service.[75]

The responsibilities required of a centurion were numerous and included duties related to various forms of policing, camp details, construction, and public ceremonies. Thus, in addition to acting as century commanders, centurions could also function as military police, temporarily keeping under guard men who had breached discipline; they also acted at times as policemen throughout the provinces, helping to maintain public order, a duty that even extended to Rome, where we hear for example of a centurion killed in a riot while trying to maintain public order at a theatre in AD 15.[76] They would also attend the councils of their high commanders, as during the Gallic Wars, when Caesar was compelled to convene a meeting of the centurions under his command, in this instance to reprimand them for their anxiety over facing Germans, something that was undermining camp morale, and for second guessing their commander's strategy.[77] Caesar also indicates that centurions would take part in scouting parties for establishing camps, and, in addition, functioned as individual commanders of ships during naval operations, along with military tribunes.[78] Centurions could also be sent to survey for preliminary plans of major infrastructure projects, as when Caligula sent a chief centurion to survey the possibility of digging a canal through the isthmus at Corinth in Greece.[79] They also played a role in public ceremonies, such as when in AD 19 a troop of centurions conveyed the ashes of Tiberius' dead nephew, the popular prince Germanicus, to Rome on a bier carried on their shoulders.[80]

The qualities needed for a centurion who had attained his office are neatly summed up by Vegetius, author of a military treatise from the fourth century AD. There he states quite succinctly the following:

> A centurion must be chosen for his great strength, his tall stature, know how to fight with a sword and to wield his shield most knowledgably, learned every skill of armament, be vigilant, sober, and dexterous, be more prepared to follow orders than to talk, keep his comrades disciplined, practised in arms, and ensure that they are well dressed and shod, that their arms are polished and shined.[81]

This strict discipline and the demands imposed made centurions formidable men indeed, as the ample testimony in our sources shows. As Pat Southern notes, these were men chosen for their dependability and clear-headedness in battle, rather than being reckless and hotheaded.[82] The historic record generally gives the impression that centurions were indeed blunt-spoken men of enormous loyalty, discipline, and courage. Our sources provide numerous examples both memorable and striking of these qualities on display, as in the frank words spoken by a nameless centurion who claims to have served in the ranks for thirty-six years, and implies most of it with Caesar: offered pardon when captured during the civil war between Caesar and Pompey by Caesar's enemy, Scipio, in North Africa, the anonymous centurion asked Scipio to his face, 'The army of he for whose honour and victory I have fought, shall I now stand in arms against?' Scipio was enraged and had the man executed on the spot.[83] Scipio was not the only one who displayed a violent pique against centurions who fought loyally for the other side in times of civil strife. After the fearsome first battle at Bedriacum near Cremona in AD 69 between the forces of Vitellius and Otho, Vitellius had all those centurions executed who had been most vigorous in their support of his rival, something that reportedly lost Vitellius support.[84] Vitellius, however, was not one to use centurions well: when his forces were defeated at what became known as the Second Battle of Cremona later in AD 69, this time against the forces of Vespasian, Julius Agrestis, a chief centurion, bravely did reconnaissance for Vitellius who refused to believe rumours of his own defeat. After Agrestis reported back the painful truth to Vitellius, he dismissed Agrestis' report. Agrestis gave him clear proof by his suicide.[85]

Competitive rivalry between centurions was also a means to show off one's courage, as Caesar illustrates, where we find Titus Pullo and Lucius Vorenus singled out for mention, a rare occurrence in Caesar's writings, therefore notable.[86] During a rebellion of the tribes of northern Gaul in the winter of 55/54 BC, Gallic rebels attacked Quintus Cicero's fortress, and his men resisted the assault bravely. Pullo goaded Vorenus into leaving the ramparts of the fortress they were defending and to lead a group of men with him to where the enemy was thickest. Vorenus accepted and Pullo then quickly came to close quarters with a Gaul who had broken rank; he transfixed the Gaul with his spear but then, as the Gaul's comrades came to the fallen warrior's assistance Titus found it impossible to withdraw. Hard pressed and his shield and sword belt transfixed with projectiles making it impossible to revert to his sword, Vorenus managed to rescue Pullo, but grew too eager in the pursuit, fell, and was surrounded. Titus then came in turn to his rescue; they killed several Gauls and returned to camp to their fellow soldiers' great acclaim. Once Caesar arrived to relieve Cicero, he singled out the centurions by name and praised their valour.

A similarly courageous act on the part of Lucius Fabius, a centurion of the eighth legion, occurred at the siege of Gergovia during another Gallic rebellion in 51 BC, this time with a gruesome and bloody conclusion. Determined to be the first to mount the wall, he scaled a ladder and led a small group of men to be first into the city.[87] He and his men were surrounded, butchered, and cast from the wall; another centurion of the same legion, Marcus Petronius, fell trying to assail a gate and attempting to save as many of his men as possible.[88] As one readily sees, the courage of centurions could save the day, but could also result in catastrophe. Hence half a dozen years before Gergovia, in 57 BC during one of the first encounters fighting a Gallic tribe called the Nervii in what is now

Belgium, Caesar lost all of the centurions of the fourth cohort of the twelfth legion, and only a few centurions from the remaining cohorts of the entire legion remained unwounded – losses could be high.[89] As noted above, when Caesar or any other source names a centurion it is often due to their noteworthy courage. Perhaps most remarkable of all of these from Caesar's works was a retired centurion, C. Crastinus, who had re-enlisted as a veteran and was the highest-ranking centurion of Caesar's tenth legion and singled out for his exceptional bravery.[90] He made the first charge from the right at the historic battle of Pharsalus on 9 August 48 BC, where Caesar defeated Pompey, leading a special force of 120 picked men, and died in the battle from a sword thrust in his face. Caesar honoured him as the bravest man to perish in that historic encounter. Another notable centurion whose name is immortalized in the historic record was Sempronius Densus, who, according to Tacitus, made a futile attempt to rescue Cn. Calpurnius Piso Scribonianus, the chosen successor of the emperor Galba, who was overthrown by the praetorians in favour of the new rival emperor, M. Otho; despite Sempronius' valiant efforts, Otho's supporters dragged Piso out of the Temple of Vesta in the Roman Forum where he was hiding and murdered him.[91] A centurion's loyalty to his commander or emperor could be impressive, to say the least: when C. Cassius, one of Caesar's assassins, committed suicide due to miscommunication at Philippi in 42 BC, where the armies of the republic clashed with those of Marc Antony and C. Octavius, the centurion whose delay caused the miscommunication slew himself over Cassius' corpse.[92]

The steadfast discipline of centurions was vital at times to control their men, when Roman discipline faltered and the troops grew mutinous. Such mutinies tended to occur during times of political instability, such as imperial succession or civil strife. When, for example, a legion called the Venacular Legion mutinied against their commander Q. Cassius, a supporter of Pompey's who fought in Spain during the civil war against Caesar, the centurions attempted to maintain discipline and several were killed by their men when they tried to resist their insubordination.[93] Consequently, as already noted (see p. 185), centurions could be the special objects of mutinous troops' wrath, as was the case during a mutiny in Lower Germany in AD 69 – among the first neutralized by the troops were four centurions of the twenty-fourth legion, who when they tried to maintain order were quickly swept up in the rush and cast into chains, and later executed. Vitellius, in whose province the mutiny occurred, further acquiesced to the savagery of the soldiery by handing over a centurion named Crispinus, whom mutinous troops blamed for the execution of Fonteius Capito, the former governor of Lower Germany.[94] At roughly the same time in Rome itself, in the midst of a confused, drunken, nocturnal riot that turned into a near mutiny, a group of soldiers attacked and killed the strictest of the centurions as a prelude to a more general riot in the city, a riot only quelled quite delicately by the prompt intervention of the emperor Otho himself.[95]

At times the duties a centurion found himself tasked with could be quite lurid, since they played a grim and bloody role in the occasionally violent politics of the empire and the imperial family. It was a centurion who allegedly carried out the murder of Agrippa Postumus, Augustus' grandson, upon Tiberius' assumption of power, thereby eliminating a potential political rival.[96] Later in his reign, during the fraught and dysfunctional family dispute over succession when Tiberius ordered his niece, Agrippina the Elder's, arrest for conspiracy, Tiberius ordered a centurion to beat her so brutally that she lost an eye before being sent into exile.[97] Suetonius reports that numerous centurions were involved in the plot to assassinate Caligula (not surprisingly, given his alienating treatment of them throughout his reign), and that centurions also carried out the murder of his wife Caesonia and their infant daughter, some of whom were subsequently executed under Caligula's successor, his uncle Claudius.[98] Centurions were also involved in the execution of Valeria Messalina, Claudius' wife and the empress who was found guilty of adultery and conspiracy in AD 47.[99] Some twelve years later, a centurion named Obaritus murdered Agrippina the Younger, daughter of Agrippina the Elder, sister to Gaius Caligula and mother of the emperor Nero, in perhaps one of the most lurid and hair-raising scenes in all of Roman history. Fearing his mother as a rival and goaded on by his mistress, Poppaea Sabina, Nero sent Obaritus, a centurion of the fleet at Misenum, to murder Agrippina after a botched attempt to assassinate her by sending her out to sea in a collapsible ship. Deserted by all of her retinue in the dark of the night, the soldiers surrounded her villa and, after a brief confrontation stabbed her to death in her bedroom.[100] After her death it was the military tribunes and centurions who helped give Nero the cover, in part, for his suspected crime, and still later had a hand in the execution of his hapless wife, Octavia, who was falsely accused of adultery and forced to suicide in AD 62.[101] Nor were these the only occasions in which centurions were ordered to carry out the execution of imperial rivals – it occurred a number of times under Nero in the wake of various conspiracies and perceived opposition. Indeed, centurions constituted one of the key instruments to Nero's tyranny, since he used them to police audience reaction and to encourage applause during his performances.[102] However, not all centurions were well disposed towards Nero, and we find one, Sulpicius Asper, involved in a plot against Nero in AD 66 known as the Pisonian Conspiracy (named for the senator who spearheaded it). Denounced and arrested, Asper's constancy and composure in the face of his imminent execution was noteworthy according to our sources, and when asked directly by Nero his reason for conspiring against him, the centurion responded tersely but ambiguously, 'I could help you in no other way.'[103]

It bears noting, as we conclude this section, that centurions, for all the virtues that many displayed, could be unscrupulous. One of the causes of a widespread and dangerous rebellion in Britain in AD 60 discussed in the previous chapter was, according to Tacitus, abusive behaviour by centurions against the Iceni and the royal house of a recently deceased local client king, Prasutagus, including the rape of his widow and queen, Boudicca, and his two daughters, not to mention the plundering of his kingdom.[104] Centurions could be rough customers. Similarly, in Apuleius' novel *The Golden Ass* a centurion demands from a small farmer his beast of burden; since the centurion spoke Latin the farmer was unable to understand, prompting the centurion to hit him with his vine rod, repeating the demand in Greek. The farmer fought back, but the centurion ultimately appropriated the animal. It is a fictional account to be sure, but taken in its larger context quite plausibly reflects a genuine experience all the same. Finally, we note that in the gospels (*Matthew* 27:54; *Mark* 15:39; *Luke* 23:47), a centurion is present at the crucifixion, likely overseeing the execution with the men under his command; this, too, was a duty of a centurion, who upon Jesus' death and the rending of the veil famously intoned, 'Truly this man was the Son of God.' This brief survey of who and what a centurion was renders the New Testament characterization all the more credible. Centurions are often portrayed in our sources as having simple values of belief in obedience, in their own authority, in discipline and order: heeding John's command to come to repentance;

the unflinching faith of the centurion with the sick servant that was as complete as any saint's; the unquestioning acceptance of Christ's divinity in the face of his death and suffering. The brief and austere depictions of the centurions one encounters in the New Testament seem more than plausible given the historic record, and their personalities, for all their laconic depiction, leave a vivid and striking impression.

* * *

> But when the morning was now come, Jesus stood on the shore: but the disciples knew not that it was Jesus … Therefore that disciple whom Jesus loved saith unto Peter, It is the Lord. Now when Simon Peter heard that it was the Lord, he girt his fisher's coat unto him (for he was naked,) and did cast himself into the sea.
>
> *John* 21:4, 7

Makers of Roman mosaics were fond of depicting fishermen, since for the Romans and the Greeks, fish was variously both an important staple protein and, as the case is today, a great luxury of the table, depending on the species. Such mosaics depict fishermen in various stages of undress, and are often, as was the case with Peter, dressed in little or nothing (see fig. 7.4). This chapter has examined three of the numerous professions mentioned in the New Testament. We have not examined the life or profession of the humble worker who plied his trade at sea, mending nets, maintaining his boat, doing the heavy and one imagines often malodorous work of hauling fish, and selling them at market. Nor is this the only profession we have elided in this chapter. We have not considered the life and work of the local advocate, the carpenter, the day labourer; nor have we considered the life and work of the steward of a great estate, the household servant (invariably a slave), or the prostitute. All of these, and more, are people whom Jesus variously encountered and mentioned in his parables and teachings, and are the sorts of people with whom Jesus consorted, conversed, and occasionally broke bread.

But the three archetypes we have examined, unlike those just cited, were ones very much within and part of the Roman power structure, a power to which the people of Judaea and its surrounding small client states had become extremely hostile by the time the New Testament was composed, and as Josephus tells us, even well before the ministry of

Fig. 7.4: A Roman mosaic with a fishing scene; ca. early third century AD from a Roman house, Sousse (Tunisia). Note the men toil at what must have been hot, hard, and sometimes very damp work, naked. (Ad Meskens via *Wikimedia Commons*)

Jesus himself. That is what makes his encounter with these characters who variously wielded or supported or were products of so much power perhaps all the more remarkable. They were all despised and feared. Yet in the context of Jesus' ministry, Jesus welcomed a *publicanus* – a man who chose a life of profit and filling Rome's coffers – to be one of his apostles. He broke bread with the *architelonēs* Zacchaeus, a man locally notorious for his, by his own admission, dishonest dealings in the courts against taxpayers. And he expressed his admiration of a man of war, the centurion, whose position of authority, requiring strength and courage, gave him his simple but superlative faith in an eccentric and puzzling charismatic who wandered the province. Jesus did not simply preach the radical notion of the forgiveness of one's enemies. For all intents and purposes he lived with them, spoke with them, ate with them, and welcomed them among his disciples. In our chapter on resistance we noted the radical nature concerning the gospels' depiction of resistance to Roman power. The centurion, informant, and tax collector represent, in a sense, the state monopoly on violence, the legal system, and the power to tax and appropriate state revenue. Jesus' response to and not so subtle undermining of the Roman power structure in the gospel narratives through his warm and generous reception of those who represent it constitutes an equally radical, unique, and moving contrast to the hostile and violent reaction to it found in other sources, such as Josephus, or for that matter, Roman sources such as Tacitus. However, we must be clear that Jesus' ministry did not undermine Roman power; it did, however, ultimately result in the destruction of one of its pillars, paganism, and in a profound reconfiguration of society through one of, if not the, most remarkable of cultural revolutions in our species' history

Chapter 8

Epilogue

Over the years I have taught my share of courses on Greek and Roman – especially Roman – history, culture, literature, and language. The religions of these two great cultures are subjects I have always found to be of particular fascination, both for myself and my students. In the course of this book, however, I must confess that I have been more cagey and less candid with my readers about my own views on religion, while in fact, I am always up front with my students in what I hope is the full interest of introducing them to historical complexities. Usually I begin with a favourite joke, a line from an old Woody Allen movie, in which a character asks his father about God to which he responds (roughly), 'I can't figure out my toaster. I'm going to figure out God?' I ask them to be open to ignorance, to try to be receptive to an agnosticism that the wide variety of human experience demands. Accept that we are not going to figure this out, and look with a jaundiced eye at any dogma. That said, there are many things about ancient religion and the three great western religions that I find attractive or compelling. The forces that a Bacchus or a Venus embodied are very real to me: go into any bar frequented by local college students in any town virtually anywhere, and you will see the two at work on a Friday or Saturday night. As one who has been in small boats on the north Pacific and been profoundly humbled if not utterly terrified by the experience, I believe the wrath of Poseidon to be very real at times. Odysseus is no myth. Can anyone observe the twentieth century and not see the hand of Ares doing his very worst as he stalks among a shivering humanity? Yet I also embrace the radical agnosticism of Socrates as concerns the ultimate nature of God and the universe. As I once said to a student who asked me outright my beliefs, I stated to her quite succinctly: 'That is easy – I'm a pagan when I read Homer, Jewish when I read the Old Testament, Christian when I read the New Testament, Muslim when I read the Qu'ran, and an atheist when I read Bertrand Russell.' Of these I was raised in the Christian

Fig. 8.1: *The Supper at Emmaus* by Caravaggio, 1606 in the Pinacoteca di Brera, Milan. (Public domain via *Wikimedia Commons*)

tradition, and while quite sceptical of the supernatural aspects of it, have, as I have aged, become intrigued by the high ethics of the Christian, Jewish, and Islamic traditions, particularly as society over my lifetime has become more secularized, and knowledge of those religious traditions turned, it seems, increasingly dim.

What I have tried to do here is to interject some historic context into one of those three great religions, the subject of Jesus' ministry, and the historical circumstances of the world around the year of his death. My hope is that, even though Jesus rarely entered the picture, this has deepened and enriched the understanding of Jesus' ministry and more importantly, given the reader a larger perspective in which to situate and appreciate his strangeness, the alienation of his message, and the eccentricity and idiosyncratic nature of his story in his time, and, in a sense, still in our own. He is a beguiling figure at times, obscure, elusive, and opaque, like his parables; perhaps that was a part of his spiritual and rhetorical method by which to attract the curious. People wonder after him, as in *John* (1:38) when two disciples follow him and Jesus turns to ask them, 'What seek ye?'

That wonder, that elusiveness is compounded for one such as myself. As a Classicist, I am aware how problematic speeches are in ancient texts. For authors such as Tacitus or Livy, these were often nothing more than rhetorical compositions, made, one suspects, out of whole cloth to suit the occasion or character they are depicting. Indeed, the only speech in an ancient text for which we have any sort of control or comparison is that of the emperor Claudius on allowing the Gauls into the Roman Senate. Tacitus relates the speech in the eleventh book of his *Annals*. A text of the actual speech, posted as an imperial decree in Lyons, France (ancient Lugdunum in the province of Gaul) and erected in bronze gives us a sense of how much liberty, even when one potentially has a text available, the ancients would take with an actual speech. How many liberties, we must ask, were taken with what Jesus actually said? And did he say it in Greek, or Aramaic? If, as is almost certainly the case, in Aramaic, how well did the writers of the gospels know to translate the Aramaic into the Greek? And how long did they wait to do so – how many days or months or years or decades, and how well did their memory serve them? One can mount a defence by noting the broad agreement of the gospel stories, but when we get into specifics, issues of translation and meaning and culture, we begin to run into a character who, if actually historical, is nonetheless elusive indeed.

Let me conclude with a magnificent exhibit at the Capodimonte Museum in Naples that I visited nearly twenty years ago. It was an exhibition of Caravaggio paintings, for whom readers will perhaps already note I have a particular fondness. I have always been drawn to him for his earthy characters and his gritty appreciation and interpretation of the Christian narrative. He knew the people who surrounded Jesus. At the time, I was not as intimately versed in New Testament narrative, but I recall being drawn to one painting in particular, his 1606 version of the *Supper at Emmaus* (fig. 8.1) – 1606, since Caravaggio had already painted one version in 1601. The story goes that after Christ's resurrection two disciples encounter him on the road to Emmaus without recognizing who he is, and he accompanies them. They are deeply impressed by his learning and ability to interpret scripture, while for their part they relate to him the recent events in Jerusalem, including presumably the crucifixion. Then they sit down at supper together: Christ breaks bread, their eyes are open, they suddenly recognize their master for whom he is, but then, at that very moment of recognition, he vanishes. That in a sense sums up for us our encounters with Christ: fascinating, charismatic, profound, transcendent. But, in the end, vanishingly elusive. It is hoped this history has provided some further context by which to make him less so, and to grasp more securely at the hem of his garment.

Appendix A

Maps

Map 1: A Map of the Mediterranean in the High Roman Empire, *ca.* AD 100. (*Reprinted from A Tacitus Reader, Bolchazy-Carducci Publishers, 2014*)

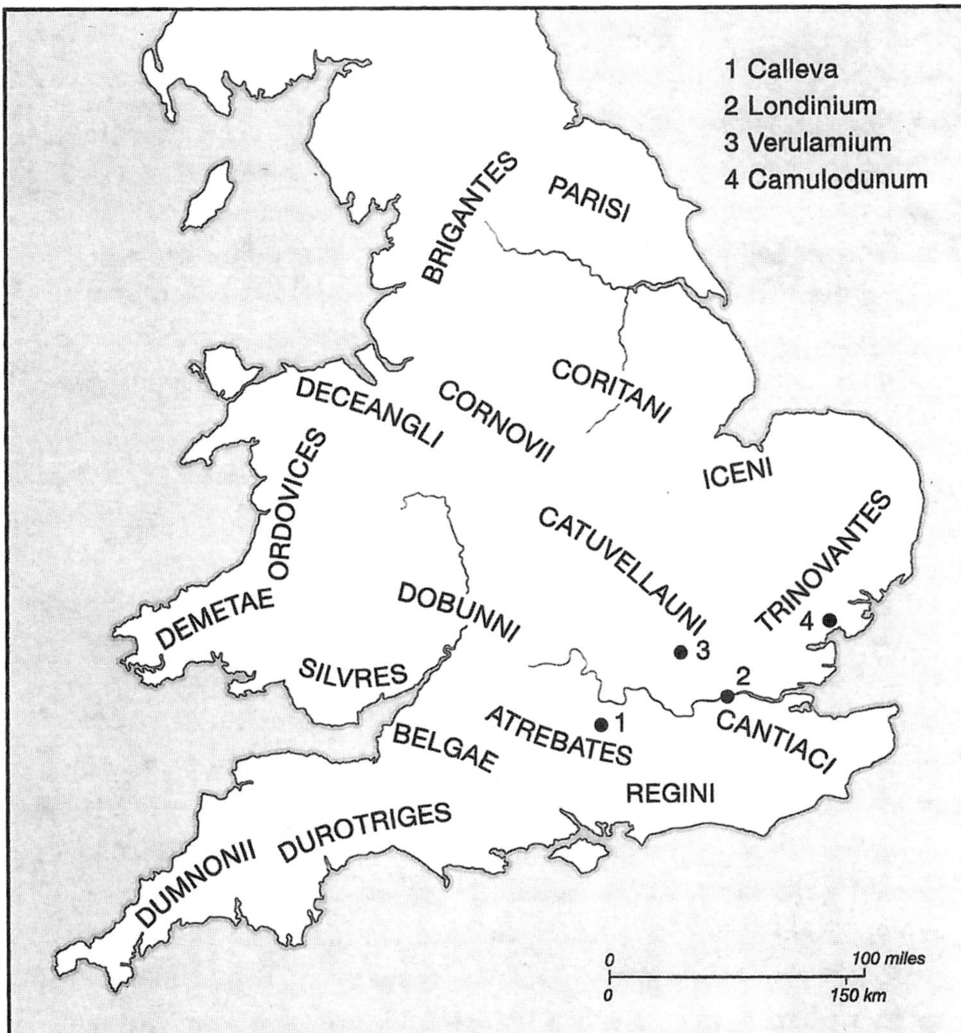

Map 2: A Map of Britain during the Revolt of Boudicca, AD 60–61. (*Reprinted from* Pax Romana. War, Peace, and Conquest in the Roman World, *by Adrian Goldsworthy, with permission of Yale University Press*)

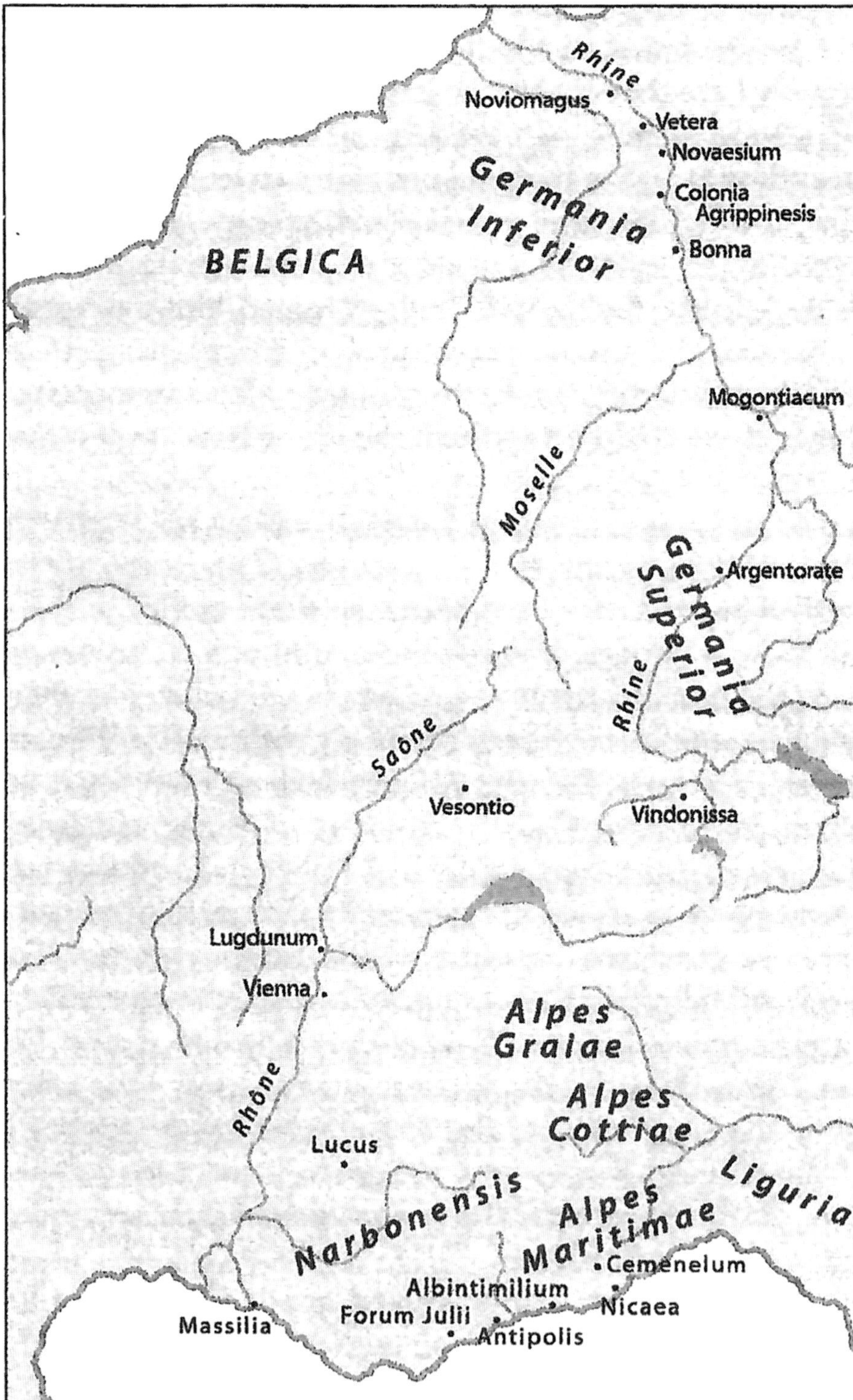

Map 3: A Map of Germany and Gaul during the first century AD. (*Reprinted from* 69 AD. The Year of the Four Emperors, *by Gwyn Morgan, with permission of Oxford University Press*)

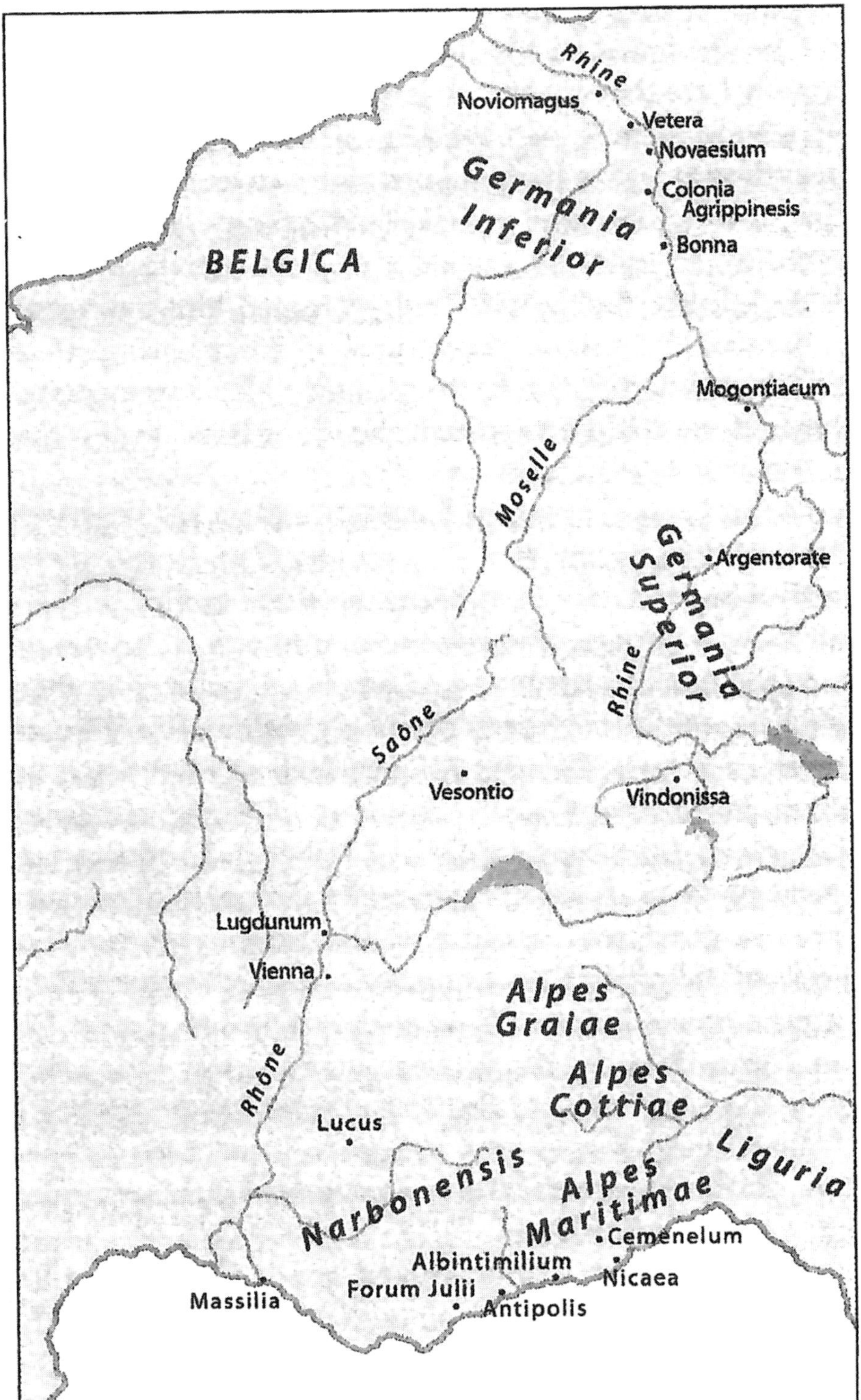

Map 4: A Map of Judaea during the Revolt of AD 66–70. (*Reprinted from* Pax Romana. War, Peace, and Conquest in the Roman World, *by Adrian Goldsworthy, with permission of Yale University Press*)

Appendix B

The Families of Tiberius and of Herod Antipas

The Family of Tiberius and the Julio-Claudian Dynasty.

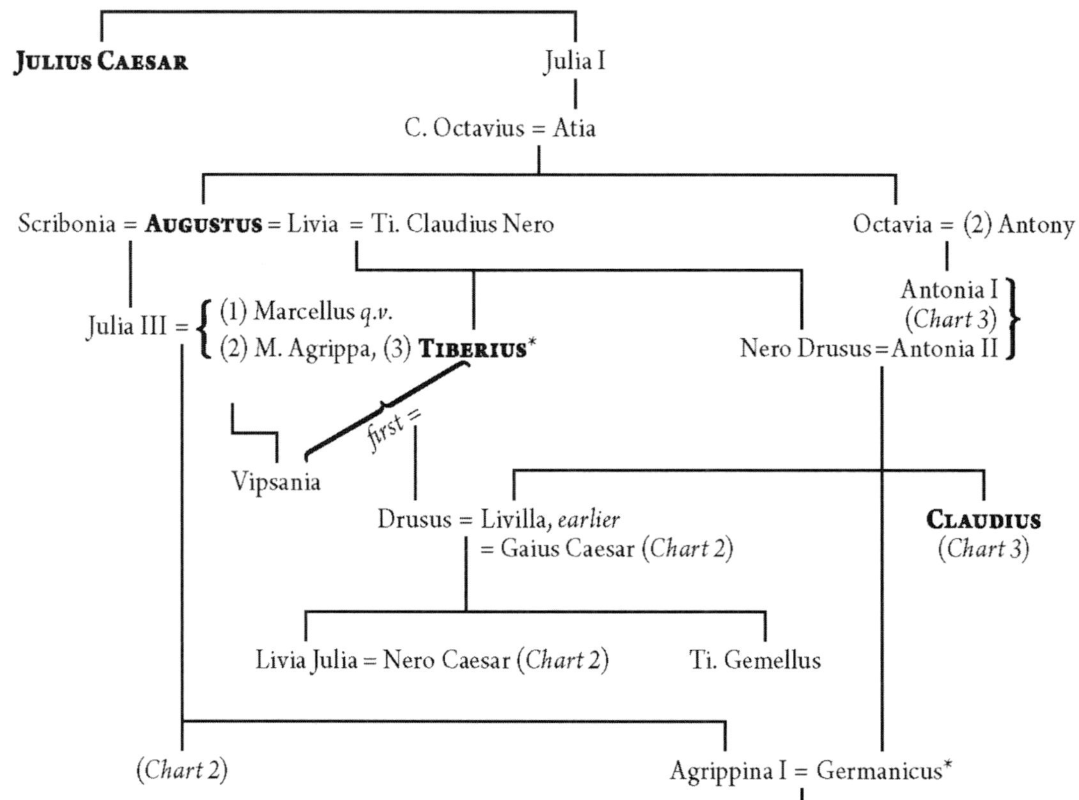

* *Tacitus refers to Tiberius and Germanicus as "sons" of Augustus and Tiberius respectively, who adopted them.*

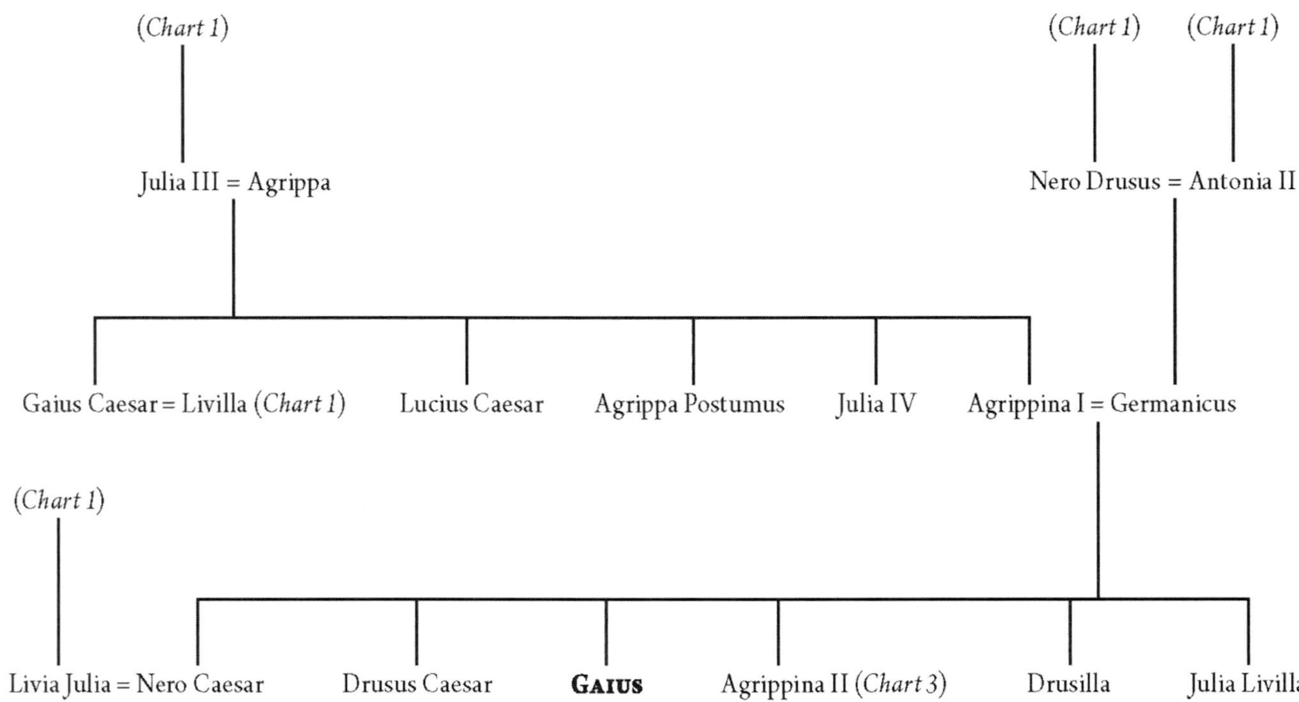
(Chart 1)
Julia III = Agrippa
(Chart 1)
(Chart 1)
Nero Drusus = Antonia II
Gaius Caesar = Livilla (Chart 1)
Lucius Caesar
Agrippa Postumus
Julia IV
Agrippina I = Germanicus
(Chart 1)
Livia Julia = Nero Caesar
Drusus Caesar
GAIUS
Agrippina II (Chart 3)
Drusilla
Julia Livilla

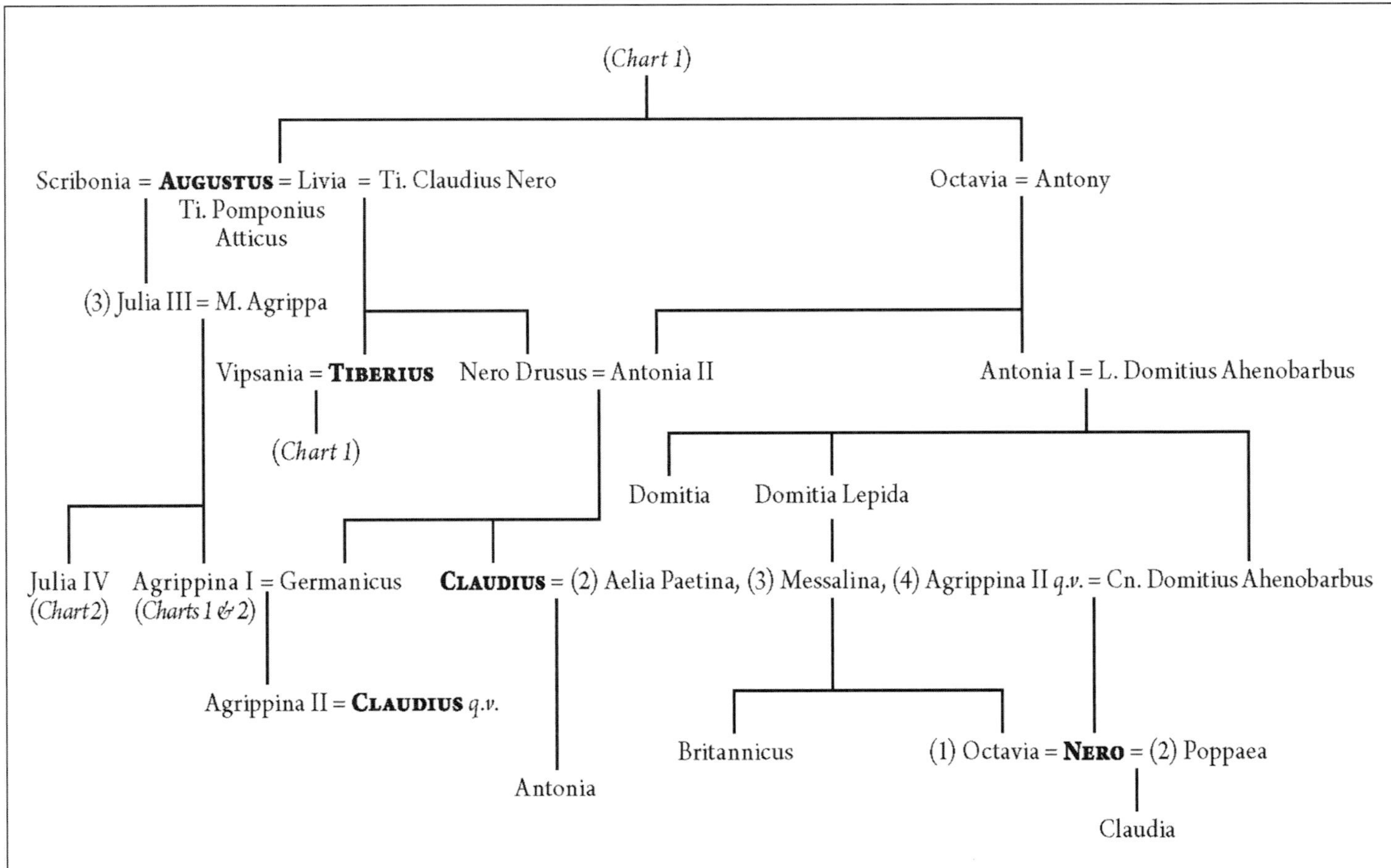
(Chart 1)
Scribonia = AUGUSTUS = Livia = Ti. Claudius Nero
Ti. Pomponius Atticus
Octavia = Antony
(3) Julia III = M. Agrippa
Vipsania = TIBERIUS
Nero Drusus = Antonia II
Antonia I = L. Domitius Ahenobarbus
(Chart 1)
Domitia
Domitia Lepida
Julia IV (Chart 2)
Agrippina I = Germanicus (Charts 1 & 2)
CLAUDIUS = (2) Aelia Paetina, (3) Messalina, (4) Agrippina II q.v. = Cn. Domitius Ahenobarbus
Agrippina II = CLAUDIUS q.v.
Britannicus
(1) Octavia = NERO = (2) Poppaea
Antonia
Claudia

The Family Tree of Herod Antipas.

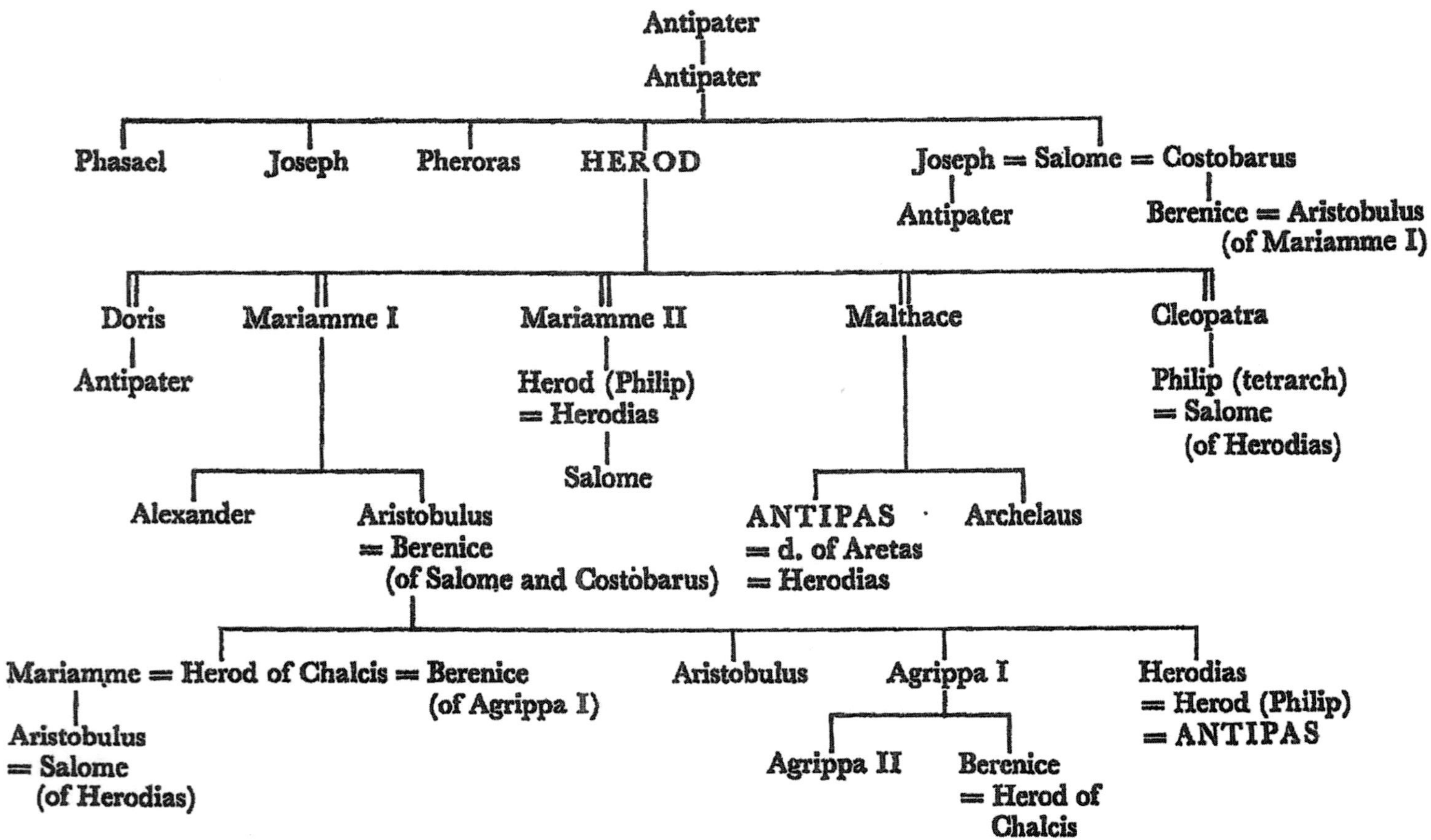

Glossary

Aedile: An elected official in charge of weights and measures in market places in Roman cities and towns; he could also be in charge of games as well as responsible for public buildings and food supplies.

Consul: The highest office of the republic; two were elected annually and they often functioned as the chief war magistrates; during the Principate it became an office for the emperor to bestow, with several consuls appointed annually usually from among senators, friends, and trusted advisors.

Consul ***suffectus***: During the Principate the two consuls from the first half of the year were known as the *consules ordinarii*; they relinquished their office generally and were followed by *consules suffecti* later in the year in order to give more senators a chance to hold high office.

Equestrian: A rank just below that of senator, in which, by the time of the empire, one had to have a minimum property requirement assessed at 400,000 sesterces; equestrians made up both a business and political class, and some men of equestrian status, such as Tiberius' praetorian prefect Sejanus, became substantially more powerful and wealthy than senators.

Magister equitum: Literally 'the master of horses', the office was a relic from the ancient republic; in times of emergency when dictators were appointed, the *magister equitum* would be the second in command, as Marc Antony was when Caesar was dictator.

Novus homo: Literally a 'new man'. A man who was usually first in his family to hold a high magistracy, usually the consulship, thereby ennobling his family. Notable *novi homines* or new men include Cato the Censor (the Elder Cato), C. Marius, and M. Tullius Cicero.

Pharisees: This is a group of Jewish spiritual leaders that will ultimately become the basis of Rabbinic Judaism. Unlike the Sadducees, they generally opposed greater cultural assimilation, recognized oral doctrine, and were receptive to the writings of the prophets and concepts such as the resurrection of the dead; there were some who were also seemingly receptive to Jesus' teachings.

Praefect (Prefect): A title of varying definition, but generally indicative of an official who had administrative duties of a certain capacity, such as the *Praefectus Praetorianus* who commanded the praetorian guard, or the *Praefectus Annonae* who was in charge of grain supply; it was also the title of governors, such as Pilate, who administered provinces over which equestrians were in charge.

Praetor: A judicial official whose numbers varied over time and who was elected annually. The position was high enough that former praetors, along with former consuls, were sent out to govern provinces.

Princeps: The term was used by Augustus from the republican institution by which a senator, through his experience, service, and standing, was recognized as among the most authoritative voices of the Senate to which others deferred. It came to be the term used for the emperor, itself derived from the term *imperator*, a salutation given to victorious generals.

Procurator: The title of a governor after AD 40 in charge of equestrian provinces; later this becomes a general term used for those who represented the interests of the emperor throughout the provinces and in the civil administration.

Quaestor: A financial official who administered Rome's *aerarium* or treasury; these varied in number over time, and they gradually came to assume other duties. During the republic each commander had a quaestor to manage the army's finances. In the late republic they could be chosen by a commander to manage finances within a province as well, and even take over his duties were he incapacitated or absent.

Sadducees: A Jewish sect that believed in the practices of the law and whose identity centred on the Temple, the high priesthood, and the sanctity of both; they appear to have been stricter about certain practices than the Pharisees. Many also appear to have belonged to aristocratic families and generally favoured good relations with the Romans.

Tribune: Ten tribunes were elected annually during the republic; they acted as champions of the people's interests and as their protectors; their persons were sacrosanct, and they had the right to introduce *rogationes* (bills) before the Senate which would 'advise and consent' on the *rogatio* before it would be voted on by the people.

tribunicia potestas: 'The power of a tribune' which Augustus assumed for himself during his rise to power, by which he posed as the people's protector, augmented the sanctity of his person, and had greater control over the legislative agenda of the Senate. The tribunate remained a step in a senator's career, but under Augustus the office was stripped of all its power.

Triumph: The military procession culminating in a sacrifice to Jupiter on the Capitoline. Under the emperors only they were allowed, with a few exceptions, to enjoy this honour in which the commander embodied Jupiter himself. While a relatively simple ceremony in the early republic, it grew increasingly elaborate over time.

Notes

Chapter 1: Introduction

1. See Drews 1984: 112–122.
2. See Van Voorst 2000: 45, n. 70.
3. See Van Voorst 2000: 45, n. 70 for his compelling argument on Book XV (*Ann.* 15.44) as the first introduction of Christians in Tacitus' work.
4. The attempt to set the date in the context of the fall of Sejanus has a particularly storied scholarly past; see e.g. Maier 1968: 3–13 for one of numerous such discussions which is not without its problems, such as an assumption that Tiberius was an on-again off-again anti-Semite.

Chapter 2: Tiberius: The Man on the Coin

1. The three standard biographies on Tiberius include Seager 1972, Levick 1976, and Shotter 1992; the most recent work on Tiberius is Van Dijk 2019.
2. Tac. *Ann.* 1.4.3.
3. For his dual descent from the Claudians see Suet. *Tib.* 3.1.
4. Suet. *Tib.* 4.
5. Suet. *Tib.* 6.
6. Tac. *Ann.* 1.10.4.
7. Suet. *Tib.* 6.7.
8. The best discussion of Augustus' rise to power and usurpation of the Roman state is still Syme's seminal 1939 work, *The Roman Revolution.*
9. For Vipsania's pedigree see Nep. *Att.* 12.1–2; for Tiberius' marriage to her see Suet. *Tib.* 7.
10. For the history of Tiberius' tragic marriage to Vipsania and his fraught relations with his second wife, Julia, see Suet. *Tib.* 7; also see Cass. Dio 54.35.4 for his marriage to Julia; for Vipsania also see Tac. *Ann.* 1.12.6, 3.19.4.
11. Suet. *Tib.* 8; Cass. Dio 53.28.3; see Raaflaub and Samons 1991 for discussion.
12. For his praetorship see Cass. Dio 54.19.6; for his consulship see 54.25.1.
13. See Tac. *Ann.* 2.3.4; Suet. *Tib.* 9; Parthia was Rome's rival empire to the East, and included virtually all of modern Iran and Iraq; it survived until the early third century AD when it succumbed to a renascent Persian empire.
14. Hor. *Od.* 4.14; Suet. *Tib.* 9; they both may have received the illustrious salutation of *imperator* for their accomplishments, see Tac. *Ann.* 1.3.1.
15. See Suet. *Tib.* 68 for a physical description of Tiberius; see Tac. *Ann.* 6.5 for the diminutive applied to Tiberius.
16. Suet. *Tib.* 68.
17. Cass. Dio 54.31.2.
18. Suet. *Tib.* 7; Cass. Dio 55.1–2.
19. See Vell. 2.97.2–4; Suet. *Tib.* 9; Cass. Dio 55.6.1.
20. See e.g., Tac. *Ann.* 3.56.1.
21. The sources are unanimous about her character; see Vell. 2.100.3; Sen. *Ben.* 6.32; Tac. *Ann.* 3.24.2; Suet. *Aug.* 65; Dio 55.10.12; for her witticisms see Macrob. *Sat.* 2.5.1–9.
22. See Vell. 2.100.4; Fulvia, herself a granddaughter of the renowned C. Gracchus, had been married to Clodius Pulcher, a famous nemesis of Cicero's, and also to C. Scribonius Curio, a supporter of Caesar's who was killed while fighting in Africa

in 49 BC; for Julia's drinking bouts see Cass. Dio 55.10.12; see 55.10.15 for Iullus Antonius' execution.

23. For the deaths of Gaius and Lucius see Tac. *Ann.* 1.3.3; Suet. *Tib.* 15.2; Dio 55.10a.9–10.
24. For Tiberius' self-imposed exile and adoption of Greek mannerisms see Suet. *Tib.* 10–13.
25. See Rutledge 2008 for discussion.
26. Suet. *Tib.* 57.1.
27. Suet. *Tib.* 8.
28. See Tac. *Ann.* 4.43 for these Greek delegations.
29. Suet. *Tib.* 70.
30. Suet. *Tib.* 56.
31. See Tac. *Ann.* 6.21 for the incident on Rhodes. For Thrasyllus' influence also see Cass. Dio 58.27.1–2; for his successful prediction to Tiberius on Rhodes (where he appears to have made his acquaintance) see Suet. *Tib.* 14.4; cf. in general Tac. *Ann.* 6.20–22; both Suetonius and Tacitus also indicate Tiberius himself was something of a dilettante astrologer. Court astrologers were by no means a remarkable phenomenon in the early Principate.
32. That is Suetonius' (*Tib.* 11) version of events; Velleius says the same but states that Tiberius dissimulated this reason out of modesty, stating that, wanting a rest from his labours and, secure in the knowledge that Gaius and Lucius would help Augustus, he requested leave to retire, Vell. 2.99.2.
33. Suet. *Tib.* 11.
34. Tacitus' Latin is particularly powerful at *Ann.* 1.4.4: *ne iis quidem annis, quibus Rhodi specie secessus exul egerit, aliud quam iram et simulationem et secretas lubidines meditatum.*
35. Suet. *Tib.* 12–13; cf. Cass Dio 55.10.19.
36. On his adoption see Vell. 2.103.3–4; Suet. *Tib.* 15; Cass. Dio 55.13.1–2.
37. For his campaigns see Vell. 2.104–109; Cass. Dio 55.13.1–2.
38. For Tiberius' campaigns in Pannonia following his campaigns in Germania see Cass. Dio 55.28.5–55.31.1.
39. See Vell. 2.117–119; Tac. *Ann.* 1.10.3; Suet. *Aug.* 23; *Tib.* 17; Cass. Dio 56.18–24; see now Peter Wells' excellent 2004 book for a general and highly readable study of the battle and the archaeology of the site; also see Tac. *Ann.* 1.60–62 for a hair-raising and macabre tour of the battle site some six years later.
40. See Tac. *Ann.* 1.3.
41. See Champlin 2012: 366–67.
42. The uncertainty is vividly portrayed in Tac. *Ann.* 1.4; 1.7.9–11; 1.13.2–3.
43. Tac. *Ann.* 1.4.3–5.
44. Vell. 2.123; Tac. *Ann.* 1.5.5; but see Cass. Dio 56.31.1 – who says contrary to the other sources that he was summoned from Dalmatia.
45. The episode is vividly described in Tac. *Ann.* 1.5.6.
46. Tac. *Ann.* 1.6.1.
47. Tac. *Ann.* 1.5.2–4, 1.6.
48. For the best most recent study of Agrippa Postumus and his place in the imperial family, and his demise see Pettinger 2012.
49. Tac. *Ann.* 1.2.1.
50. Tacitus' description of the funeral at *Ann.* 1.9–10 attributes to the crowd two opinions concerning Augustus' life and career, the first favourable but short, the second longer, decidedly negative, and likely intended to leave the more lasting impression; for Augustus' vanity in choosing Tiberius see Tac. *Ann.* 1.10.6.
51. Tac. *Ann.* 1.7.3–10.
52. Tac. *Ann.* 1.11–12; cf. Suet. *Tib.* 24.
53. Tac. *Ann.* 1.13.4–7.
54. Suet. *Tib.* 24.1.
55. For the mutinies upon the death of Augustus and Germanicus' expedition see Tac. *Ann.* 1.16–52, 55–71; *Ann.* 2.5–26; Vell. 2.125.

56. Tac. *Ann.* 2.39–40; Suet. *Tib.* 25; Cass. Dio 57.16.3–4.
57. See p. 132 for a more detailed discussion of Tacfarinas.
58. See p. 132 for a more detailed discussion of Julius Florus' and Julius Sacrovir's rebellion in Gaul.
59. See p. 48 for a more detailed discussion.
60. Tac. *Ann.* 4.59.1–4.
61. For a good discussion of the sculptures see Stewart 1977: 76–90; Ridgeway 2000: 78–91.
62. Ulysses in Latin; his popularity is perhaps attested by the simple fact that as nearly as we can tell Homer's *Odyssey* was one of the first Greek works to be translated into Latin when the early poet, Livius Andronicus, undertook to write his verse translation *The Odussia*.
63. See Pliny *HN* 34.62.
64. Rutledge 2012: 266–71.
65. Cass. Dio 58.1.1.
66. See Saviano: 2006.
67. For Tiberius' retirement to Capri see Houston 1985: 179–96.
68. See Suet. *Tib.* 60.
69. For an excellent discussion of the villa see McHugh 2020: 138–41.
70. For Tiberius' personal appearance as he grew older and his ulcerated complexion see Suet. *Tib.* 68.2; his baldness was mocked publicly by some, see Cass. Dio 58.19.1–2; the Caesars tended to be hypersensitive about their hair or lack thereof, as was the case with Julius Caesar (Suet. *Caes.* 45.2; cf. 51.1) and possibly Gaius Caligula (Suet. *Cal.* 50.1).
71. See Tac. *Ann.* 4.57 for the various reasons proffered.
72. Suet. *Tib.* 42; mocking someone with drinking pure wine was to imply they were a barbarian, since civilized peoples drank their wine mixed with water.
73. See Suet. *Tib.* 43–45 for the very explicit description of Tiberius' alleged sexual perversions and proclivities; see Champlin 2011 for a good discussion of Tiberius on Capri.
74. See Tac. *Ann.* 6.1.2–5.
75. Tacitus states in Latin, *suo tantum ingenio utebatur*, *Ann.* 6.51.6: the phrase is subject to much argument and interpretation by Tacitean scholars; for the best discussion and summation of this passage see Woodman 1989: 197–205.
76. See p. 85.
77. See Jos. *AJ* 18.81–84: the story goes that four disreputable Jews in Rome took advantage of a Jewish proselyte of noble standing, Fulvia, to swindle her out of purple cloth and gold, telling her that they would send the offerings to the Temple in Jerusalem but selling and pocketing the earnings from the offering for themselves; her husband, a certain Saturninus, reported this to Tiberius who was his friend, and the whole Jewish population was then reportedly expelled from Rome out of concern for excess proselytizing. The expulsion is well documented in our sources; see Sen. *Epist.* 108.22; Tac. *Ann.* 2.85; Suet. *Tib.* 36; Cass. Dio 57.18.5a.
78. Philo *Leg.* 299–305.
79. Jos. *AJ* 18.65–80; cf. Tac. *Ann.* 2.85; Suet. *Tib.* 36.
80. Tac. *Hist.* 5.8, 5.13; cf. Tac. *Ann.* 15.44.4 for Christianity as a *superstitio*.
81. Suet. *Tib.* 31.
82. Suet. *Tib.* 33–35.
83. Suet. *Tib.* 59.
84. Tac. *Ann.* 6.6.1–2.
85. Tac. *Ann.* 6.6.3.
86. We know of their existence and get a bare glimpse of their content from Suet. *Tib.* 61.1 and *Dom.* 20 where we learn that the emperor Domitian was an avid reader of Tiberius' memoirs. In addition to Tiberius, Claudius, although he did not leave memoirs, did write history, while Claudius' niece, Agrippina the Younger, Nero's mother, left memoirs that Tacitus consulted for the Neronian books of his *Annals*,

while later Vespasian wrote war commentaries on his campaigns in Judaea. None of these survive, and the loss of Agrippina's works is perhaps particularly regrettable.

87. There are a number of instances of Tiberius' biting wit and sarcasm throughout our sources. See e.g., Suet. *Tib.* 52.2, 61.5; Cass. Dio 57.14.1–2, 57.18.2.

Chapter 3: The Praetorian Prefect: Lucius Aelius Sejanus

1. The two major individual studies on Sejanus include Hennig 1975 and now McHugh 2020; also see Woodman 1977: 245–63 and Champlin 2010 and 2012 as excellent supplements.
2. For the ill omens that attended Sejanus assuming office on New Year's Day AD 31 see Cass. Dio 58.5.5–7.
3. Tac. *Ann.* 4.2.4.
4. See Champlin 2012.
5. Tac. *Ann.* 1.24; for Sejanus' early life in general see McHugh 2020: 1–23; for his role in helping to crush the mutinies of AD 14 see McHugh 2020: 33, 36–40.
6. For a conjectural assessment of Sejanus' early career path, see McHugh 2020: 20–21.
7. See McHugh 2020: 4–7 for a discussion of its development.
8. Tac. *Ann.* 1.69.7.
9. Cass. Dio 57.19.6; the post was reserved for men of equestrian status and an indication, given the importance of Egypt for Rome's grain supply, of a high level of trust by the emperor.
10. Tac. *Ann.* 4.2.1–4; Suet. *Tib.* 37.1; Cass. Dio 57.19.6; see McHugh 2020: 56–58, 71–74 for a good discussion about the consolidation of the camp and its organization.
11. Cass. Dio 57.19.7.
12. See Tac. *Ann.* 4.2.2–4; Cass. Dio 57.19.6–7 for Sejanus' motives in uniting the separate units into one large headquarter.
13. Tac. *Ann.* 4.2.3–4.
14. For his father and familial origins from the originally Etruscan town see McHugh 2020: 3–12.
15. See Champlin 2012: 367–68 for the nature of the praetorian prefect's office and the skills required in this period to administer it competently; for Sejanus' ties to the senatorial class in Rome, which included familial ones, see Champlin 2012: 368–70; for his connections to Roman men of letters see now Champlin 2012: 375–78.
16. Tac. *Ann.* 4.1.4.
17. For Hannibal's character sketch in Livy see 21.4; for Catiline's in Sallust see *Cat.* 5.1–5; see Martin and Woodman 1989: 84–5 for discussion of the influence of Livy and Sallust on this passage.
18. See Champlin's fine summation of his career, 2012: 387, where Champlin places him in the context of powerful Roman ministers and grandees who preceeded him.
19. For the whole episode of Sejanus' seduction of Livilla and the murder of her husband, Drusus, see Tac. *Ann.* 4.3, 7–8; cf. Suet. *Tib.* 62.1; Cass. Dio 57.22.2, 57.22.4b; for an analysis of Sejanus' sexual liaisons and their context see Champlin 2012: 378–81.
20. Cass. Dio 55.10.18.
21. Tac. *Ann.* 4.1.3; see McHugh 2020: 12 for Sejanus' place on Gaius' staff.
22. See Tac. *Ann.* 2.84 for the birth of the twins.
23. Cass. Dio 58.3.8; for Cicero's use of spies and intelligence gathering during the Catilinarian Conspiracy see Sall. *Cat.* 26.1–3, 28.1–2.
24. Tac. *Ann.* 4.1.3; Cass Dio 57.19.5; see McHugh 2020: 13–14.
25. Tac. *Ann.* 4.3.3–4; for Livilla's seduction also see Cass. Dio 57.22.2.
26. Suet. *Aug.* 69.1.
27. Tac. *Ann.* 4.8.1.
28. For Claudius' poisoning and those involved see Tac. *Ann.* 12.66–67; Suet. *Claud.* 44.2–3; Cass. Dio 61.34.2–3; for the suspicion of the poisoning of Germanicus (almost certainly untrue) see Tac. *Ann.* 2.74.2, 3.7.2; Cass. Dio 57.18.9–10. For the 'bewitching' of Germanicus see Tac. *Ann.* 2.69.5.

29. For Livia's alleged removal of Gaius see Tac. *Ann.* 1.3.3; for Augustus' possible involvement in the death of C. Pansa see Tac. *Ann.* 1.10.1; Suet. *Aug.* 11; cf. Pseudo-Brutus *Epist. ad Cic.* 1.6; for rumours of poisoning surrounding Drusus' death see Feldherr 2009: 175–89.
30. Tac. *Ann.* 4.11.4; for Eudemus see Tac. *Ann.* 4.3.5.
31. See Martin and Woodman 1989: 128–29; McHugh 2020: 76–77, 83; McHugh 2020: 93–97 has an excellent summation of the arguments and remains along with the current consensus a sceptic of our ancient sources' claims of poisoning.
32. For discussion of the case of Clutorius Priscus and bibliography see Rutledge 2001: 92–93; McHugh 2020: 77–78.
33. For Drusus' deep resentment of Sejanus see Tac. *Ann.* 4.7.2–3; Cass. Dio 57.22.1; for discussion see McHugh 2020: 92–94.
34. See McHugh 2020: 55–56.
35. Tac. *Ann.* 4.7.4; Levick 1990: 23 conjectures that the two will have clashed in AD 15 over the quelling of one of Rome's many fires as well, citing Cass. Dio 57.14.10; cf. McHugh 2020: 89–90. For Drusus' ill-tempered nature and heavy drinking see Tac. *Ann.* 1.29.4, 1.76.5; Cass. Dio 57.14.9–10.
36. Tac. *Ann.* 4.8.3–5; for Tiberius' response to his son's death cf. Cass. Dio 57.22.4a; Suet. *Tib.* 52.1–2; cf. Tac. *Ann.* 3.6 where Tiberius rebukes the Roman people for what was viewed as their excessive displays of grief and mourning in the wake of Germanicus' death.
37. See McHugh 2020: 102–103 for the motives and commencement of Sejanus' moves against Agrippina.
38. Tac. *Ann.* 4.12.
39. See Cass. Dio 57.22.4b for his general remarks concerning Sejanus' attack on Agrippina and her supporters.
40. Tac. *Ann.* 4.18–20; see Rutledge 2001: 141–42 for discussion and a detailed bibliography; McHugh 2020: 105–107.
41. See Champlin 2012: 363 citing Hennig 1975: 41–67.
42. For Sejanus' attack against Cordus see Tac. *Ann.* 4.34–35; Cass. Dio 57.24.1–4; cf. Sen. *Dial.* 6.1.2, 6.22.4; Suet. *Aug.* 35; for discussion with bibliography see Rutledge 2001: 94–96; McHugh 2020: 110–111.
43. Tac. *Ann.* 4.39.1.
44. Tacitus cites the letter in a summary; see *Ann.* 4.39.2–6.
45. Tac. *Ann.* 4.40.5–7; for a good discussion of the letter see McHugh 2020: 114–116.
46. For the rest of Tiberius' reply see Tac. *Ann.* 4.40.8–12; for the betrothal of Claudius' son to Sejanus' daughter see Suet. *Claud.* 27.1; Cass. Dio 58.11.5.
47. Tac. *Ann.* 4.41.2.
48. For the need to court Sejanus due to his control of imperial access see McHugh 2020: 91–93.
49. Tac. *Ann.* 3.65.3.
50. See pp. 33–4.
51. See Tac. *Ann.* 4.52–54; for discussion of the case with bibliography see Rutledge 2001: 142–44; McHugh 2020: 122–24.
52. See Tac. *Ann.* 4.52.3–6; Suet. *Tib.* 53.1.
53. Tac. *Ann.* 4.53.1–3.
54. Tac. *Ann.* 4.54; Suet. *Tib.* 53.1; see McHugh 2020: 125–26 for discussion.
55. Tac. *Ann.* 4.59.2–4; see Chapter 2, pp. 25–7 for a discussion of Tiberius' imperial villa at Sperlonga; for Tiberius' increased confidence in Sejanus after this incident see McHugh 2020: 134–35.
56. See Tac. *Ann.* 4.59.5–4.60; Suet. *Tib.* 54 treats in brief the persecution and destruction of Nero and Drusus; for discussion see McHugh 2020: 136–37.
57. Tac. *Ann.* 4.17.1–3; see McHugh 2020: 104–105 for discussion.
58. Tac. *Ann.* 4.17.4.
59. Tac. *Ann.* 4.60.4–6; see McHugh 2020: 142 for discussion.

60. Tac. *Ann.* 4.67.5–6.
61. The case is related in Tac. *Ann.* 4.66. For the case in the context of Sejanus' rise see McHugh 2020: 142–43.
62. See Tac. *Ann.* 4.68–70; cf. Cass. Dio 58.1.1–3; see Rutledge 2001: 144–46; McHugh 2020: 143–46 for discussion of the case.
63. See Cass. Dio 58.1.3; cf. Plin. *HN* 8.145 where Pliny recounts not just the loyalty of Sabinus' dog, but also gives unpleasant details about his execution and mutilation.
64. Tac. *Ann.* 4.70.7.
65. Tac. *Ann.* 4.74.3; on the numerous statues set up to Sejanus throughout Rome and their significance see Champlin 2012: 373.
66. Tac. *Ann.* 4.76; as Martin and Woodman 1989: 262–63, note, this union mirrors and contrasts the seduction of Livilla by Sejanus at the opening of the book and stands in contrast to the imperial disapproval given to any marriage connection between them.
67. Tac. *Ann.* 5.3.1; for her obituary notice see Tac. *Ann.* 5.1.
68. For the whole episode in which the final moves are made to eliminate Nero, Agrippina, and Drusus, see Tac. *Ann.* 5.3–5.
69. The Roman attitude towards homosexuality was a complicated one, and depended on status as well as whether one was the passive or active partner. The best general study of the phenomenon is Williams 1999.
70. Suet. *Tib.* 53.2. An ancient Roman form of asylum was to take refuge at the statue of a god or (later) emperor if the emperor were considered a *divus*, i.e., of divine status. Agrippina and her family were widely popular and this extended to the armies of the Rhine that Germanicus had formerly led into battle; they even affectionately imposed the name Caligula on his son Gaius, a diminutive meaning 'little boots' after the baby military *caligae* (boots) he wore as a toddler.
71. Cotta Messalinus, a man of high standing, stood out for his craven viciousness in his opinion against Agrippina and Nero, Tac. *Ann.* 5.3, while Junius Rusticus (Tac. *Ann.* 5.4) stood out for his brave but futile opposition.
72. For the arrest, sentencing, exile, and death of Agrippina see Suet. *Tib.* 53; Philo's nemesis Flaccus Avillius appears to have been one of her accusers, see Philo *Flacc.* 9; for Nero's declaration as a public enemy see Suet. *Tib.* 54.2, *Cal.* 7. See McHugh 2020: 156–58 for the arrests of Agrippina and Nero.
73. Suet. *Tib.* 64.
74. Cass. Dio 58.2.7–8.
75. Tac. *Ann.* 6.40.4; see McHugh 2020: 159–60 for the elimination of Drusus.
76. Suet. *Tib.* 54.2, *Cal.* 7; Cass. Dio 58.3.8.
77. For Tiberius' intimate monikers see Cass. Dio 58.4.3; for his betrothal to a member of the imperial family see Tac. *Ann.* 4.40.11; Cass. Dio 58.7.5. We are uncertain precisely who this was – Livilla, the widow of Tiberius' son Drusus, is one suggestion despite Tiberius' previous refusal; so too is the ex-wife of the now exiled Nero, Julia, daughter of Livilla and Drusus. Both have been suggested but the issue is by no means certain, despite Dio's claim at 58.3.9 that it was indeed Julia, daughter of Drusus and Livilla. Whether Sejanus was connected to the imperial house upon his death is problematic, since he is referred to as *gener* which can mean both son-in-law and future son-in-law; see Tac. *Ann.* 5.6.2, 6.8.6; cf. Suet. *Tib.* 65.1 where he notes that this was a part of Tiberius' deception as he started to move against Sejanus. For discussion of the significance of the titles heaped on Sejanus see Champlin 2012: 373–74; McHugh 2020: 153–55.
78. Cass. Dio 58.4.4.
79. Cass. Dio 58.4.1–2; McHugh 2020: 166–67 views this otherwise, arguing that it was not until well into 31 that Tiberius began to plan Sejanus' fall.
80. Roman emperors – and senators – were consummate actors when they had to be. Nero reportedly gave a *tour de force* performance when he bid his mother farewell for the last time as he prepared to murder her, Tac. *Ann.* 14.4. For an outstanding study of the role of theatricality in Roman imperial politics, where senators had to put on the proper 'mask' as it were in appeasing the emperor, see Bartsch 1994.

81. See Jos. *AJ* 18.181–82. Pallas was to go on to be very powerful at the court of the emperor Claudius and to survive early into Nero's reign, becoming one of the richest men in the empire; his brother, Antonius Felix, was to become procurator of Judaea (AD 52–60) and oversee in part the case against Paul. For Pallas' career see Oost 1958.
82. Jos. *AJ* 18.181.
83. Cass. Dio 65.14.1; Caenis was later to become the mistress of Vespasian, Suet. *Vesp.* 3, 21; Cass. Dio 65.14.1–4.
84. Jos. *AJ* 18.180; cf. Val. Max. 4.3.3.
85. See Levick 1990: 25; for a detailed discussion of the relationship between Antonia and Sejanus, and Antonia's role – or lack thereof – in Sejanus' demise see Nichols 1975: *passim*; for Sejanus' taking aim at Gaius Caligula see Nichols 1975: 55, citing Tac. *Ann.* 6.3.4; Suet. *Tib.* 61; cf. McHugh 2020: 170–76 for Tiberius, Gaius, and the struggle over Gaius' succession; for Antonia's role in Sejanus' fall see McHugh 2020: 172–74 who argues that Antonia's affection for her grandson did indeed motivate her involvement in imperial politics at this juncture.
86. Tac. *Ann.* 6.3.4.
87. See Cass. Dio 58.5.1–4.
88. See Levick 1990: 106; also see Syme 1956: *passim*; Ehrenberg and Jones 1976: 53 = *CIL* 6.10213; see McHugh 2020: 167–68 for discussion.
89. Cass. Dio 58.5.1.
90. On Sejanus' assumption of the office of consul and the ill omens that attended see McHugh 2020: 130–31.
91. For the psychological game Tiberius played in order to keep Sejanus off balance see Cass. Dio 58.6.2–5.
92. Cass. Dio 58.7.1–3; see McHugh 2020: 98 and Champlin 2012: 381–86 for discussion of Sejanus and his relationship with Fortuna; Champlin includes in his discussion the significant connections, too, between Sejanus and King Servius.
93. Cass. Dio 58.7.4–58.8.1; see McHugh 2020: 175–76 for discussion – to ally suspicion Sejanus and his son Strabo were elevated to the same priesthood.
94. See Cass. Dio 58.8.3–4; for his death see Suet. *Tib.* 54; see McHugh 2020: 177 for discussion.
95. See McHugh 2020: 177–78.
96. See McHugh 2020: 168–72 for Sejanus' own popularity and for his moves against Gaius, the future emperor Caligula, who was also a popular figure.
97. Cass. Dio 58.8.2.
98. Cass. Dio 58.8.3.
99. Cass. Dio 58.8.4.
100. Cass. Dio 58.8.4; on Macro, his family, career, and connections, see McHugh 2020: 181; he was married to Ennia Thrasylla, granddaughter of Thrasyllus, Tiberius' court astrologer.
101. This included the use of Drusus, still in prison, as commander-in-chief of armed forces to oppose Sejanus; see Suet. *Tib.* 65.1–2 for Tiberius' alternate plans in case of failure; for the significance of this see McHugh 2020: 160-61.
102. For Macro as Sejanus' successor see Jos. *AJ* 18.186; see Cass. Dio 58.9.2–3 for Sertorius' deception of Sejanus.
103. For the detailed events of the morning leading up to the reading of the letter in the Senate see Cass. Dio 58.9.4–6; for discussion of his arrest and imprisonment see McHugh 2020: 183–87.
104. Suet. *Tib.* 65.1.
105. See Cass. Dio 58.10.1–5 for the reading and contents of the letter.
106. The same concern as that mentioned in Cassius Dio is also mentioned in Suet. *Tib.* 65.1.
107. For the scene of his arrest in the Senate see Cass. Dio 58.10.6–8.
108. Cass. Dio 58.11.3.
109. For the scene in which he is led to prison and the reflection on human fortune see Cass. Dio 58.11.1–2.

110. Cass Dio 58.11.4–5.
111. Cass. Dio 58.11.5.
112. Bleasus' two sons were also later executed, see Tac. *Ann.* 6.40.3. Sejanus had had three children with his ex-wife Apicata, Tac. *Ann.* 4.3.5; the identity of the third child is a matter of some dispute, but one can safely assume his eldest son Strabo who had already come of age. That all of them were executed in the wake of their father's demise is indicated in Tac. *Ann.* 6.4.1 and Dio 58.11.6; for the bloody aftermath of Sejanus' fall see McHugh 2020: 196–204.
113. Tac. *Ann.* 6.4; the horrifying sexual details are also noted in Suet. *Tib.* 61.5 and in Cass. Dio 58.11.5.
114. Cass. Dio 58.11.6.
115. That Livilla was quickly and soon executed after Sejanus and certainly dead by New Year of 32 is indicated at Tac. *Ann.* 6.2.1.
116. Cass. Dio 58.11.7.
117. See Tac. *Ann.* 6.23–24 for the ultimate fate of Drusus; cf. Suet. *Tib.* 65.2.
118. Tac. *Ann.* 6.23.6; cf. Cass. Dio 58.22.4 who gives a similar motive in connection with the continued persecution and confinement of Drusus and his mother Agrippina; for Theodorus' remark see Suet. *Tib.* 57.1.
119. For Agrippina's end and Tiberius' response see Tac. *Ann.* 6.25.
120. Asinius Gallus was arrested under mysterious circumstances and was subsequently starved to death or starved himself to death while under house arrest; see Tac. *Ann.* 6.23.1; Cass. Dio 58.3.1–7; for discussion see McHugh 2020: 124–25.

Chapter 4: A Roman Governor: Pontius Pilate

1. See Wroe 1999.
2. See Carter 2003: 3–11, whose study also includes a succinct but solid discussion of Roman governors in their provinces, see 2003: 35–54. Carter's study consists as well of four individual chapters, each of which is an individual study of the characterization of Pilate in each of the four gospels.
3. See Plin. *Ep.* 10.97 for Trajan's response.
4. For Tacitus' ethnography of the Jewish people, their origins, and the history of Rome's relationship with them, see *Hist.* 5.1–13; for discussion of Tacitus' representation of Judaism see Gruen 2016: 265–82; Bruce 1984: 33–44.
5. Aniconic, meaning that they did not allow images, although there were some stunning exceptions, as for example the synagogue at Dura Europas on the Euphrates in Syria, which has now been moved to the National Museum in Damascus. Images such as scenes from the life of Moses (in Roman garb) abound in the frescoes from Dura.
6. For a good general discussion with further references see Beard, North, and Price 1998: 80, 92, 96–98, 160, 164–66, 260, 272, 298, 337–38 (for the Great Mother); see 91–96 (for the cult of Bacchus and its suppression); see 161, 180, 222, 230, 250, 264, 266, 269, 277, 279, 281–84, 287–89, 291–92, 294, 296, 298, 301–302, 307–309, 383–84 (for the cult of Isis).
7. For Cicero's governorship of Cilicia we have a first-hand account with reports scattered among correspondents with his friends. See Cic. *ad fam.* 2.7, 2.9–13, 2.15, 2.17, 2.19, 3.2, 3.5–12, 13.56–7, 13.64–65, 15.1–4, 15.6, 15.9, 15.14 – this is by no means a complete list of his correspondence to friends (and from friends) while governor of Cilicia, but are those letters most nearly concerned with governing his province, though there are plenty of extraneous subjects in them as well – e.g. financial concerns or concerns over politics back in Rome. Of these the longest and one of the most informative is 15.4 to Cato the Younger, which gives us a sense of Cicero's actions in the provinces and a good taste of Ciceronian vanity.
8. Set down now in studied detail in an excellent monograph by Miles: 2010.
9. Cicero, *Verr.* 2.4.30; cf. 2.4.47; see Miles 2010: (n. 2), 175, 205–206 for discussion; cf. Rutledge 2012: 50.
10. A renowned general of the republic, Titus Flamininus took one of the remaining three from Macedonia in the 190s BC, but had the decency to dedicate it to Jupiter on the Capitoline, making it public property, Cicero, *Verr.* 2.4.128–30.

11. *Verr.* 2.4.122; cf. 2.2.50 where Cicero accuses Verres of plundering Syracuse's temples of every artwork imaginable.
12. Cic. *Verr.* 2.4.32.
13. Cic. *Verr.* 2.4.1–2.
14. Cic. *Verr.* 2.4.12–14.
15. For discussion see Vasaly 1993: 111–14; Bounia 2004: 277; cf. Stewart 2003: 142, who notes that Heius' house was something of a public museum in its own right, citing Cicero, *Verr.* 2.4.3–7; cf. Miles 2010: 155, 206–8 on Heius' collection.
16. For the whole episode of Verres' sojourn at Lampsacus see Cic. *Verr.* 2.1.63–85.
17. See p. 130 for Galba's crime and a more detailed account of its results.
18. Juv. 1.48–50.
19. See Plin. *Ep.* 2.11–12.
20. Suet. *Galb.* 9.1.
21. *Acts* 25:12.
22. See Rudich 2015: 110 for discussion of Pilate's forebears in this office; see Rudich 2015: 110–114 for a summary of Pilate's reign which only briefly touches on his encounter with Jesus.
23. Schiavone 2016: 59–60 notes that *procurator* was the term given to Judaea's governor only from the time of the emperor Claudius (AD 41–54) onward. The inscription concerning Pilate reads … S TIBERIEUM/ … NTIUS PILATUS/ … ECTUS IUDAE[A]E/ … E … – first published in 1961, it has been restored and conjectured to have fully read as follows: CAESARIENSIBUS TIBERIEVM PONTIVS PILATVS PRAEFECTVS IVDAEAE DEDIT, which translated reads literally, 'Pontius Pilate the prefect of Judaea gave the Tibereium to the people of Caesarea.'
24. Schiavone 2016: 53; see Wroe 1999: 13–16 for the Pontii, who came from Samnium in south central Italy.
25. See Schiavone 2016: 56.
26. See e.g., *BJ* 2.169–77 and *AJ* 18.55–62, 85–89.
27. For this episode see Jos. *AJ* 18.55; cf. *BJ* 2.169–77 where Pilate receives considerably less expanded discussion and attention than in *AJ* – a scant two paragraphs is all the space he is allotted in the *BJ*. Josephus there notes, in addition to his marching the images into Jerusalem, his appropriation of the sacred treasury for the construction of an aqueduct and his massacre of those protesting his actions, see pp. 82–3.
28. See Jos. *AJ* 18.56.
29. For the disturbance this caused and Pilate's ultimate capitulation see Jos. *AJ* 18.57–59.
30. As astutely noted by Rudich 2015: 112, 115.
31. Schiavone 2016: 86–90; it should be noted that in contrast Rudich 2015: 110–114 takes a very dim view of Pilate's actions in Judaea.
32. Jos. *AJ* 18.120–23.
33. For the whole incident and the ensuing disastrous Roman response see Jos. *AJ* 18.60–62; for discussion see Schiavone 2016: 90–93.
34. See e.g., Schiavone 2016: 91.
35. Schiavone 2016: 84–85 does not accept Philo's characterization of Pilate as the malignant Verrine type governor that he is made out to be; he bases this on what he views as a schematic and not terribly specific depiction of his misdeeds, and argues that the reason for Philo's depiction is Pilate's lack of sensitivity towards Jewish religion and culture. He does grant, though, that Pilate was insensitive to Jewish religious practice and custom. Carter 2003: 15–19 looks at how the three major and roughly contemporary sources for Pilate, Philo, Josephus, and the gospels, each present Pilate. Carter 2003: 15–16 like Schiavone sees Philo's negative spin on Pilate as a stock or stereotypic caricature of a bad Roman governor, and both are inclined to dismiss it. The problem is that Philo is our closest source to Pilate – closer than the New Testament by far, and our other sources that criticize Roman governors tend to be Roman ones themselves. These, too, are schematic. However, just because we do not have specific, incisive details does not mean corruption and mismanagement were

absent. What would we know specifically of Verres' misdeeds, after all, but not for the survival of Cicero?

36. For the whole incident see Philo, *Leg.* 299–305; for the shields see Schiavone 2016: 174–75; see Hoehner 1972: 179–80 concerning why even aniconic shields with inscriptions would have been a religious violation for the Jewish community and for the timing of the incident which he dates to after AD 31.
37. See Philo *Leg.* 300; for discussion see Hoehner 1972: 176–78; Wroe 1999: 110–113.
38. Philo *Leg.* 302.
39. Schiavone 2016: 58–59 remains unconvinced of a close relationship between the two, rightly noting that Pilate survived the fall of the prefect in AD 31.
40. See Eus. *Hist. Eccl.* 2.5; Philo *Flacc.* 1.
41. For the expulsion of AD 19 see Jos. *AJ* 18.65–84; Tac. *Ann.* 2.85; Suet. *Tib.* 36; Cass. Dio 57.18.5a; see pp. 36–7.
42. See Jos. *AJ* 18.65–84 for details concerning the case: Tiberius also disallowed Jewish worship in Rome and forced them to burn their sacred vestments and implements; Jews of military age under the pretext of conscription were sent off to 'unhealthy' regions, and any Jew disobeying Tiberius' edict to leave the city was threatened with slavery. Also see pp. 36–7 for the episode, which is closely associated with the temporary shutdown of the cult of Isis as well. See Schiavone 2016: 58–59 for discussion; as Rudich 2015: 107–108 notes, it is hard, apart from Caligula's absurd desire to impose imperial worship on Jews, to detect any anti-Semitic policies among the Julio-Claudians.
43. Jos. *AJ* 18.63–64. For a good current discussion of the passage see Wallace-Hadrill 2011: 353. Schiavone 2016: 93–94 accepts the passage as authentic and uses it to argue for the cooperation of Jewish and Roman authorities in the arrest and execution of Jesus.
44. Also see Eus. *Hist. Eccl.* 2.2; cf. Tert. *Apol.* 21.24; see Schiavone 2016: 170–71 who argues that Pilate's report to Tiberius about Christ should not be downplayed or dismissed, arguing that Pilate will have wanted to have preempted any possible bad reports from local Jewish leadership over his response to the situation, and Tiberius had a close relationship with Herod's family, which was still ruling in the region.
45. For the entire episode see Jos. *AJ* 18.85–89.
46. See Hoehner 1972: 174 n. 6.
47. Tac. *Ann.* 6.32.6.
48. Schiavone 2016: 179.
49. See Jos. *AJ* 18.172–77 for the story; for discussion see Carter 2003: 50–52.
50. As Schiavone 2016: 13 phrases it in a series of questions, 'what was Pilate's role really? That of a despot? An accomplice? A bungler?'
51. Ovid's exile remains one of the more controversial mysteries of antiquity and has given rise to what one scholar once referred to as the 'Ovid in exile' industry; the poet tells us of his night of exile but not the reason, vaguely attributing it to a *carmen et error* – a poem and a mistake, *Trist.* 2.207.
52. See p. 18.
53. For a detailed history of Scribonius' conspiracy see Andrew Pettinger's provocative and fascinating 2012 study.
54. See Tac. *Ann.* 2.69.5 and cf. Suet. *Cal.* 3.3 for magic and witchcraft in Germanicus' case; see Tac. *Ann.* 2.71–72 for Germanicus' death; see Tac. *Ann.* 3.10–18 for Piso's trial and suicide; see Bodel 1999; Damon 1999; Talbert 1999, all in a special edition of *AJP* dedicated to the discussion of the punishment of Piso in light of new evidence from an inscription discovered in Spain.
55. See Tac. *Ann.* 3.49–51 for Clutorius' case; cf. Cass. Dio 57.20.3–4.
56. Philostr. *VA* 8.3.
57. See pp. 49, 51 for Pulchra's case.
58. Schiavone 2016: 38–42 is right to avoid the term trial, given the lack of strict legal niceties that were present. It is more accurate to term Jesus' encounter with the Roman legal system as more of a hearing rather than anything that followed normal civil or

criminal proceedings which was the exclusive right of a citizen, so I avoid the use of the word 'trial' in the context of Jesus' ordeal. Wroe 1999: 227–28 sees it as a trial, but given the example of Pliny and others in terms of their treatment of non-citizens this almost certainly would not have been the case.

59. *Matthew* 21:8–10; *Mark* 11:8–10; *Luke* 19:37–39; *John* 12:12–15. In *Luke's* version it should be noted that his entrance is somewhat more muted than in *Mark* and *Matthew*, but he is still attended by a 'multitude'.
60. *Mark* 11:18; cf. *Mark* 12:12 where he states 'they sought to lay hold on him, but feared the people'; similarly see *Luke* 20:19; 22:2.
61. See Schiavone 2016: 41–43 where he also notes that they likely met in haste to quickly make up a credible charge against Jesus to present to the Romans; Schiavone also assumes plausibly some form of cooperation, though it may have been limited, between Pilate, Caiaphas, and Annas. Also see Schiavone 2016: 80 who notes this body probably 'served as a court for religious matters'.
62. For Caiaphas' appointment and deposition see Jos. *AJ* 18.35, 95. For discussion see Schiavone 2016: 79–80 who notes that governors had the right to appoint the high priest (usually chosen from among the Sadducees since there was good cooperation between them and the Roman authorities) and Pilate kept on Caiaphas for the entire length of his tenure (Caiaphas had been nominated by Valerius Gratus and confirmed by Pilate). Governors had discretion to decide the amount of power high priests could wield, and had complete jurisdiction over religious affairs with the possible though likely exception of imposing the death penalty. The high priest would also have had pretty much complete control of the Temple, including the finances of it, and as Schiavone points out, the Temple functioned as a type of autonomous city-state within Jerusalem and Judaea, including having its own police force such as possibly the very one that arrested Jesus.
63. Schiavone 2016: 47–48 who also notes that in *John* (18:14) Caiaphas had said that 'it was expedient that one man should die for the people'; cf. *John* 11:50.
64. The whole episode of Jesus' interrogation at Pilate's hands is related in *Matthew* 27:1–25, *Mark* 15:1–15, and *Luke* 23:1–25.
65. *Luke* 23:2; the Greek verb for 'to pervert' or 'to overthrow' is *diatrepō*, a verb that is vague enough but even more so in the circumstances; *Christos* in this instance refers to an anointed king (*chriō* translates 'I anoint'), looking back to the ceremonies of Solomon and David, a ceremony that would be adopted for religious reasons by the Medieval kings of Europe, starting in earnest with Charlemagne, as a statement about both their royal and religious authority. Schiavone 2016: 100 notes that in *Luke* Jesus is accused of wanting the Jews not to pay tax to Caesar and of making himself king, both grave offences against the Roman state. See Wroe 1999: 197–99 for the negative opinion Romans had of kings, but this is a well-documented antipathy. For interpreters on a governor's staff see e.g., Caes. *BGall.* 1.47.4.
66. *Matthew* 27:11; *Mark* 15:2; *Luke* 23:3.
67. *Matthew* 27:11; cf. *Mark* 15:2; *Luke* 23:3.
68. *Matthew* 27:13; cf. *Mark* 15:4.
69. See pp. 123–4 for discussion.
70. See *Matthew*. 27:14–16; *Mark* 15:6–11, who adds the detail at 15:7 not found in *Matthew* that Barabbas 'had made insurrection with him, who had committed murder in the insurrection'; cf. *Luke* 23:19 who says Barabbas had been cast into prison for sedition and murder. Schiavone 2016: 133–34 sees the presentation of Jesus to the crowd and the attempt to exchange Jesus with Barabbas as the result of a dangerous impasse between the Jewish and Roman authorities at this juncture in Jesus' hearing, Pilate veering towards release, the Sanhedrin believing that its prestige would be seriously damaged were Jesus set free.
71. *Matthew* 27:17; *Mark* 15:7–11.
72. Also noted by Schiavone 2016: 138.
73. The word *ho ochlos* in both the singular and plural (*hoi ochloi*) is used e.g. at *Mark* 15:8, and *Matthew* 27: 20.

74. The precise word used in both gospels – *Matthew* 27:18 and *Mark* 15:10 is *phthonos*, which can be translated as malice, spite, envy, or ill will.
75. Indeed, Schiavone 2016: 135–38 postulates that the 'multitude' was more or less the Sanhedrin and its staff of guards and other administrative officials; both the *Matthew* and *Mark* passages agree that the authorities could find none to bear false witness against Jesus, until in *Matthew* two are found, while *Mark* more vaguely states 'many' were found but notes that 'their witness agreed not together'.
76. See Schiavone 2016: 139.
77. *Matthew* 27:19. Schiavone 2016: 128 casts doubt on even the existence of Pilate's wife, and argues that wives were usually not permitted to go with their husbands when they were given an imperial post, but this changed between the republic and the empire, and all the more considering the extended appointments – recall ten years in the case of Pilate – under Tiberius; see Marshall 1975: 11–18 for a good discussion of this phenomenon. A debate in the Senate in AD 22 related in Tac. *Ann.* 3.33–34 certainly implies wives were, by that date, accompanying their husbands to the provinces they were assigned to govern.
78. Suet. *Caes.* 81.3.
79. Plin. *Ep.* 5.5; see Syme 1968: 148 for Fannius and his origins.
80. The demand for Jesus' crucifixion is a suspicious one, given Jewish attitudes towards it as a punishment, see Maccoby 1980: 35–37; Schiavone 2016: 148.
81. Annas himself had been a high priest from AD 6 until 15, appointed to the post by Quirinius, governor of Syria and deposed by Valerius Gratus; for discussion see Schiavone 2016: 37–38.
82. See Schiavone 2016: 146–48 for Pilate's intent in scourging Jesus. In *John* Pilate's flagellation of Christ is attempted as an alternative to execution, an alternative that ultimately fails, while in *Matthew* and *Mark* it is a preliminary to execution.
83. Schiavone 2016: 159–60.
84. See Schiavone 2016: 10 for the non-historical nature and intent of the gospels.
85. Tert. *Apol.* 21.24; see Schiavone 2016: 170–71.
86. See Schiavone 2016: 142–43.
87. See Schiavone 2016: 141–44.

Chapter 5: The Tetrarch: Herod Antipas

1. There are no less than three discrete monographs devoted exclusively to Herod Antipas, including Webb 2018; Jensen 2006; and Hoehner 1972. Among these Jensen 2006: 35–44 has an excellent summary of the history of the scholarship on Antipas.
2. In the gospels and local parlance he was often referred to as *basileus* or king, but this may have been nothing more than a local courtesy and traditional title among the Jewish population, see Hoehner 1972: 149–51.
3. Josephus is our main and essential literary source for the history of Antipas, his family and reign; see Jensen 2006: 53–68; for a survey of the remaining sources see Jensen 2006: 101–103, of which Nicolaus of Damascus, who lived during the reign of Augustus, is among our more important, although his work survives in mere fragments.
4. Tac. *Ann.* 4.5–6.
5. Tac. *Hist.* 5.9–10.1.
6. For an excellent summation of the history of the province from initial Roman involvement under Pompey the Great to the advent of Herod see Rudich 2015: 89–94.
7. Not very long afterwards in 57 BC Aulus Gabinius, the governor of Syria and a political ally of Pompey the Great, divided Judaea into five discrete administrative regions governed by Sanhedrins and maintained Hyrcanus as high priest. See Schiavone 2016: 71 for discussion.
8. Tac. *Ann.* 2.42.7.
9. For the rebellions in Africa and Gaul see p. 132.
10. For a general study of Rome and client kingship see Braund 1984; for a good succinct summation of the reign of Herod the Great see Rudich 2015: 94–101.

11. See Jos. *AJ* 17.20; *BJ* 1.562; for his birth and parentage see Hoehner 1972: 11–12.
12. For Herod Antipas' early upbringing in Judaea and then Rome see Hoehner 1972: 12–17.
13. For a good succinct discussion see Jensen 2006: 181–4; also see Holum 1993 and 1997 for summaries of the excavations conducted at Caesarea.
14. See *AJ* 15.267–76.
15. See especially *AJ* 15.275–76.
16. For the whole episode see Jos. *AJ* 17.149–65; cf. *BJ* 1.648, 650.
17. For the execution of Matthias and his followers see Jos. *AJ* 17.167; *BJ* 1.650 he does not mention Judas by name but we can guess he was among those who shared Matthias' fate.
18. Jos. *AJ* 16.201–205.
19. Jos. *AJ* 16.206–208.
20. Jos. *AJ* 16.244–53, 16.300–312; cf. *BJ* 1.467–75, 495, 516–27, for Antipater's intrigues.
21. Jos. *AJ* 16.313–24.
22. See Jos. *AJ* 16.328–94 for this whole extended and detailed episode; cf. *BJ* 1.538–51; see Hoehner 1972: 9 for discussion.
23. Jos. *AJ* 17.185–87; *BJ* 1.661–64.
24. Macrob. *Sat.* 2.4.11.
25. Jos. *AJ* 17.188; cf. Jos. *BJ* 1.646, 664, 668; for Herod's change of heart see Hoehner 1972: 10–11, 18–19; see Rudich 2015: 101–105 for Archelaus' reign.
26. For the episode see Jos. *AJ* 17.206–209, 213–18; cf. Jos. *BJ* 2.10–13.
27. For the slaughter inside the Temple see Jos. *AJ* 17.237; see Hoehner 1972: 28.
28. For a good discussion of the hearing before Augustus and the parties' claims, see Hoehner 1972: 18–39.
29. For the whole episode of the embassy to Rome and the competing claims of Archelaus and Antipas see Jos. *AJ* 17.220–49; cf. *BJ* 2.20–38; for Salome's role in the trial see Hoehner 1972: 22–27.
30. See Jos. *AJ* 17.227.
31. *Ibid.*
32. Jos. *AJ* 17.230–39.
33. For Nicolas' speech see Jos. *AJ* 17.240–47; for his influence with Augustus see Hoehner 1972: 28–30.
34. For the entirety of the revolt see Jos. *AJ* 17.250–98; *BJ* 2.39–79; see Hoehner 1972: 35–38 for discussion.
35. For the entire episode, including Sabinus' taking control of the citadels see Jos. *AJ* 17.220–23; *BJ* 2.39–41.
36. Jos. *AJ* 17.252–53.
37. Jos. *AJ* 17.254; *BJ* 2.42–44.
38. Jos. *AJ* 17.271.
39. Jos. *AJ* 17.273–74.
40. Jos. *AJ* 17.283.
41. Jos. *AJ* 17.278–84; Jos. *BJ* 2.60–65 where he is called Anthrongaeus; see Hoehner 1972: 83 for discussion.
42. Romans were not shy about mass crucifixion; M. Licinius Crassus, the wealthiest man in Rome who was given command to crush the Spartacus rebellion in 71 BC crucified 6,000 slave and gladiator rebels, lining the Via Appia from Rome to Capua, App. *BCiv.* 1.120.
43. See Jos. *AJ* 17.299–316; *BJ* 2.79–100.
44. See Jos. *AJ* 17.303 who tells us that Philip was friendly with Varus who wanted to help Philip have a share of the rule in the region once the partition he saw coming was effected.
45. For the delegation and its complaints see Jos. *AJ* 17.304–14.
46. See Mason 2016: 250. He notes in general throughout his study that much of what drove ostensible conflict between Rome and Judaea had often to do with inter-ethnic

conflict within the regions of Judaea, Samaria, Galilee, Peraea, and the various other small regions of the area.

47. For the precise details of the settlement see Jos. *BJ* 2.93–100.
48. See Hoehner 1972: 23–31; cf. Jensen 2006: 222–24.
49. See Hoehner 1972: 31–32.
50. See Jos. *AJ* 17.350; *BJ* 2.114–16; cf. Strabo 17.3.7 for Juba's death in AD 23.
51. See *Leviticus* 18:16, 20:21 for the prohibition.
52. See Jos. *AJ* 17.342–44 for Archelaus' trial before Caesar and his downfall; cf. Strabo 16.2.46; Jos. *BJ* 2.111–12; Cass. Dio 55.27.6; see Hoehner 1972: 103–109; Jensen 2006: 104–106 for discussion.
53. See Jos. *BJ* 2.167; see Hoehner 1972: 105–109 for discussion.
54. See Jos. *AJ* 17.355; 18.1–2; *BJ* 2.117; Quirinius moved in very high circles and was friends with Tiberius who delivered his funeral eulogy in AD 21, see Tac. *Ann.* 3.48.
55. Schiavone 2016: 60 notes that the governor of Judaea was independent from the governor of Syria but that Judaea was demilitarized while Syria was not, and so Syria's governor had greater heft. Pilate had ultimate power in his province, but the governor of Judaea came over time to consider the governor of Syria 'a senior colleague' in the administration of the region in particular circumstances. For the full authority given to governors of Judaea starting with Coponius see Jos. *AJ* 18.2.
56. See Jos. *AJ* 18.3–4; *BJ* 2.118; cf. *Acts* 5:37; see Hoehner 1972: 83 for a brief discussion; see Mason 2016: 245–57 for Judas, who Mason argues was targeting Judaeans, not Romans per se, and notes part of the motive for their unrest was the potential loss of Jerusalem's pre-eminence.
57. Jos. *AJ* 18.5–10 for Judas' notions concerning Roman rule.
58. Jos. *AJ* 18.23–25; cf. *BJ* 2.118.
59. For the Pharisees, Sadducees, and Essenes see Jos. *AJ* 18.11–22; *BJ* 2.119–66; the existence of this fourth school has been questioned by some, but for Josephus' reference to the movements of Judas and Saddok as such see Jos. *AJ* 18.9. For a discussion on Josephus' digression see Jensen 2006: 79–80.
60. Livias was later renamed Julias when Livia was adopted officially into the Julian clan after AD 14, though after the first century it appears to have reverted back to the name Livias; for Antipas' building programmes see Jos. *AJ* 18.27–28; for the geography of Galilee under Antipas see Hoehner 1972: 43–46; for Livias see Hoehner 1972: 87–91; for Sepphoris see Hoehner 1972: 84–87 who notes that its proximity as a major centre makes it likely that Jesus will have plied his trade as a carpenter there. For a good discussion on the archaeology of Sepphoris with bibliography see Jensen 2006: 149–62.
61. See Jos. *AJ* 18.36–38; cf. *BJ* 2.168; for Tiberias see Hoehner 1972: 91–100; Jensen 2006: 94–96, 135–49 which includes a detailed discussion of Tiberias' archaeology.
62. See Hoehner 1972: 56–61 for the reputation of the people of Galilee; for the economic state of Galilee see Hoehner 1972: 65–73.
63. See Jensen 2006: 106–109 for discussion; see pp. 83–84 for the incident under Pilate.
64. Chronology can be one of the more vexatious issues in dealing with events in Josephus; see, e.g., Hoehner 1972: 125–31, 170–71 for the problem with the date of John the Baptist's death, Antipas' marriage to Herodias, and the death of Jesus. He concludes plausibly that Antipas married Herodias in 29 or 30 and that John's death occurred in 30 or 31.
65. See Jos. *AJ* 18.109–112 for Antipas' relationship with Herodias; for the problems with the identity of Herodias' husband see Hoehner 1972: 131–36 who concludes that the Herod of Josephus and the Philip of *Matthew* and *Mark* are one and the same.
66. Jos. *AJ* 18.116–19. On John the Baptist in Josephus see now Evans 2007; see also Hoehner 1972: 122–23 who postulates that Josephus' sources for John would have included records kept by the high priest; see Hoehner 1972: 136–46 for discussion of Antipas' motives in arresting John, the nature of his message, and his audience. Jensen 2006: 98–99 sees the execution of John the Baptist as simply an example in Josephus of yet another member of the House of Herod behaving tyrannically.

67. See *Matthew* 3.7–10; *Luke* 3:1–21 for his fire and brimstone preaching; for the representation of John the Baptist in the gospel accounts see Hoehner 1972: 110–122.
68. See *Mark* 6:17–19; *Luke* 3:19; see *Lev.* 20:21 for the Judaic prohibition. Hoehner 1972: 144–45 notes that Josephus may have also implied a connection between Herod's marriage to Herodias and the denunciation of the Baptist, since he relates their marriage immediately before he discusses his preaching.
69. Jos. *AJ* 18.118; according to Hoehner 1972: 136–37 concern over incitement of the people was a prime motive for John's arrest.
70. See *Matthew* 14:5; *Mark* 6:20; Jos. *AJ* 18.117–19.
71. Jos. *AJ* 18.119 says this is where he was executed though the gospels imply he was executed at Tiberias; see Hoehner 1972: 146–49 for discussion.
72. *Mark* and *Matthew* only mention Antipas sporadically, *John* not at all, while it is only in *Luke* that Jesus stands before Antipas in the course of his hearing; for Antipas in *Luke* see Jensen 2006: 114–122.
73. On Herodias' daughter, her identity, and her dancing before Antipas see Hoehner 1972: 151–57.
74. See Hoehner 1972: 158–62 for discussion concerning on whom the burden of responsibility fell for John's death.
75. Hoehner 1972: 161.
76. For Antipas on Jesus as John resurrected see *Matthew* 14.2; *Mark* 6: 14; see Hoehner 1972: 189–91 for discussion.
77. See Hoehner 1972: 199–202.
78. For discussion of the passage in *Luke* see Hoehner 1972: 214–224.
79. See *Luke* 13:31–33; see Hoehner 1972: 224 for discussion. Schiavone doubts the meeting between Herod and Jesus during Jesus' hearing, see Schiavone 2016: 128–30, and argues that Judaea would have been beyond Herod Antipas' jurisdiction. Schiavone suggests that the story is a fiction intended to parallel Herod Agrippa's later persecution of Paul and an effort by the writers of the gospel to load the scales against the Jewish authorities.
80. For a detailed discussion of *Luke's* narrative see Hoehner 1972: 224–32; for the question of jurisdiction see Hoehner 1972: 233–39, who argues Pilate was by no means obliged to relinquish Jesus to Antipas and that it was likely a gesture of diplomacy.
81. For discussion of their enmity see Hoehner 1972: 180–81.
82. See Hoehner 1972: 182–83 who argues the simple courtesy of Pilate's act may have served to reconcile the two and that their enmity mentioned in *Luke* could have arisen over any number of Pilate's actions.
83. See Hoehner 1972: 244–45.
84. See Jensen 2006: 122–24 for discussion of the passage in *Acts*.
85. Jos. *AJ* 18.109–115; for discussion of the conflict between Antipas and Aretas see Hoehner 1972: 142–44 who notes that relations between the Nabataeans and Judaea had been generally good.
86. See Hoehner 1972: 254–56 for Antipas' struggle with Aretas.
87. Jos. *AJ* 18.101–105; see Hoehner 1972: 252–53; Jensen 2006: 92–93 for discussion; presumably Vitellius got his revenge when he assisted Herod Agrippa in deposing Antipas in some way; for Vitellius' stint as governor of Syria see Rudich 2015: 114–115; for a general overview of Tiberius' and Antipas' relationship see Jensen 2006: 224–26.
88. For the breaking off of Vitellius' campaign see Hoehner 1972: 256.
89. See pp. 149–150.
90. Jos. *AJ* 18.116–17.
91. For Aristobulus and his execution, see n. 22; see Jos. *AJ* 18.126–27, 242 for Agrippa's parentage; for Agrippa's machinations against Antipas see Hoehner 1972: 257–63; for Agrippa in the context of Josephus and in relation to Antipas see Jensen 2006: 83–86. The friendship between Claudius and Agrippa is a running thread through Robert Graves' famous treatment of the fourth Roman emperor in his two historical novels of the period, *I, Claudius* and *Claudius the God*.

92. See Jos. *AJ* 18.145–46.
93. See Jos. *AJ* 18.149.
94. See Jos. *AJ* 18.150.
95. Flaccus was a highly placed drinking companion of Tiberius', (see Suet. *Tib.* 42.1) who has a relatively prominent place in his reign – and in Tacitus' *Annals*; see e.g. 2.32, 41, 66–67; he died while governing his province, see Tac. *Ann.* 6.27; also see Ovid *Ex Pont.* 1.10 where the poet addresses a poem to him from his exile.
96. See *AJ* 18.161–62, 18.165–66; we are unsure what motivated Tiberius' change of heart.
97. For Tiberius Gemellus, son of Drusus and Livilla, and grandson of Tiberius, see Jos. *AJ* 18.214–15, 18.219–21; Tac. *Ann.* 6.46; Suet. *Cal.* 23.3; Cass. Dio 59.8.1 – he was put to death suddenly and without warning. Tacitus tells us Tiberius predicted it once when tearfully embracing his grandson in front of Caligula – 'You will kill him' he said to Caligula in reference to Gemellus, 'and another you'. Gemellus may in fact have been Sejanus' son, see p. 44.
98. See Jos. *AJ* 18.185–93; cf. *BJ* 2.179–80.
99. See Jos. *AJ* 18.203–204.
100. See Jos. *AJ* 18.229.
101. See Jos. *AJ* 18.236–37; Lysinias was Iturea in the Lebanon, Jos. *AJ* 15.344.
102. See Jos. *AJ* 18.238.
103. See Jos. *AJ* 18.240–44.
104. See Jos. *AJ* 18.245–47.
105. For the episode of Antipas, Fortunatus, and the letters, see Jos. *AJ* 18.249–52.
106. Jos. *AJ* 18.250; see Hoehner 1972: 101 for discussion; cf. Jensen 2006: 226–27 which includes a brief survey the relationship between Antipas and Caligula.
107. For the possibility of Gaul see Jos. *AJ* 18.252; for Spain see Jos. *BJ* 2.183; see Jos. *BJ* 2.182–83 in general for Antipas' fall from grace.
108. See Jos. *AJ* 18.253–55.
109. See Jensen's 'balance sheet' 2006: 241.

Chapter 6: The Resistance

1. For Galba's command in Spain and his treachery see App. *Hisp.* 58–60; for his defence see Cic. *Brut.* 89–90; Livy *Per.* 49. For Variathus and the war in general see App. *Hisp.* 60–75; Vell. 2.1.3; Front. *Str.* 2.5.7, 2.13.4, 3.10.6, 3.11.4, 4.5.22; Aur. Vict. *De Vir. Ill.* 71; Val. Max. 9.6.4; Eutrop. *Brev.* 4.16; Flor. *Epit.* 1.33; Oros. 5.4; Livy *Per.* 52; Diod. Sic. 33.1 (fragment); Cass. Dio 22.73, 75, 78 (fragments); for a general study of Variathus (sometimes called Viriathus) see Silva 2013.
2. For Andriscus' rebellion see Polyb. 36.10; Livy *Per.* 49–50, 52; Vell. 1.11.1–2; Diod. Sic. 31.40 (fragment); Paus. 7.13.1; Flor. 1.30.
3. The ancient bibliography on Mithridates is ample, but our most significant ancient sources include Appian's history of Rome's war with Mithridates, while substantial portions of Plutarch's lives of Sulla, Lucullus, and Pompey the Great are taken up with the subject; Cicero's speech *De Lege Manilia* (On the Manilian Law) is exclusively about honouring Pompey the Great with an extraordinary command against Mithridates; there are now no less than three major recent studies on Mithridates and his kingdom of Pontus; see Mayor 2011; Roller 2020; Matyszak 2020.
4. A war related in detail in Sallust's war monograph the *Bellum Jugurthinum*, or *War with Jugurtha*.
5. Perhaps to the delight of its residents – his father, also Manius Aquillius, had been over-zealous in his extraction of taxes from the provincials; for Manius' death see App. *Mith.* 21.
6. See App. *Mith.* 22.
7. See Tac. *Ann.* 4.24.1; cf. Tac. *Hist.* 4.54.
8. There is a possibility that there was a religious element to Arminius' ambush though this is conjectural: during the punitive expeditions against him conducted by Germanicus we hear that the German peoples gathered in a forest sacred to their ancient German version of Hercules, Tac. *Ann.* 2.12.1–2; for the special place of Hercules among the

Germans see Tac. *Germ.* 3.1; see Dyson 1971: 257 for discussion. The sacrifice at altars of some of Arminius' Roman captives indicates a religious element may well have been standard practice of northern peoples; see e.g. Heather 2006: 92–93. For a good general study of Arminius and his ambush see Wells 2004.

9. For the revolt see Tac. *Ann.* 3.40–47.
10. For Tacfarinas' revolt see Tac. *Ann.* 2.52, 3.20–21, 3.32.1, 4.23–26.
11. For an excellent recent commentary on the *Agricola*, whose introduction is accessible to the non-Latin reader, see Woodman (with Kraus) 2014.
12. For the speech see Tac. *Agr.* 30–32.
13. The following is not a precise word-for-word translation, but a paraphrased summary that gives the sense of the remainder of Calgacus' speech from Tac. *Agr.* 31–32.
14. The Brigantes reference is problematic; for discussion see Ogilvie and Richmond 1967: 260; Woodman 2014: 248.
15. The Latin word for 'instruments' in the Latin text is *manus*, and I follow Woodman's translation (2014: 253), but it often literally means a band of men, and refers to the auxiliaries Romans employed in their armies.
16. Tac. *Agr.* 33.1.
17. Tac. *Agr.* 38.1–2.
18. For discussion of how this phrase recalls Calgacus', see Woodman 2014: 282.
19. Rudich 2015: 267–85 sees Masada as an instance of extreme religious dissidence led by the *sicarii*.
20. Livy 28.22–23.
21. App. *Hisp.* 97; for a good general discussion over the preferable fate of death to slavery see Bradley 1994: 44.
22. Cass. Dio 54.5.1–3.
23. App. *BCiv.* 4.80.
24. App. *Pun.* 130–31.
25. Flor. *Epit.* 1.31.
26. E.g., an argument could be made for the Second Sacred War of the early 440s BC, when in central Greece Phokis attempted to wrest control of the Delphic Oracle from Delphi itself, as a possible exception, though this became something of a proxy war between Athens and Sparta and little is known about the conflict; similarly there were hostilities over the control of Elis which determined the control over the Olympic Games and the site of Olympia that was sacred to Zeus and Hera, but this too appears to have occurred in the context of a conflict whose motives were by no means religious, see Xen. *Hell.* 7.4.29–32.
27. As in the case of Julius Caesar who secured his election as Pontifex Maximus through shameless bribery; however, although people were indignant at his methods, they did not contend his investiture with that office; see e.g. Plut. *Caes.* 7.1–4; Suet. *Caes.* 13; Cass. Dio 37.37.
28. Hence Socrates is attacked for introducing 'new gods' into Athens, but also charged with atheism, while in Rome the cult of Bacchus took a populist approach, usurping the elite's role in the cult for which its members paid dearly; for the whole episode of the suppression of Bacchus' cult see Livy 39.8–19; for discussion see Beard, North, and Price 1998: 91–96.
29. See Beard 2009 for an outstanding history of the Roman triumph and how it changed and developed over time.
30. For Herodotus' religious attitudes see the monumental study by Harrison 2000.
31. Interestingly both deities were Juno; for the *evocatio* at, e.g., Veii see Livy 5.21.1–4, 5.22.3–8; cf. Lactant. *Div. Inst.* 2.7.11; cf. 2.16.11; see Rutledge 2007: 181 for discussion and bibliography.
32. For contentions specifically over the Delphic Oracle in Athens see Hdt. 7.140–43; for Ajax see Hdt. 8.64; cf. 8.121.
33. For the miracle of the olive tree see Hdt. 8.55.
34. See Thuc. 2.54.

35. Our main sources for which include Livy 29.10.4–11.8, 29.14.5–14; Ovid *Fast.* 4.247–348; cf. Cic. *De Har. Resp.* 27–28.
36. For a good recent discussion and summary of Boudicca's revolt see Goldsworthy 2016: 190–97; cf. Dyson 1971: 258–64.
37. See Tac. *Ann.* 14.29–39; Dio Cass. 62.1–12 for the most complete ancient accounts of Boudicca's rebellion.
38. See Braund 2015: 21; cf. Rutledge 2013: 232–33. Financial stress during Nero's regime may also have been a factor in the situation in Judaea when it revolted in AD 66, see p. 156.
39. See Crummy 1997 for a general discussion of the Roman site.
40. Tacitus in fact blames the rapacity of this agent for causing the rebellion in the first place; nothing more is known of Catus.
41. For her speech see Cass. Dio 62.3–5.
42. Cass. Dio 62.6.4–5.
43. For Boudicca emphasizing her role as a religious leader or persona see Dyson 1971: 261.
44. For the Roman destruction of sacred sites see Rutledge 2007: 179–95.
45. Tac. *Ann.* 14.30.3: *agenti haec Suetonio repetina defectio provinciae nuntiatur*, 'News of the province's sudden defection was conveyed to Suetonius while he was in the midst of these operations.'
46. Dyson 1971: 260.
47. *Agr.* 14.3. The difficulty here is his remark appears somewhat out of left field and is followed by a digression about the lead up to Boudicca's revolt in chapter fifteen, followed in chapter sixteen by the actual rebellion, with no explicit connection made between the final sentence at 14.3 and what follows.
48. See Cunliffe 2018: 282–83 for discussion; see Caes. *BGall.* 6.13.4–10 for Druidic leadership among the ancient inhabitants of Gaul and for the region of the Carnutes (in the region around Orléans); see Caes. *BGall.* 7.1–3, 7.11 for Cenabum as a central point in the outbreak of the rebellion in 52 and Caesar's assault against it.
49. Cass. Dio 62.7; see Cunliffe 2018: 283 who certainly thinks impaling a form of religious sacrifice.
50. Cass. Dio 62.11.4.
51. For the Germans sacrificing Roman captives as offerings see Tac. *Ann.* 1.61.4–5; cf. Caes. *BGall.* 6.16; Tac. *Ann.* 13.57; for a discussion of this phenomenon and the archaeology of it see Heather 2009: 44–45.
52. Tac. *Hist.* 1.59, 4.13; Tacitus' manuscript of the *Annals*, in which he would have related Vindex's revolt breaks off in the year 66, but Cassius Dio has a brief account, see 63.22–24; however, Dio gives only the briefest mention of the disorders in Germany under Civilis, whose name he does not even mention, only briefly noting that Petilius Cerealis put an end to the disorder in the German provinces, 65.3.1–3.
53. Tac. *Hist.* 4.14.
54. Tac. *Hist.* 4.61.
55. Tac. *Hist.* 4.19.
56. Tac. *Hist.* 4.25–27, 34.
57. For his support of Vespasian see Tac. *Hist.* 4.13, 4.31.
58. For his servility under Caligula and Claudius see *Vit.* 2.5.
59. For his exploits as a charioteer under Caligula see Suet. *Vit.* 17.2; for his dicing under Claudius, flattery of Nero, and his intimacy with Caligula see *Vit.* 4.1.
60. Too close: Otho boasted of his wife's, Poppaea Sabina's, beauty, and Nero ended up taking her as a mistress and sending Otho off to his distant governorship early in his reign.
61. The conflict between Galba and Otho, then between Otho and Vitellius, are related in Tacitus' *Historiae*, Books I–II.
62. Suet. *Vit.* 10.3.
63. For his gluttony and heavy drinking see Suet. *Vit.* 13, 17.2.
64. For Minerva's Shield see *Vit.* 13.2.

65. Tac. *Hist.* 3.83.
66. Tac. *Hist.* 3.70–72; see Sailor 2008: 203–249 for an interesting and excellent discussion of the destruction of the Capitoline temple.
67. For Flavius Sabinus' horrific execution at the hands of the degenerate Vitellius see Tac. *Hist.* 3.74 – it is one of many painful moments in Tacitus' narrative.
68. Suet. *Vit.* 17; cf. Tac. *Hist.* 3.84–85 who is our source for the 'latrine' version of the story.
69. See Tac. *Hist.* 4.54 for the revitalization of Civilis' rebellion.
70. See Sailor 2008: 243 for discussion.
71. For their introduction see Tac. *Hist.* 4.55.
72. Tac. *Hist.* 4.59.
73. Tac. *Hist.* 4.59–60.
74. Tac. *Hist.* 4.61; killing by bow and arrow was one of several forms of religious sacrifice and was one means of honouring the gods among the neighbouring Gauls; see Strabo citing Posidonius, 4.4.5; see Cunliffe 2018: 283 for discussion.
75. Tac. *Hist.* 4.61; on Veleda as a religious leader in this rebellion see Dyson 1971: 263–67 and for the revolt of the Batavians more generally; he notes a distinctly nativist and religious element to this rebellion and also that Lupercus may well have been a demarcated victim for human sacrifice.
76. Tac. *Hist.* 4.64–65.
77. Tac. *Hist.* 4.65.
78. Tac. *Hist.* 5.22.
79. Tac. *Hist.* 4.71.
80. For the defeat at Trier see Tac. *Hist.* 4.75–78; for that at Vetera see Tac. *Hist.* 5.14–18.
81. Tac. *Hist.* 5.24.
82. See Strabo 7.3.5; for discussion see Cunliffe 2018: 327; Strabo at 7.3.13 states that the Dacians lived in the region of the upper Danube towards Germania while the Getae lived on the lower Danube, but that the two were identical linguistically.
83. The institution also apparently still held to the Pythagorean doctrine of abstention from meat according to Strabo 7.3.5.
84. Strabo 7.3.11; see Cunliffe 2018: 327–28 for discussion.
85. Suet. *Caes.* 44.3.
86. Mason 2016: 199. His book constitutes the most detailed current study of the context, causes, and course of the Jewish rebellion of AD 66–70; for his summary of scholarship on the causes of the rebellion see 201–208; also see Rudich 2015: 76–85 for the events that led to the initial outbreak of hostilities and ultimately led to Eleazar's prohibition of imperial sacrifice in the Temple.
87. See Mason 2016: 200, 278–80 for discussion where he admonishes against any sort of innate animus between Rome and Judaea.
88. For the ethnic aspects of the conflict see Mason 2016: 217 where he begins an argument for the regional nature of the conflict rather than one driven by hatred of Rome; for his excellent breakdown of the localized and idiosyncratic nature of the regions and its cities prior to the advent of Rome see 226–39.
89. For Caligula's attempt to introduce the imperial cult and the ultimate frustration of the plan see Rudich 2015: 115–20.
90. See Jos. *BJ* 2.285–88; for discussion see Goldsworthy 2016: 232 who notes that there may have been genuine commercial reasons for the construction of the workshop and that it may not have been intended as an intentional slight.
91. For Gessius Florus' early actions as governor of Judaea see Jos. *BJ* 2.277–80.
92. See Mason 2016: 315–318 for discussion of the fiscal constraints Rome faced under Nero; for the culpability of both Florus and Cestus in the outbreak of the rebellion see Rudich 2015: 85–88, who argues that action by Cestus against Florus could have potentially saved the situation.
93. See Jos. *BJ* 2.280.
94. See Jos. *BJ* 2.266–70; the Jewish disputants claimed governance since it had been Herod the Great who had established the city, while the Greek population argued that

Herod would never have constructed the pagan temples and erected pagan idols had it been intended for the Jews.
95. See Jos. *BJ* 2.289; see Goldsworthy 2016: 233 for discussion.
96. See Jos. *BJ* 2.291–92.
97. Jos. *BJ* 2.293–96.
98. Jos. *BJ* 2.321.
99. For the response to Florus inside Jerusalem see Jos. *BJ* 2.325–32.
100. See Mason 2016: 508–509 for discussion.
101. Jos. *BJ* 2.334–35.
102. Jos. *BJ* 2.336–41.
103. Herod Agrippa II had inherited the small kingdom of Chalcis upon his father Herod Agrippa's death in AD 48, but in 53 was forced to relinquish it and given, in exchange, territory once ruled by Philip the tetrarch which was increased under Nero to include certain cities in Galilee, including Tiberias and Livias; his sister was Queen Berenice, a noted love interest of the future emperor Titus; it was before Agrippa and Berenice that Paul pleaded his case in AD 59 or 60, see *Acts* 25–26.
104. See Jos. *BJ* 342–404; for Agrippa II's lengthy speech see 2.345–401.
105. For the taking of Masada see Jos. *BJ* 2.408–409; for the violence in Syria see Jos. *BJ* 2.457–65; for its spread into the kingdom of Agrippa II and Alexandria see Jos. *BJ* 2.487–506.
106. Jos. *BJ* 2.409–10; the temple captain was next in rank to the high priest; Rudich 2015: 68–71 sees this as the most immediate and precise reason for the outbreak of the war for Josephus. Sacrifices were offered twice a day for the nation and the emperor (so Jos. *BJ* 2.197, 409), and consisted of two lambs and a bull in honour of Caesar according to Philo *Leg.* 157, 317; Philo says that the emperor covered the expense but Josephus asserts the Jews paid for it (Jos. *Ap.* 2.77).
107. Jos. *BJ* 2.411–17.
108. Jos. *BJ* 2.421–24.
109. See Jos. *BJ* 2.425–41.
110. Jos. *BJ* 2.457–65.
111. See Jos. *BJ* 2.499–509; see Mason 2016: 281–90 for an analysis of Cestius' actions; for Cestius' reputation as an incompetent bungler see Mason 2016: 282–84.
112. Jos. *BJ* 2.527–48; for discussion of Cestius' march on Jerusalem see Mason 2016: 296–99; see 301–309 for discussion of the chronology of Cestius' actions.
113. Jos. *BJ* 2.562–66.
114. Jos. *BJ* 2.647–52; for the role of the Zealots in the conflict see now Rudich's excellent discussion which comprises chapter five of his study, 2015: 210–52.
115. Jos. *BJ* 4.155–61.
116. Jos. *BJ* 4.162–96.
117. Jos. *BJ* 4.197–207.
118. Jos. *BJ* 4.216–24.
119. Jos. *BJ* 4.305–25.
120. See Mason 2016: 491–502; cf. Rives 2005: 145–66.
121. For a history of the *fiscus Judaicus* and its larger implications see Heemstra 2010.
122. For the *sicarii* as constituting a significant religious group in this conflict see Rudich 2015: 253–85.

Chapter 7: The Collaborators: Informants, Tax Collectors, and Centurions

1. It is also inevitably problematic for us now due to its use of an anti-Semitic slur as well.
2. For a general study and biographical survey concerning what we know of *delatores* from the first century AD see Rutledge 2001.
3. Tac. *Ann.* 1.74.1–3.
4. The nature of the Latin here renders it controversial whether the Latin refers to Romanus Hispo or Caepio Crispinus; see Sinclair 1995: 11–12, 118–119 for discussion.
5. Against Marius Priscus, a corrupt governor of Africa; see p. 77.

6. For Eprius Marcellus see Rutledge 2001: 225–28; for Vibius Crispus see Rutledge 2001: 278–82; for Fabricius Veiento see Rutledge 2001: 229–32.
7. Quint. *Inst.* 12.7.1–3.
8. Cic. *Verr.* 2.2.134.
9. Cic. *Verr.* 2.1.64.
10. For Naevius' actions against Dio see Cic. *Verr.* 2.2.19–24; for Naevius' further activities see Cic. *Verr.* 2.3.90–91; 2.5.108.
11. Cic. *Verr.* 2.4.100.
12. See Philo *Flacc.* 20–24, 125–36 for Lampo's and Isodorus' activities and Flaccus' antipathy towards the Jewish population in his province; cf. *Flacc.* 136–45 for Philo's particular hatred of Isidorus.
13. Jos. *BJ* 7.437–53.
14. Sherwin-White 1963: 47.
15. Sherwin-White 1963: 100.
16. Scholarly discussion of *publicani* is ample and includes: Badian 1972; Brunt 1990: 354–432; McLeister 2016 (a doctoral thesis devoted exclusively to the subject of *publicani* in the Principate); cf. Davenport 2019: esp. 197–201; Wilson 2018; also see Nicolet 2000: 335–84 for the Ephesus Decree or *Monumentum Ephesenum*, an important document for our understanding the complexities of *publicani* and taxation; cf. Engelman and Knibbe 1989. See Julius Pollux, *Onomasticum* 6.30.128 for *publicanus* (*telonēs* in Pollux's Greek) as a term of abuse listed under *vitarum infamium nomina*, or 'Names of infamous livelihoods', where it finds company with such terms as pimp (*pornoboskos* in Greek), and bar tender (*kapēlos*). See Youtie 1967 for an attempt to reconstruct Jesus' attitude towards *publicani*.
17. Badian 1972: 15.
18. See Jones 1974: 26 for the breakdown in revenue classification for Rome.
19. Badian 1972: 24.
20. Cic. *Verr.* 2.2.7; 2.3.12; see Maccoby 1973: 41 for discussion.
21. Tac. *Hist.* 4.74; Maccoby *ibid.*
22. Livy 25.3.
23. See e.g., Cic. *Att.* 1.17.9; 2.1.8.
24. Andreau 1999: 21–22.
25. Davenport 2019: 199 notes that our literary sources concerning *publicani* are sparse and problematic and often tied into the moral characterization of emperors and how they collected taxes; more substantial, however, is information about *publicani* in legal writings from the empire supplemented with some evidence from inscription, see van Nijf 2008.
26. Davenport 2019: 199–200. Davenport cites for this an interesting bit of evidence from the letters of Cornelius Fronto, who wrote on behalf of Q. Saenius Pompeianus (*Ad M. Caes.* 5.49) to Antoninus Pius in the 150s AD whose contract for the collection of public taxes in Africa was approved (and likely renewed) by Antoninus Pius.
27. Brunt 1990: 360 notes *societates* of *publicani* who farmed taxes were still active under Tiberius and Nero. Leases of five years are attested not just in the late republic, but under Hadrian (AD 117–138) and Alexander Severus (AD 222–35); cf. Brunt 1990: 421–22 where he concludes that tax farming persisted until the late empire at least for indirect taxes.
28. Brunt 1990: 356.
29. Brunt 1990: 382–83 notes that there was an extensive accounting system in place to ensure the honest dealings of tax farmers and procurators were put in place in part for stricter control of *publicani*.
30. For discussion see Brunt 1990: 381–83.
31. See Brunt 1990: 382–83 for discussion where he notes: 'They might collect 100, on which their proper percentage was 10, but declare only 80, retaining 8 as their due and embezzling 20. Or they might bargain with the taxpayers to receive openly 50 instead of 100, obtaining another 25 on the side. Such possibilities made it more essential to scrutinize their accounts.'

32. See Tac. *Ann.* 13.50; see Nicolet 2000: 111 for discussion.
33. See Brunt 1990: 385.
34. See e.g. Graf 2018: 489 on two freedmen *publicani* installed in Palmyra in Syria as tax collectors of foreign goods, and Gawlikowski 1998: 145–51 (for L. Spedius Chrysanthus as a tax collector in AD 58).
35. See Maccoby 1973: 57–60. In the case of Judaea this was the wealthy, propertied, and entrenched class known as the Sadducees, from whom the high priest was appointed to the Temple by the Romans, though religious authority was in the hands of Rabbis who were also leaders of the Pharisees. Also see Youtie 1967: 17 for his conjecture concerning the sort of people associated with tax farming whom Jesus might have encountered.
36. Suet. *Vesp.* 1.2.
37. Juv. 3.29–40; for discussion of this passage see Armstrong 2012: *passim*; Davenport 2019: 243–44. For Roman equestrians as *publicani* during the early empire see Demougin 1988: 103–112. As was the case with Cicero, Tacitus seems to attest that *publicani* and equestrians were similarly equated (see *Ann.* 4.6.3–5), but the extent of equestrian involvement in this activity is difficult to assess (Davenport citing Demougin 1988: 109–110 found only one Julio-Claudian equestrian acting as a *publicanus*).
38. Davenport 2019: 244–45, citing inscriptions from Illyria, Moesia, and elsewhere; for example T. Julius Capito, 'farmer of public taxes for the *portorium Illyrici et ripa Thraciae*, was honoured with a public statue, the *ornamenta* of a *IIvir* and *decurio* at Oescus in Moesia Inferior.'
39. See Brunt 1990: 387; he postulates that this may have been done for excise taxes but about these – as Brunt notes – almost nothing is known.
40. It is by no means clear what the term *architelonēs* signifies, but it is likely that as such he coordinated a number of other *publicani* or *telonēs*, so perhaps we need to imagine Zacchaeus as leading a large corporation of tax collectors of which he was the chief coordinator, although this remains conjectural.
41. See *Luke* 19:1–10 for the Zacchaeus episode.
42. *Or.* 46.8.
43. See Maccoby 1973: 40; as Davenport 2019: 179 notes, after 27 BC and Augustus' settlement there were two types of procuratorial provinces – first public provinces such as Achaea, Africa, or Asia governed by senatorial proconsuls, and second, imperial provinces allocated to Augustus himself that he governed through legates – these were the *procuratores Augusti* who had authority for managing Augustus' own affairs and state finances (see e.g., Cass. Dio 53.15.3; Strabo 17.1.12). These provincial *procuratores* were in charge of collecting direct taxes and managing the collection of indirect taxes from *publicani* in addition to paying and supplying the army.
44. See Davenport 2019: 197–98 for discussion; see Cass. Dio 55.25.5 who reports on the Augustan system of taxation.
45. The records were extensive, but few survive, though we know they existed and some do come down to us in fragments; see Youtie 1967: 1 citing three day books of tax payments from Karanis in the second century.
46. See Udoh's exhaustive and excellent 2006 study on taxation and imperial administration in the region for a detailed study of the sources for and history of taxation in Judaea.
47. Macobby 1973: 38. For *publicani* in general in the province of Judaea see Maccoby 1973: 38–42; Hoehner 1972: 73–79 who notes that Julius Caesar abolished tax farming in the region of Judaea (although it returned in the early empire).
48. Brunt 1990: 409.
49. A *diminutionem tributi*, Tac. *Ann.* 2.42.6. For Valerius Gratus see Jos. *AJ* 18.33–35, 177; also see Philo *Leg.* 199 for his complaints about the *publicanus* Capito and his extortionate collection of taxes in Judaea.
50. Suet. *Tib.* 32.2; For an excellent discussion on this passage see Champlin: 2008: 416.
51. See Brunt 1990: 389, citing Jos. *AJ* 14.201, *BJ* 2.405–407. As Davenport 2019: 198 notes (cf. Brunt 1990: 380–81 for discussion), the collection of *tributum* in the province

of Asia was taken away in 47 BC from the *publicani* and given directly to the cities – though we cannot be sure this is applicable as a general principle to other provinces.

52. Tac. *Ann.* 1.17.
53. Tac. *Ann.* 1.20.
54. Tac. *Ann.* 1.23.
55. Tac. *Ann.* 1.26.
56. Tac. *Ann.* 1.30.
57. Tac. *Ann.* 1.31–32.
58. Tac. *Ann.* 1.44.
59. Tac. *Hist.* 3.6; see Rutledge 2001: 198–200 for Arrius.
60. *ILS* 2656.
61. Emphasis on title, since, as Goldsworthy 2003: 69–70 has noted, a centurion did not constitute so much a rank as an office.
62. For Fortunatus see *ILS* 2658.
63. Caes. *BGall.* 6.40.7.
64. Caes. *BCiv.* 3.53.4.
65. Suet. *Caes.* 68.3–4.
66. *CIL* 8.2354.
67. Tac. *Hist.* 4.61.
68. Goldsworthy 2003: 73; we might wonder whether the centurion seeking help for his servant was from a local elite, given that he will have presumably spoken to Jesus in Aramaic, although this raises the question concerning whether Greek might not have been used as a local language, given its cultural and linguistic domination in the East. Doubtless though centurions when moved from place to place, as many were, will have learned a smattering of the local dialect while in the West Latin will have been the *lingua franca* for administrative purposes.
69. See e.g., Cass. Dio 49.14.3.
70. See Goldsworthy 2003: 50.
71. See Breeze 2016: 101.
72. Tac. *Ann.* 1.61.4–6; cf. p. 132 n. 8
73. See Southern 2006: 108.
74. Tac. *Hist.* 3.19.
75. See Tac. *Hist.* 4.5 for Helvidius' background.
76. For their function as military police see Caes. *BAf.* 54; for their role in maintaining public order see e.g. Tac. *Ann.* 1.77.
77. Caes. *BGall.* 1.39–40.
78. Caes. *BGall.* 3.14.
79. Suet. *Cal.* 21.
80. Tac. *Ann.* 3.2.2.
81. Veg. *De Re Mil.* 2.14.
82. Southern 2006: 93.
83. Caes. *BAf.* 45–46.
84. Tac. *Hist.* 2.60.
85. Tac. *Hist.* 3.54.
86. Caes. *BGall.* 5.44.
87. See Caes. *BGall.* 7.47.
88. Caes. *BGall.* 7.50.
89. Caes. *BGall.* 2.25.
90. Caes. *BCiv.* 3.91, 99.
91. Tac. *Hist.* 1.43.
92. Cass. Dio 47.46.5.
93. Caes. *BAlex.* 57.
94. See Tac. *Hist.* 1.56–59.
95. Tac. *Hist.* 1.80–82.
96. Tac. *Ann.* 1.6.
97. Suet. *Tib.* 53.2.

98. Suet. *Cal.* 58–59; *Claud.* 11.1.
99. Tac. *Ann.* 11.37.3.
100. Tac. *Ann.* 14.8.
101. For their cover up of Nero's crime see Tac. *Ann.* 14.10; for their involvement in Octavia's punishment see Tac. *Ann.* 14.64.
102. Tac. *Ann.* 14.15.6–9.
103. Dio 62.24.2; Tac. *Ann.* 15.68.1.
104. Tac. *Ann.* 14.31.1–5.

Bibliography

Abbreviations:
AJAH = American Journal of Ancient History
AJP = American Journal of Philology
CW = Classical World
CQ = Classical Quarterly
JRS = Journal of Roman Studies
TAPA = Transactions of the American Philological Association
ZPE = Zeitschrift für Papyrologie und Epigraphik

Andreau, Jean. 1999. *Banking and Business in the Roman World.* Translated by Janet Lloyd. (Cambridge University Press).

Armstrong, D. 2012. '*Juvenalis eques*: a dissident voice from the lower tier of the Roman elite', in S. Braund and J. Osgood (eds.), *A Companion to Persius and Juvenal*, (Oxford and Malden MA). 59–78.

Badian, E. 1972. *Publicans and Sinners. Private Enterprise in the Service of the Roman Republic* (Cornell University Press).

Bartsch, S. 1994. *Actors in the Audience. Theatricality and Doublespeak from Nero to Hadrian.* (Harvard University Press, Cambridge Massachusetts).

Beard, Mary. 2009. *Roman Triumph.* (Harvard University Press).

Beard, M., North, J., Price, S. 1998. *Religions of Rome. Volume 1: A History.* (Cambridge University Press).

Bodel, J. 1999. 'Punishing Piso', *AJP* 120: 43–62.

Bounia, A. 2004. *The Nature of Classical Collecting. Collectors and Collections, 100 BCE–100 CE* (Ashgate).

Bradley, Keith. 1994. *Slavery and Society at Rome.* (Cambridge University Press).

Braund, David. 1984. *Rome and the Friendly King: The Character of the Client Kingship.* (London, Croom Helm).

Braund, Susan. 2015. 'Seneca Multiplex', in *The Cambridge Companion to Seneca*, Shadi Bartsch and Alessandero Schiesaro (eds.). (Cambridge University Press). 15–28.

Breeze, David. 2016. *The Roman Army.* (Bloomsbury).

Bruce, F. F. 1984. 'Tacitus on Jewish History', *Journal of Semitic Studies* 29.1: 33–44.

Brunt, P. A. 1990. *Roman Imperial Themes.* (Oxford University Press).

Carter, Warren. 2003. *Pontius Pilate. Portraits of a Roman Governor.* (Liturgical Press, Collegeville Minnesota).

Champlin, E. 2008. 'Tiberius the Wise', *Historia* 57.4: 408–425.

—— 2010. 'My Sejanus', *Humanities* 31.5: 18–21, 52–53.

—— 2011. 'Sex on Capri', *TAPA* 141: 315–332.

—— 2012. 'Seianus Augustus', *Chiron* 42: 359–86.

Crummy, Philip. 1997. *City of Victory: The Story of Colchester, Britain's First Roman Town.* (Colchester Archaeological Trust).

Cunliffe, Barry. 2018. *The Ancient Celts.* (2nd edition, Oxford University Press).

Damon, C. 1999. 'The Trial of Cn. Piso in Tacitus' *Annales* and the *Senatus Consultum de Cn. Pisone Patre*: 'New light on narrative technique', *AJP* 120: 143–62.

Davenport, C. 2019. *A History of the Equestrian Order.* (Cambridge University Press).

Demougin, S. 1988. *L'ordre équestre sous les Julio-Claudiens.* (Rome).
Drews, Robert. 1984. 'The Lacuna in Tacitus' *Annales* Book V in Light of Christian Traditions', *AJAH* 9: 112–122.
Dyson, Stephen L. 1971. 'Native Revolts in the Roman Empire', *Historia* 20: 239–74.
Ehrenberg, V., and Jones, A. H. M. 1976. *Documents Illustrating the Reigns of Augustus and Tiberius.* (David Stockton [ed.], 2nd. Edition, Oxford).
Engelman, Helmut and Knibbe, Dieter. 1989. 'Das Sollgesetz der Provinz Asia: Eine neue Inschrift aus Ephesos', *Epigraphica Anatolica* 14.
Evans, Craig. 2007. 'Josephus on John the Baptist', in Levine, Amy-Jill, et al. *The Historical Jesus in Context.* (Princeton University Press).
Feldherr, A. 2009. 'The Poisoned Chalice: Rumour and Historiography in Tacitus' Account of the Death of Drusus', in *Materiali e discussioni per l'analisi dei testi classici* 61. *Callida Musa: Papers on Latin Literature: In Honor of R. Elaine Fanthom.* 175–89.
Galinksy, K. 1998. *Augustan Culture.* (Princeton University Press).
Gawlikowski, M. 1998. 'Deux publicans et leur tombeau', *Syria* 75: 145–51.
Goldsworthy, A. 2003. *The Complete Roman Army.* (Thames and Hudson Ltd., London).
—— 2016. *Pax Romana. War, Peace and Conquest in the Roman World.* (Yale University Press).
Graf, David F. 2018. 'The Silk Road between Syria and China', in *Trade, Commerce, and the State in the Roman World*, A. Wilson and A. Bowman (eds.). (Oxford University Press). 443–530.
Gruen, Erich. 2016. *The Construction of Identity in Hellenic Judaism: Essays on Jewish Literature and History.* (DeGruyter).
Harrison, Thomas. 2000. *Divinity and History. The Religion of Herodotus.* (Oxford University Press).
Heather, P. 2006. *The Fall of the Roman Empire. A New History of Rome and the Barbarians.* (Oxford University Press).
—— 2009. *Empires and Barbarians. The Fall of Rome and the Birth of Europe.* (Oxford University Press).
Heemstra, Marius. 2010. *The Fiscus Judaicus and the Parting of the Ways.* (Tübingen: Mohr Siebeck).
Hennig, D. 1975. *L. Aelius Seianus.* (Munich).
Hoehner, Harold W. 1972. *Herod Antipas. A Contemporary of Jesus Christ.* (Cambridge University Press, republished in 1999, Zondervan Academic).
Holum, K. 1997. 'Caesarea', in *The Oxford Encyclopedia of Archaeology in the Near East vol. 1*, Eric M. Meyers (ed.). (Oxford University Press). 399–404.
Holum, K., and Raban, A. 1993. 'Caesarea: The Joint Expedition's Excavations, Excavations in the 1980s and 1990s, and Summary', in *The New Encyclopedia of Archaeological Excavations in the Holy Land*, Ephraim Stern (ed.). (Jerusalem: The Israel Exploration Society & Carta). 282–86.
Houston, George. 1985. 'Tiberius on Capri', *Greece and Rome* 32.2: 179–96.
Hughes, John. 1996. *Pan's Travail. Environmental Problems of the Greeks and Romans.* (Johns Hopkins University Press).
Jensen, Morten H. 2006. *Herod Antipas in Galilee. The Literary and Archaeological Sources in the Reign of Herod Antipas and its Socio-Economic Impact in Galilee.* (Wissenschaftliche Untersuchungen zum Neuen Testament 2.Reihe). (Mohr Siebeck).
Jones, A. H. M. 1974. *The Roman Economy.* (Totowa, NJ: Rowman and Littlefield).
Levick, Barbara. 1976. *Tiberius the Politician.* (London).
—— 1990. *Claudius.* (Yale University Press).
Maccoby, Hyam. 1973. *Revolution in Judaea. Jesus and the Jewish Resistance.* (Taplinger Publishing).
MacMullen, Ramsey. 1990. *Changes in the Roman Empire: Essays in the Ordinary.* (Princeton University Press).
Maier, Paul L. 1968. 'Sejanus, Pilate, and the Date of the Crucifixion', *Church History* 37.1.3–13.

Marshall, A. J. 1975. 'Tacitus and the Governor's Lady: A Note on Tacitus III.33–34', *Greece & Rome* 22.1: 11–18.

Martin, R. H. and Woodman, A. J. 1989. *Tacitus. Annals Book IV.* (Cambridge University Press).

Mason, Steve. 2016. *A History of the Jewish War.* (Cambridge University Press).

Matyszak, Philip. 2020. *Mithridates the Great. Rome's Indomitable Enemy.* (Pen and Sword, Barnsley).

Mayor, Adrienne. 2011. *The Poison King. The Life and Legend of Mithridates, Rome's Deadliest Enemy.* (Princeton University Press).

McHugh, John S. 2020. *Sejanus: Regent of Rome.* (Pen and Sword, Barnsley).

McLeister, Kyle. 2016. *Publicani in the Roman Principate.* Doctorial Thesis, McMaster University.

Miles, Margaret M. 2010. *Art as Plunder. The Ancient Origins of Debate about Cultural Property.* (Cambridge University Press).

Nicols, John. 1975. 'Antonia and Sejanus', *Historia. Zeitschrift für Alte Geschichte*, 24.1: 48–58.

Oost, S. V. 1958. 'The Career of Marcus Antonius Pallas', *AJP* 79: 113–39.

Pettinger, Andrew. 2012. *The Republic in Danger. Drusus Libo and the Succession of Tiberius.* (Oxford University Press).

Raaflaub, K. and Samons, J. 1991. 'Opposition to Augustus', in *Between Republic and Principate: Interpretations of Augustus and His Principate*, K. Raaflaub and M. Toher (eds.). (University of California Press, Berkeley). 417–454.

Ridgeway, B. S. 2000. 'The Sperlonga Sculptures; The Current State of Research', in *From Pergamum to Sperlonga: Sculpture in Context*, T. De Grummond and B. S. Ridgeway (eds.). (University of California Press, Berkeley). 78–91.

Rives, J. B. 2005. 'Flavian religious policy and the destruction of the Jerusalem Temple', in *Flavius Josephus and Flavian Rome*, Jonathan Edmondson, Steve Mason, and James Rives (eds.). (Oxford University Press). 145–66.

Roller, Duane W. 2020. *Empire of the Black Sea: The Rise and Fall of the Mithridatic World.* (Oxford University Press).

Rudich, Vasily. 2015. *Religious Dissent in the Roman Empire: Violence in Judaea at the Time of Nero.* (Routledge).

Rutledge, S. 2001. *Imperial Inquisitions. Prosecutors and Informants from Tiberius to Domitian.* (Routledge).

—— 2007. 'The Roman Destruction of Sacred Sites', *Historia* 56: 179–95.

—— 2008. 'Tiberius' Philhellenism', *CW* 101.4: 453–67.

—— 2012. *Ancient Rome as a Museum: Power, Identity, and the Culture of Collecting.* (Oxford University Press).

—— 2013. 'The Slow Annexation of Britain', in *A Companion to Roman Imperialism*, Dexter Hoyos (ed.). (Brill). 223–36.

Sailor, Dylan. 2008. *Writing and Empire in Tacitus.* (Cambridge University Press).

Saviano, Roberto. 2007. *Gomorrah. A Personal Journey into the Violent International Empire of Naples Organized Crime System.* (Farrar, Straus and Giroux).

Schiavone, Aldo. 2016. *Pontius Pilate. Deciphering a Memory.* (Norton, trans. 2017 by Jeremy Carden).

Seager, R. 1972. *Tiberius.* (Blackwell).

Sherwin-White, A. N. 1963. *Roman Law and Society in the New Testament.* (Oxford University Press).

Shotter, David. 1992. *Tiberius Caesar.* (Routledge).

Silva, Luis. 2013. *Viriathus and the Lusitanian Resistance to Rome 155–139 BC.* (Pen and Sword, Barnsley).

Sinclair, Patrick. 1995. *Tacitus the Sententious Historian: A Sociology of Rhetoric in Annales 1–6.* (Penn State University Press, University Park).

Southern, Pat. 2006. *The Roman Army. A Social and Institutional History.* (ABC-CLIO. Inc., Santa Barbara)

Stewart, A. 1977. 'To Entertain an Emperor: Sperlonga, Laokōon, and Tiberius at the Dinner-Table', *JRS* 67: 76–90.

Stewart, P. 2003. *Statues in Roman Society. Representation and Response* (Oxford University Press).

Syme, Sir Ronald. 1939. *The Roman Revolution*. (Oxford University Press).

—— 1956. 'Seianus on the Aventine', *Hermes* 84.3: 257–66.

—— 1968. 'People in Pliny', *JRS* 58: 135–51.

Talbert, R. J. A. 1999. 'Tacitus and the *Senatus Consultum de Cn. Pisone Patre*', *AJP* 120: 89–98.

Udoh, F. E. 2006. *To Caesar What Is Caesar's: Tribute, Taxes, and Imperial Administration in Early Roman Palestine*. (Brown Judaic Studies).

Van Dijk, W. 2019. *The Successor: Tiberius and the Triumph of the Roman Empire*. (Trans. By Kathleen Brandt-Carey, Baylor University Press).

Van Nijf, O. 2008. 'The social world of Roman tax-farmers and their personnel', in *The Customs Laws of Asia*, M. Cottier et al. (eds.). (Oxford University Press). 279–311.

Van Voorst, Robert E. 2000. *Jesus Outside the New Testament: An Introduction to the Ancient Evidence*. (William B. Eerdmans Publishing).

Vasaly, A. 1993. *Representation: Images of the World in Ciceronian Oratory*. (University of California Press, Berkeley).

Wallace-Hadrill, D. S. 2011. 'Eusebius of Caesarea and the *Testimonium Flavianum* (Josephus, *Antiquities*, XVIII. 63f.)', *The Journal of Ecclesiastical History* 25.4: 353–62.

Webb, Simon. 2018. *What Do We Know About Herod Antipas?* (The Langley Press).

Wells, Peter. 2004. *The Battle that Stopped Rome: Emperor Augustus, Arminius, and the Slaughter of the Legions in the Teutoberg Forest*. (W. W. Norton and Co.).

Williams, Craig. 1999. *Roman Homosexuality*. (Oxford University Press).

Wilson, Andrew. 2018. *Trade, Commerce, and State in the Roman World. Oxford Studies on the Roman Economy*. (Oxford University Press).

Woodman, A. J. 1977. *Velleius Paterculus. The Tiberian Narrative* (2.94–132). (Cambridge University Press).

—— 1989. 'Tacitus' Obituary of Tiberius', *CQ* 39.1: 197–205.

—— Woodman, A. J. (with C. S. Kraus). 2014. *Tacitus: Agricola*. (Cambridge University Press).

Wroe, Ann. 1999. *Pontius Pilate*. (Random House).

Yonge, C. D. 1854–90. *The Works of Philo*. (London).

Youtie, H. C. 1967. 'Publicans and Sinners', *ZPE* 1: 1–20.

Index

Note: Proper Roman names are listed alphabetically according to their *gentilicium* (their second or clan name), if known. The names of emperors and more famous (or notorious) Romans are generally referred to by their better-known *cognomina* or last names.